264 West 40th Street

Jim Gath

Copyright © 2015 by Jim Gath
All rights reserved. No part of this publication may be reproduced, distributed, or transmitted in any form or by any means, including photocopying, recording, or other electronic or mechanical methods, without the prior written permission of the publisher, except in the noncommercial uses permitted by copyright law. For permission requests, write to the publisher, addressed "Attention: Permissions Coordinator," at the address below or email sealofterspress@gmail.com.

Sealofters Press, Inc.
1061 East Indiantown Rd, Suite #104
Jupiter, FL 33477

Sealofters Press, Inc. was established in 2008 as a publishing alternative to the large, commercial publishing houses currently dominating the book publishing industry. Sealofters Press, Inc. is committed to publishing works of educational, cultural and community value.

ONE

"Smolinski?"

"Nope", I shrugged. "Fiberglass room?"

"Ah, sonofabitch", John Bubniak said in Polish. Bubniak was our foreman.

"Seventh floor? Pouring pumps? Maybe on twelve", I offered.

"Nah, I look all places", said Bubniak.

"Okay, I'll go." I got up and walked around the desk, turning sideways so I wouldn't ram my thigh on the corner and add to the already existing bruise that never seemed to leave.

Goddam desk.

I went into the hall, hit the elevator "up" button and lit a cigarette. Twenty seconds later the bell rang and the little green "up" arrow lit up over the middle elevator car. I walked on and hit '20'. A couple of other people were already in there, an old Jewish guy who sold buttons from his cubby hole-sized place on the sixth floor and a messenger with a bag of food. I cupped the cigarette and neither said anything, not that they would. I got off on twenty, made a left, walked into the stairwell and started down.

I found Smolinski on the eighth floor landing, drunk as a skunk and coughing blood. He started some harangue in Polish and I opened the door so we could get the elevator back down to the second floor. He kept coughing and spouting off but he followed me peaceably.

"John, we gotta get this guy to a hospital or doctor or something. I don't want him dying here and I don't want any of us to catch whatever it is he's got."

"No money", Bubniak said simply. He sat two boxes on the floor next to the door. "XK- 1000 and fleur-de-lis", he said, pointing to each of the two boxes. I got up, walked around the desk again and wrote the information John had given me on the boxes. Why he couldn't write what was in the boxes before he brought them out of the shop was beyond me. He never did, though. I think it was his version of a cat bringing a dead mouse into the house and dropping it at your feet. Sort of a pride thing.

Jeanne and Dale were at lunch with Jim Lucey, the vice president of the bank. They wouldn't be any help by the time they got back. Lunch with Lucey meant martinis and that would effectively end their productivity for the day.

"John, why don't you get him in a cab and take him up to St. Vincent's emergency room? Just drop him off - they'll do something with him."

"Money?"

"Here", I said, handing him a ten. "Take a cab back, too."

Off they went, John holding him more or less vertical and Smolinski still railing and coughing.

I found the invoices and COD tags and labels for the pump and fountainhead John had brought in, wrote the information in the UPS book and put everything back in about the same pile as John had left them.

Tiger was rousing herself from her midday nap and made her way over to sniff the pile. I caught her with her eye on the open door. "Tige! Get away from that door! Come on - let's get you something to eat." I picked her up and walked around to the "kitchen" area in the next room, the room with the printing presses, collating machine, paper cutter, boxes of paper, file cabinets and a couple of old grey steel desks.

The "kitchen" consisted of a refrigerator - one of those that dispensed water and ice cubes, but that feature hadn't worked in about five years - and a microwave oven, the pride and joy of the whole place.

I put Tiger down on the table. Bubniak had taken a rolling steel cart, had put cheap Formica on the top and wall paneling on the sides, all held together with ill-fitting aluminum strips. I swept a couple of cockroaches onto the floor, nailed one with my foot while the other escaped under the refrigerator, and presented Tige with an already opened half-can of cat food from the fridge. I really loved that cat.

I had met Tige a few years prior, when Jeanne rescued her from somewhere. I had been staying at the Hotel Landseer on West 51st Street just off Eighth Avenue and Tige stayed with me for a few days because Jeanne and Dale had a couple of cats of their own at home and she couldn't go there. The three days she spent with me were spent under the radiator.

The Landseer's manager didn't really care. It was a dump anyway, one step up from a Single Room Occupancy joint. When I checked in and put my stuff in the closet, I found a paperback picture book on the closet shelf, entitled "Fellatio". How thoughtful of the Landseer management. Behind his back, we referred to the manager as "Wingie". He had one of those thalidomide-type arms that was about eighteen inches long, total. I only stayed there a couple of weeks, upgrading during week two to a two-room "suite".

In the "living room" I counted four layers of linoleum through the holes worn in the traffic pattern.

"Fellatio" moved with me. By then, Tiger had moved to the office on 40th Street.

I heard the elevator ring, and then the electric eye bell at the front office door went off. Jeanne and Dale were back from lunch, with Lucey in tow.

"What's happenin'? Any checks in the mail?" Dale loved it when the mailman came and always went immediately to the self-addressed business reply envelopes. Those were the ones that generally held checks in advance for one or more models of the water display fountains that were the basis of our business.

As a matter of fact, we were the largest manufacturers of self-contained water display fountains in the country. You know, the kind where there's a round bowl from which jets of water shoot up and are lit by one or more waterproof lights in the middle. We literally sold thousands of them, in sizes that ranged from 20 inches in diameter to eight feet in diameter.

I was the national sales manager.

I usually just left the mail in a pile and let Dale have his fun of opening the ones with the checks in them. He would toss any other piece of correspondence onto the floor next to the easy chair that was his base of operations. Usually, that other correspondence consisted of past-due bills, but Dale wanted none of that. That was Jeanne's purview.

"Thirty-two hundred! Hot damn! This calls for a drink!" Dale wheeled around the corner toward the kitchen area. The kitchen area also usually had a couple of half-dead half- gallon jugs of Johnny Walker Red laying around. He reached into the fridge and brought out four Styrofoam cups, filling them with ice from the ice maker that wouldn't deliver ice but made it just fine.

"Whoa, I gotta get back to the office", said Lucey.

"Here. Have a couple of hot dogs with your drink. They'll sober you up." Dale had it down to a science.

He'd wrap a hot dog in one of those industrial brown paper towels, slap it into the microwave for thirty seconds, put the dog in a bun, wrap it up again and give it another thirty seconds. Voila.

As I recall, those hot dogs were great. Really. Whatever, we'd go through a dozen or more a day. They were the specialty of the house.

Lucey sat on the couch in the front office, a hot dog in one hand and a Styrofoam cup full of Johnnie Red in the other. Natch, he slopped mustard on his suit. "Shit."

We had a nickname for Jim Lucey, too. My grandfather, Newt, called him "Hole-in-the- head". Not to him, of course, just behind his back. Lucey had this weird looking scar right in the middle of his forehead. It *was* like a hole and it wasn't reddish or anything - it was kind of black. Looked like a hole. Nobody ever asked him what it was.

Dale and Jeanne couldn't have made it without Lucey. He loved them and bent scores of the rules of banking for them. They never cheated him, though. It was a real, solid relationship that worked out well for both parties.

When I'd see him in the bank, stone cold sober, he always had a stern, banker's countenance. Get him over to our office, though, lay three or four Johnnie bombs on him, and he always sat there grinning like a banshee.

I was, more often than not, the "bartender". I loved to bomb people. Fill the cup with scotch (or whatever), splash a half-ounce of water on top and away we'd go. I think that's why a lot of people came to visit. They'd show up sober as a judge and less than an hour later would have a major buzz going. Oh, they'd complain a little once in a while, but only perfunctorily. Nobody ever turned down a drink that I can remember.

Bubniak came back in. "They put Smolinski in room by himself. Put red sign outside door - nobody go in." Shrug. "Must go make crate for eight-footer." Off he went.

I guess Dale and Jeanne and Lucey had been talking about the building again. The real estate company that handled the building had told Dale he could get it for around $600,000, which seemed like a pretty good deal to the three of them sitting there sipping their scotch. Actually, Jeanne was also trying to herd up the checks from around Dale's chair so she could get the deposit in before the bank closed. I told her I'd take care of it and did.

Once I had the deposit ready to go, I offered to run down the two blocks to the bank. It was about a quarter to three. It'd give me a chance to see daylight.

"Nah, have one of John's guys go", said Dale. "Sit down. Relax. Have a drink."

I walked next door to the shop. "John, can you have one of your guys go to the bank?"

"Sure. Piotrowski! Hutch-pon!" Now, I realize 'hutch-pon' is a phonetic spelling for some Polish phrase meaning "hurry up", but John was always yelling it to one of his guys or the other.

"Hutch! Hutch!" Piotrowski, a little skinny guy with a big nose, hustled himself front and center.

"Na bank!", ordered John. 'Na' meant 'to', spelling aside. I could speak quite a bit of Polish, mostly swear words that always amazed the new guys, but I'll be damned if I ever learned to spell anything.

Piotrowski grabbed the checks and deposit slip and headed for the hallway, John and me in tow. He reached for the elevator button. "No!", said John, saying something in Polish and motioning toward the stairs. Piotrowski hit the door running. Ten minutes to three.

Plenty of time.

"What do you suppose is the matter with Smolinski?" I asked John as we made our way back down the hall. "Ah, he is pijac", John said with a dismissive wave of the hand. 'Pijac', pronounced pee-yak, means drunk. It's one of the two or three Polish words I know how to spell. Off he rushed into the fiberglass room.

I walked back into the office and Dale asked me, "Jim, how'd it be if we three fountain tycoons owned this building? The General Fountain Building. We could put the name up in lights on the roof like the 666 Building or the Pan Am Building. Should we use red or blue lights?"

I voted for blue. Jeanne giggled and took a sip of her drink. Lucey stood unsteadily, wiping at his mustard stain and said, "I gotta get back to the salt mine."

TWO

This all happened in the mid-1970s, at least my time as a fountain tycoon. I was there nine years before I realized the place was only big enough for two fountain tycoons, but I'm getting a little ahead of myself.

Jeanne was my aunt, my mother's sister. She and Dale had hooked up in the late '50s and had, according to them, been married somewhere in Ohio, but there was always a question as to whether the ceremony actually took place.

Jeanne had been a flight attendant – called a stewardess back then - beginning after World War II, ferrying soldiers around the country. Sometime in the late 40s, she married (at least I think she married) the love of her life, a pilot named CJ. CJ died in a plane wreck right around the time their only daughter, Diane, was born. CJ's death completely devastated Jeanne and I don't think she ever got over it. My cousin, Diane, is about a year and a half younger than I am and we were always close. Dale gave her a nickname a few years later that always stuck among many in the family: Iz. Her real name was Diane Adele, but as a youngster she'd say "My name is Diane Izadel". She became Iz, at least to Jeanne and Dale and me.

Dale came from Marion, Indiana. He and his brothers, Paul and Jack, grew up pretty much with their mother only. Their father, Roy, was always anywhere but Marion, Indiana.

Roy made an absolute fortune by founding and developing the original magazine crew concept. You don't see much of it anymore, but I know it's out there because I still see classified ads in newspapers touting "TRAVEL. Get paid to travel. All expenses paid. Great commissions. Call XXX-XXX-XXXX".

Magazine crews would travel the country, from city to city and town to town, selling magazine subscriptions door to door. These crews could be populated by quite a conglomeration of wandering souls. You'd have wizened old veterans in their early thirties, a fairly nice bunch in their mid- to late-twenties and a bunch of starry-eyed kids who always claimed to be twenty-one, but never quite were.

There was always – and still probably is – an overabundance of booze, pills, grass, fast food, cigarettes, lies, fights and arrests around these crews. I used to visit some of them as a kid, though, and it seemed like a perfect, exciting lifestyle. They got to live in motels, drive around in nice cars, listen to rock 'n roll and country and western music all day and never really work.

Dale's family – his father and brother Paul (of whom it was said his crews "scorched the earth they walked on") – made quite a lot of money early on, especially Roy. Their home office was in that hotbed of magazine crew-dom, Terre Haute, Indiana.

Roy had his own plane (I saw pictures of him with it and in it), big fancy cars, and squads of lackeys always in his wake. A millionaire back when a million bucks was really something. He kept suites in hotels in cities across the country, had a stable of pretty good racehorses, even had daily manicures with clear nail polish. Always wore an ascot and carried himself like royalty.

But, at the time, the magazine business was all about cash.

And, somehow, Roy's partner blew him in to the IRS right at the peak of his time at the top.

Roy was ruined. He escaped prison, but the IRS had him right by the shorthairs and he had to give them everything he had – everything. Hell, ol' Roy was still paying the IRS when he died, nearly thirty years later. Still always wore an ascot, though, and had the occasional manicure, albeit without the daily clear nail polish.

Dale had a Dodge/Chrysler dealership in Marion and a wife and two boys, Dale, Jr. and Earl (aka Little Earl). He was doing real well, belonged to the country club, went to Rotary and Lions meetings. Then, somehow, he met Jeanne.

Here again the story becomes murky, but in no time at all, Dale had left his family, gotten rid of the dealership, quit the country club and probably turned in his Rotary and Lions pins. He took up with Jeanne and off they went.

How to make money?

Why, a magazine crew, naturally.

Dale became a hero to a young boy – me. Quite a bit younger than my folks, good looking, charming and always seemed to be having a real good time, he drove a brand new 1955 powder blue Caddy convertible – the kind with the big bullets on the front bumper. He was like rock 'n roll before there was rock 'n roll, if you know what I mean.

Anyway, Dale and Jeanne and little Iz would travel around the country – mostly the Midwest, east and partway down south. The paid attention to try and hire pretty nice kids. One of their managers, Fred Schifferly, even gave me the only bible I ever owned, not that he or I were religious or anything, it was just a nice gesture to a kid of nine or ten.

Oh, they had their fair share of weirdos around at any given time, it was part of the culture.

Bob Woerner, one of the original beatniks, called Dale at the motel one afternoon, saying, "Dale! You gotta come and get me. The heat's got me!"

Dale said, "Woerner, are you drunk? It's November. We're in Timonium, Maryland and it's forty-five degrees!"

"No, man. The *heat!* The heat's got me!" Woerner meant he had been arrested for some such thing and, like all good beatniks of the time, referred to the local constabulary as "the heat". Woerner was good people, though.

Jackie Hinkle idolized Dale. He was one of Dale's "car handlers", meaning he'd take four or five kids out from the motel in the morning and drop them off in some unsuspecting neighborhood for the morning. They'd all meet up again around noon, Hinkle would buy them each a cheap lunch, and off they'd go for the afternoon, 'til he picked them up around four or five. Hinkle was always watching out for Dale's best interests.

Cash-in time was always good for some excitement. As all the car crews would converge on the motel at the end of the day, everybody had to hand Dale the cash they'd taken in. The cash they'd taken in had to match the receipts, which were also handed in. The car handlers also had copies of their charges' receipts and everything had to match: cash, receipts and receipts.

They never did.

There were always honest mistakes: some kid would hit his cash for a pack of cigarettes or gum or candy or something and that didn't generally cause anything other than minor chaos.

Sometimes, though, some real money – like, say twenty or thirty bucks would be unaccounted for. Dale would catch it. The car handler would scream at whomever came up short. The kid would scream back that he'd given all his money to the handler for safe-keeping. Full-fledged ruckuses were always a part of cash-in, fistfights often ensued, furniture would be trashed and the money would sometimes reappear. Not often, though. Sometimes it had been wired home. Sometimes, the telltale fragrance of booze was on somebody's breath. Sometimes, a kid had a new shirt in a bag carefully tucked under his mattress. Whatever, it was always good entertainment. We young'uns weren't allowed into cash-in time very often. Too dangerous. Shit.

One time it was Dale's birthday and Hinkle had spent his own good money to buy Dale a birthday cake with a lot of red icing on it. He sat it proudly on the table right next to Dale. One of the car handlers, it could have been Tom Dooley, was already half in the bag and clumsily backed into the cake, Hinkle's pride and joy.

Dale remembered seeing Hinkle's hand slide under the plate just before Dooley took the whole cake right smack in the face. A free-for-all ensued, primarily because there was a camp that thought the world of Dale and another that couldn't care if school kept. Pretty soon, the whole room was fighting, chairs were being thrown, windows broken, tables overturned. A real melee, right in the middle of a tidy little motel owned by a nice middle-aged couple, who had the audacity to call the police.

In troops four or five Barney Fifes, replete with their Smokey the Bear hats. One cop got on his walkie-talkie and called for two or three ambulances. He thought there was blood everywhere. Out came the guns and the fighters abruptly became friends once again. Dale had to explain, quite carefully and diplomatically, that there wasn't really any blood at all – it was just the red icing from his birthday cake from Hinkle that had gotten thrown around in everybody's faces.

The cops, not really wanting to deal with thirty or thirty-five half-drunken misfits, decided to buy Dale's story, called off the ambulances and made for the nearest doughnut shop. Dale sent somebody to the nearest drugstore for mercurochrome, gauze, tape and band aids.

Hinkle was still pissed.

A few years later, Dale and Jeanne had the crew at a pretty nice hotel in Memphis. There was a little pool in the middle of the lobby. As guys who run magazine crews spend a whole lot of time sitting around lobbies, Dale thought some sort of splashing water display would look nice in the middle of that pool.

He went to a hardware store, bought some copper tubing, a hand drill and bits, a few couplings and a submersible pump. Back in the room, he fashioned his raw materials into something that looked like it would shoot water into the air.

He took it down to the lobby, put it in the water and plugged in the pump. Damned if it didn't work. Looked pretty nice, actually. He called the manager over and showed it to him. About two minutes later, Dale had sold his first fountain.

He realized then and there that there was a market for water display fountains, particularly for hotels, motels and restaurants. At the time, no such inexpensive display of water existed, particularly one that would recycle the same water over and over again.

Over the next few months, he would spend a lot of his free time putting together his rudimentary little fountains and selling them in whatever city they happened to be in, mostly to restaurants who'd put them in their lobbies. Pretty soon, he realized he might really have a business here and the magazine crew life never really appealed to him or Jeanne anyway.

OK, thought Dale, let's build fountains.

And, in 1960, there was no other place to become a manufacturer of cosmopolitan, sophisticated display equipment like New York City. Especially for a kid from Marion, Indiana.

THREE

They called the company Real Fountains, Inc. and took a small space on the eleventh floor of 264 West 40th Street, just off Eighth Avenue, in the heart of the Garment Center.

It was a twenty story building that looked just like every other building in the Garment Center. Some were a little bigger, some a little smaller, but they were all originally built of sandy-colored bricks sometime in the 1910s and 20s. By the 1960s the sandy colored bricks had all turned kind of a dull brown.

The Garment Center moves a little bit this way and that, but generally is thought to consist of the area bordered by 40th Street on the north, 36th Street on the south, Eighth Avenue on the west and Broadway on the east. It's mostly two blocks wide, though, because Seventh Avenue runs between Broadway and Eighth Avenues.

The area hasn't changed all that much since the early 60s. There are still guys pushing carts laden with bolts of cloth, semi-finished clothing and brand spanking new duds on hangers and wrapped in plastic. Guys push around carts of buttons, collars, elastic, thread, accents of all kinds, sewing machines and everything else that moves from one small factory to another within a couple of city blocks. Back in the 60s, most of the pushcart guys were Puerto Rican, but since that time, guys from all over Central and South America, Africa and Asia have moved in and that part of the industry is nicely integrated.

Trucks still dominate the narrow streets, everything from tractor trailers to vans to step-ups to the ubiquitous overnight delivery trucks. Traffic was horrendous then and has remained that way to this day.

The Polish guys called it 'korek'. I'll say this one more time: I'll spell everything Polish in phonetics. Please forgive me. If any Polish people are reading this, they can take it up with Tovarish Piltsultski.

When they wanted to curse the traffic, they'd say, "Korek, kuravamotch!" 'Kuravamotch' means 'sonofabitch' or something really close to it. I learned to use it all the time. The other word we'd use to curse something was 'skurivassin', which means roughly the same thing, I think, only worse. Even among the new Polish recruits, kuravamotch would be greeted by raised eyebrows and a chuckle, but skurivassin would bring wide-eyed surprise and howls of laughter.

All the big fashion houses have quarters in the Garment Center, but most of those are over on Seventh Avenue, in the high rent district. Over where we were, there are little mom 'n pop operations, button guys, ribbon guys, shoulder pad guys, accent guys. People who have lived month-to-month their entire lives from the time they were (mostly) young immigrants until they've shriveled up and walk all bent over.

They all look poor, but I know better. If you look poor, you can negotiate far better deals – on both ends – than if you look like you're flush. We had a bunch of these people in the building that looked like they couldn't buy a canary bird a lunch, but would spend six weeks in Miami every winter. The elevators were always full of people crying poormouth, except for six weeks during the winter.

264 West 40th Street had three passenger elevators and an ancient manually-controlled freight elevator. It had two entrances, one for people and one for freight, albeit with people attached to the freight. Hand trucks were everywhere.

Back when Dale and Jeanne moved in, there was a little lunch counter in the back of the freight entrance.

Because there was only one freight elevator, guys would line up, sometimes seven or eight deep to be taken upstairs. I don't know why that little lunch counter closed. Seemed like a little gold mine to me. And I don't think a health inspector ever even knew it was there, let alone inspected it. At least the roaches didn't seem to worry, scurrying about on the counter with impunity. And the mouse droppings could be cleared off every morning with a single swipe of a greasy old rag. I'm sure the old guy who ran the counter was selling shots of booze, too, because there were always those little white paper cups laying around, like the kind you get in a dentist's chair.

I figured the old guy who ran it either died or decided to live full time in Bal Harbour.

The first few years Dale and Jeanne were at 264, the super was an elderly gentleman by the name of Mr. Edgar. Mr. Edgar was a true gentleman who hailed from Britain. He had a terrific accent and spoke softly. His clothes were always neat and pressed and everybody thought the world of him.

At the time, we were kids, maybe nine to thirteen years old, me and Iz and my sister, Jean. She was nine, I was thirteen. Iz was somewhere in between. My mom and Jean and I were visiting from Syracuse. Liverpool, actually. My dad had died suddenly of a heart attack while we were eating lunch the prior July. Bang. Dead.

Brutal.

Anyway, Dale and Jeanne and my mom and us kids invited Mr. Edgar around the corner to Smith's for a drink and/or some food.

He probably had coffee.

Smith's was great.

Eighty-five cents for a shot at the bar and a huge steam table full of what I now realize was fat-and-cholesterol-laden food at the back.

Jean got a knockwurst. And, just like all kids, took too big a bite. Next thing we all knew, she was choking, right there in front of us. "Ohmigod!", cried Mr. Edgar in his finest British accent. As we all sat there on our hands, mouths agape, Dale reached into her mouth, pulled out the offending wurst and all was well. Mr. Edgar sat there and wiped his brow with an immaculate handkerchief, saying, "Oh deah. Oh deah me." He had really cared. And this was the Garment Center.

He also cared a lot about another guy that used to hang around Real Fountains on the eleventh floor. His name was Max Kamp and he was a pretty young guy at the time, probably thirty or so. Max had taken shrapnel to the head in Korea and they'd had to put a metal plate in his head where his skull used to be.

Jeanne and Dale knew him from the magazine business and he was a nice, polite, hardworking guy. Along the way, that plate in his head started to sour or something because he began to lose his mind. Not in a bad way, he just gradually shut out the world.

Jeanne and Dale took pity on him (they took pity on everybody) and would pay him piecework for assembling little parts that went into the fountains. Pretty soon, though, ol' Max began just sitting there, staring off into space. Being who they were, Jeanne and Dale would give him money anyway, so he could eat and pay whatever paltry sum his flea-bitten hotel room cost.

Max went downhill from there. He'd taken to laying on the garbage bags in the hallway in front of the freight elevator. In those days, before plastic bags, the garbage bags were made out of heavy meshed twine and had to be emptied every night into a large dumpster. That was one of Mr. Edgar's jobs, too. Max would lie on those garbage bags all day and sleep. It troubled Mr. Edgar no end. Jeanne and Dale, too. But nobody knew where he'd come from or whether he had any family anywhere or not. And nobody had the money or real inclination to deal with what was, obviously, a real problem.

Mr. Edgar would go to the lunch counter in the freight entrance and bring Max lunch and coffee and things. Every day. With his own money. For months. Never said a thing, just did it. He'd go into the office and commiserate with Jeanne and Dale about Max's deteriorating condition, shake his head and "tut-tut" a few times. You could tell he really cared and did what he could to help the poor guy.

It all took care of itself, though, like so many things do. One day, Max just didn't show up. Never showed up again. Just disappeared. Mr. Edgar felt bad.

Just a little while after that, Dale and Jeanne got their first big order.

There was a guy named Joe Kipness who was opening a first-rate, high class Polynesian restaurant in the same building as the Winter Garden Theater up on Broadway between 50th and 51st Streets, across from Jack Dempsey's.

It was to be called The Lanai.

Kipness spared no expense. It was an absolute showplace, with a huge mural of Polynesia behind the bar that had lighting that would change the scene from day to night, even had lightning and thunder as special effects. There were aquariums (aquaria?) everywhere, full of exotic fish. Huge bamboo poles running everywhere among what looked like a jungle. A number of different levels so you never felt like you were in a restaurant – like you were in your own Lanai, as it were.

By the way, as the bamboo poles dried, they'd sometimes split at inopportune times, like when diners were present. It sounded like a gunshot going off, people would scream and waiters, properly dressed in South Sea attire, would scurry around calming everyone's nerves. At least it gave the people who'd come in from Des Moines something to talk about when they got home.

Dale had invented this little candle thing, with a spring hidden under the candle that would push up the candle continuously while not causing any wax to drip. It had a little marble base and a milk glass chimney. Kipness ordered a slew of them – one for each table with probably two or three back-ups for each. He also ordered all kinds of flowing streams and dripping water effects. The whole order was well over ten thousand dollars. Kipness became rich because he knew all the tricks.

He bought the restaurant, the finest kitchen equipment, all the furnishings, silverware, uniforms – everything – on credit.

He held a huge grand opening, complete with celebrities and press coverage out the wazoo. It was a smashing success.

The next day he declared bankruptcy.

Back in those days, the bankruptcy laws were a lot more lax than they are today. Kipness got the bankruptcy court to rule that he'd have to pay four cents on every dollar he owed.

He paid everybody their four percent and set up another corporation to buy all the assets. He changed the name to the Hawaii Kai, got a new sign, printed new stationery and menus and the Lanai was reborn as the Hawaii Kai in just under six weeks. All for four percent of the original budget. Sweet.

He did have a heart, though. He told Dale and Jeanne he didn't want to cheat a couple of kids who were from out of town and were just starting out. The other companies he owed money to, fine. Hey – he was dealing with those companies on a regular basis with his other properties. It was just business and he figured they were cheating him anyway. Fuck 'em.

He told Dale and Jeanne he couldn't pay them cash for what he owed them, but they were more than welcome to eat and drink until they were paid in full. I think they would have preferred cash over pupu platters, but what were they gonna do?

I spent some very fine hours there as a teenager, devouring flaming pupu platters and egg rolls and listening to the bamboo explode overhead.

Kipness went on to make a fortune on the Hawaii Kai and, a few years later, opened Joe's Pier Fifty-Two on 52nd Street, just east of Seventh Avenue. I spent many a night at that bar. Too many nights. He should've had better bar snacks than those nasty little Pepperidge Farms Goldfish, though. I wonder if it's still there. Probably not.

FOUR

Dale was really a pretty good inventor who had an excellent mechanical mind. Just the idea of manufacturing water display fountains, with all the little parts and fittings and things that went into making them would be pretty daunting for most people. Well, the idea of making fountains at all probably hasn't crossed the minds of more than a handful of people anyway, daunting or not.

The fountains were all self-contained and were in the shape of bowls, in different diameters. Each fountain had one or two round copper spray rings with little copper 'jets' sticking up every inch-and-a-half all the way around the ring. Each of these jets had a little brass 'jet cap' at the top. The water spouted through the jet cap. The way it worked was that water would course through the copper ring, and then through the smaller diameter jets through the even smaller jet caps. That three-time restriction of the water flow would enable the water to shoot up into the air. The water would be recycled by a submersible pump attached to the bottom of the bowl.

He invented a way to house 150-watt PAR 38 light bulbs in the middle of the fountain so they would light up the water rising through the air above the bowl.

Over time, he added a cam-type timing device attached to three different colored lights in the fountain: red, blue and green. This way the lights would turn on and off in different combinations during a one-minute cycle. The different combination of the colored lights going on and off would provide eleven different colors during the cycle, prompting the infamous selling point, "Eleven exciting and dramatic color changes per minute".

At first, the bowls were made of anodized aluminum. He had to have molds made and a spinning factory would make the raw aluminum bowls. The bowls would then be shipped to the anodizer before being shipped back to 264. Anodizing somehow infuses a colored protectorant into the aluminum and makes it shine. Real Fountains used gold and silver colored anodizing.

Dale always hated paying someone else to build his stuff, even the raw materials, so he was always inventing ways to bring the manufacturing process in-house.

Pretty soon he had the idea that the bowls could be made of fiberglass, not aluminum. For one thing, the hardness or softness of the water in different parts of the country would cause the aluminum bowls to 'pit', a nice way of saying that holes would appear in the bowls. A number of fine establishments began complaining that water was leaking all over their counters, tabletops and other set decorations that held their fountains.

Dale also was quite averse to refunds.

Fiberglass wouldn't pit nor would holes appear. He had the molds, all he had to do was to learn how to work with fiberglass.

Raw fiberglass really sucks.

It comes in rolls and is actually glass fibers, hence the name. If you get some of that fiber on your body, tiny pieces of glass embed themselves in your skin. It itches like hell. You can't wash it off, it's down in your little pores. Get some of that stuff on you and you'll itch for a good eight hours, if not longer.

The thing is, once you're used to working with fiberglass, it doesn't bother your skin at all. Maybe you build up a tolerance or something. Until you do, though, it's brutal. You have to wear a long-sleeved shirt and gloves and good, heavy pants and you have to change in and out of them before and after working with the stuff.

Little Joe Lipkowski became the fiberglass expert. Joe was a young guy, short (hence the name) and bull-strong. Real nice guy and one of the only normal people in the operation.

Joe was pretty much relegated to the fiberglass room and a nastier room was hard to find, even in the Garment Center.

It was full of rolls of glass, 55-gallon drums of polyester resins, acetone and methyl-ethyl ketone, along with various and sundry paints, lacquers and glass dusts. The room measured about forty feet by twenty-five feet and there wasn't a more environmentally lethal thousand square feet in Manhattan.

Acetone is a particularly interesting chemical. It's what fingernail polish remover is made of, only it smells far worse in its native state. It eats anything that has a polyester base, meaning plastics, fabrics, or any other myriad things we take for granted.

My sister, Jean, had bought a new blouse. Being a kid, she slopped something on it one day – I think it was ink. No problem, said Dale, acetone will take it out. Off he went into the fiberglass room with Jean's new blouse, poured some acetone into an aluminum bucket and dunked the blouse in it. Ten seconds later he pulled it out. Or, he pulled the collar out. That's all that was left of the blouse.

A few years later, I would drive through the Lincoln Tunnel to Fort Lee and fill up four 55-gallon drums with acetone and drive them back to 264, not realizing an errant spark would've lit me, the van and anything else in a half-block area up like a three-ton roman candle. I could have, unknowingly, become the first of the suicide bombers.

During my tenure, though having absolutely nothing to do with me, we progressed from "hand layup" fiberglassing to spray fiberglassing. The difference is that, instead of cutting up pieces of fiberglass rolls and laying them on the molds by hand, spray fiberglass consists of the glass in rope-like form that is fed through an automatic chopper along with the chemicals and sprayed onto the mold.

We got the new equipment from Fritz.

Fritz Lechner was a Nazi. A real Nazi. He had been in the Hitler Youth Corps back in Germany toward the end of World War II, but I think he was too young to fight. Boy, he believed in ol' Adolph, though.

Fritz lived down in Kennett Square, Pennsylvania, was one of Real Fountains' competitors and a friend of Jeanne and Dale. By 'friend', I mean they had a love/hate relationship. You kind of couldn't help but like Fritz once in a while, but at heart he was an asshole. A Nazi asshole.

To wit, his Kennett Square neighbors contacted the local authorities who presented Fritz with a cease and desist order for flying the Nazi flag from a fifty-foot flagpole in his back yard. He had a couple of lovely aquariums but they were filled with little sharks. He'd get drunk at our office and start singing loud Nazi songs out in the hallway. The Garment Center, in general, and our building, in particular, was probably ninety percent populated with Jews, many of whom still had tattoos on their forearms. Fritz could be such an asshole.

Fritz was also as thick through the head as a bull through the ass. When he came to America, he refused to learn English. German was the mother tongue. The stupid bastard ate nothing but hamburgers for the first year-and-a-half he was here because that's all he knew how to order.

I think Dale was originally introduced to Fritz by Roy, Dale's dad. At some point, Roy thought he'd sell more magazine subscriptions if his salespeople were more "continental" – in other words, European. He figured Mr. and Mrs. America would be wowed by a French or German or Norwegian or Swedish accent or something and would jump at the chance to buy Life, Look and Readers' Digest from them. He put ads in newspapers seeking out young, attractive Europeans and I guess Fritz answered an ad.

Fritz wasn't getting with the program, though. Seems every time somebody answered the door and a conversation was struck up, Fritz would expound the virtues of Nazism and how the Germans should have won the war. "Everybody would be beautiful! Look at me – blonde, blue-eyed, muscular build, strong jaw – a perfect specimen of humanity!" Pretty soon Roy pawned off Fritz on Dale. A real solid father-son relationship.

Anyway, we bought the fiberglass spray equipment from Fritz.

I got the assignment to go pick it up.

I rented a truck with an eighteen-foot bed – a huge thing – from Ajax Rental or something like that, one of those places down on Eleventh Avenue in the meat-packing district. I had never driven anything that big before – I felt like one of those delivery guys that always double-parked on 40th Street.

I took John and several of the Polish guys. John and I sat in the front and the Polish guys stood or sat in the back of the truck – in the dark and fumes all the way from midtown to Kennett Square and back. Today, people who drive trucks with a slew of immigrants in the back get charged with human trafficking and sent away for up to twenty years.

The whole trip was pretty uneventful, but we did have one kind of nerve-wracking incident. We stalled out and came to a complete stop in the middle lane of seven lanes on the New Jersey Turnpike. The truck had a manual choke that I had no idea how to use and I guess I hadn't disengaged it all the way or something. The damned truck started coughing and pitching and I couldn't get any power and John started screaming and semis were rolling past us at seventy, three or four feet from our doors and we finally just came to a complete stop. I had the very real expectation of us getting rear-ended by some fuel tanker out of Port Elizabeth and disappearing forever in a giant ball of flame. John was apoplectic – screaming *kuravamotch!, skurivassin!* and a whole lot of other words I didn't know, but I bet the guys in the back simply thought we'd arrived at our destination early. I finally got the truck started again and the rest came off without a hitch.

I think the fiberglass eventually killed Dale, but nobody quite knows.

FIVE

Almost every guy who worked for us was Polish.

At the very beginning, Dale hired Old John. At the time he wasn't Old John, he was just John. I can't remember his last name, but he was originally from Poland. He was the foreman of the place.

I was just a kid, so I don't remember him too well. I remember he used to smoke cigar butts stuck into a pipe, though. I don't ever remember seeing him smoke a full cigar, just the butts in the pipe. He'd stick the end that goes in your mouth into the pipe and light the other end, which stuck straight up. It looked like a mini-locomotive in his mouth. John was built like a bullet, or a fire hydrant. He had a big round head, gaps between all his teeth and no neck. He always had a leer on his face. Not a smile, but a leer. Freaked the shit out of my sister and Iz, I know that.

He hired John Bubniak as his second-in-command. Bubniak was heads and tails a better worker than Old John, who always made a very visible point of doing as little as he could. He thought he was indispensable and every time Dale or Jeanne would encourage him to put a nickel in it, he'd just sit there with that leer and the pipe with the cigar in it and say, "Meester, meester, meester" or "Meesus, meesus, meesus" and slow down even more.

Dale fired his ass and Bubniak got his job. Actually, Dale had a little fun firing Old John. One day he said to him, "John, I don't know how we'd ever get along without you, but starting tomorrow morning, we're going to try." Old John gave him the leer and it took him half an hour before he figured out that Dale had fired his sorry ass.

The way it worked is that John Bubniak had some friends back in Poland. At the time, a certain number of people could come to this country on a six-month work visa. Those were the guys we hired. John's friends and friends of John's friends and so on.

We usually had seven or eight of them on the payroll at any given time. They'd all live together in a cheap one or two bedroom apartment in Greenpoint, Brooklyn. They all brought their own lunches and I swear they all lived on Wonder Bread and bologna for the entire six months they were here.

We paid them minimum wage (hell, I was paid minimum wage for a long time!) and they (we) made time-and-a-half for everything over forty hours a week. These guys would work from seven in the morning 'til eight at night six days a week. I usually did the payroll on Fridays and it was nothing to see guys with 75-80 hours in a week.

They'd spend next to nothing to live for the six months and go home to Poland with up to five grand in their pockets. That five grand would buy them an apartment and a car and would mean that they had moved to the upper middle class. Amazing.

I really like most of them a lot. A lot of them were smart, as educated as one could get in Poland in the early 70s, and hard-working. Great senses of humor, too.

We always greeted each other with "chesch", which is Polish for hello and goodbye, like 'aloha'. "Naygoose" meant somebody who claimed to be working hard but was really nothing but a goldbrick. I wish we had an English word for "naygoose", We certainly have enough people who fit the profile. "Naygoosey" was plural for "naygoose".

So, I'd always walk into the shop, announcing, "Chesch, naygoosey", which brought any of the new guys up short. I'd go up to a new guy and say "Chesch, kuravamotch" (hello, you sonofabitch). "Robitch! Robitch!" (work!, work!). They either got it or they didn't. Eventually, though, they knew I was on their side (I worked as hard as any of them). Plus, I did their payroll and could flip 'em an hour or two if the mood struck me. "Shtoddy" means "boss". Actually, it means "old man", but 'old man' like in the navy: "Hurry up, the old man's coming." Dale was Shtoddy.

"Shtodda" is the same, but the feminine form. Jeanne was "Shtodda".

We all referred to Dale as Shtoddy Naygoose, the boss who doesn't do anything but talks a good game.

"Peeyock" means drunk. "Peeyonni" means in the process of drinking.

After one of those martini lunches, Bubniak would seek me out, in front of Dale and Jeanne or not. "Shtoddy?"

"Peeyock", I'd reply, Dale and Jeanne being none the wiser.

If John came looking for Dale during the lunch hour, it would be, "Shtoddy?"

"Peeyonni."

Went on like that for years.

Don't get me wrong. Dale and Jeanne worked hard, real hard, to build up the fountain business.

When they first moved to New York, they rented a one bedroom apartment in a four story walk-up at 136 West 48th Street, up over the Monte Rosa Italian Restaurant, owned and operated by Jack Lipschitz, a Jewish guy.

They were on the fourth floor.

The Chefs des Cuisine had an office on the second floor. I never quite knew what The Chefs des Cuisine was but I think it was an organization of French chefs, or so the name implied. They were a bunch of stuffy old Frenchmen, I knew that. If you ever ran into one of them on the stairs, they pretended not to notice you but got a look on their face like they smelled something distasteful. I figured they were probably old guys out of work and everything seemed distasteful.

Jack – we called him Jack Monte Rosa – lived on the third floor with his wife Viola, who demanded everyone refer to her as *Miss* Viola. Miss Viola was crazy as a shithouse rat.

She'd wear this orange straw hat that had the word *Cuernavaca* embroidered onto it and would come out on the landing, naked as a jaybird except for the hat, and scream the longest litany of profanity I've ever heard in my life – even to this day. We had to tiptoe and duck down past her apartment on the way up or down because she would lurk in her apartment, looking through the peephole. If she heard or saw you, out she'd pop, naked and in the hat, screaming like a fucking banshee. She'd get all foamy at the mouth and the veins in her forehead would pop out. She scared the shit out of me and Jean, but Iz would just laugh like hell and egg her on.

Jack could generally hear the screaming from his post at the front of the Monte Rosa and would climb the stairs and calm Miss Viola and herd her back into the apartment.

Poor old bat.

Bill Ruben lived across the hall from Jeanne and Dale with his much younger, very English wife, Cynthia. Billy Ruben's claim to fame was that he'd written a book about Alger Hiss, Whitaker Chambers and the Pumpkin Papers case. Billy was a died-in-the wool communist and conspiracy theorist. Man, the arguments he used to have with Dale about JFK's death and the Warren Commission. His and Cynthia's place was full of books.

Ruben was about five-nine, weighed in about 240, was bug-eyed and had a Ben Franklin-type hairdo – nothing on top, but pretty long on the sides and back. He had the biggest bulbous nose you ever saw. Always carried a sheaf of unruly papers under his arm, ostensibly working on his next great book which, of course, never got written.

I really thought the world of Billy Ruben. He could drive you nuts, though.

He always asked a bazillion questions about the most mundane shit.

"I saw Joe Jaboni walking down 56th Street yesterday. Hadn't seen him in four or five years."

Billy: "Which side of the street was he walking on?"

"Uh, the uptown side, I think. Anyway, he lost his job and is living at the 'Y'."

Billy: "The 'Y'?" Which one?"

"I don't have any idea."

"How did he lose his job?"

"I didn't ask him."

"Where was he going?"

"I don't know."

"Did he look like he was in a hurry?"

"How the hell do I know if he looked like he was in a hurry? He was walking down the street."

"East 56th or West 56th?"

That type of thing. Conversation with Billy Ruben could go on for hours, if you let them.

Ruben, never having any money had, by the mid-seventies, perfected the art of eating and drinking for free. Cynthia, after receiving her citizenship papers, had dropped him like a bad habit years earlier. Most of the saloons and bars in the area used to serve hot and cold hors d'oeuvres during happy hour that generally lasted from five o'clock until 7:30 or until the grub was gone.

Billy would saunter in to one of the joints, grab a plate of food, and see if anybody he knew was at the bar. If there was, he'd set his plate down next to the person and maybe, *maybe*, order a drink. But only if his buddy hadn't offered to buy him one in the first five or ten minutes. Billy would ask his friend if he was meeting any of the 'gang' at this particular establishment a little later. If the answer was 'yes', Billy was in clover. He could just hang out 'til others arrived, swish his nearly empty glass around a few times and each of the 'gang' would end up buying him drinks. Several platefuls and seven or eight scotches later, Billy would head home. All for about three bucks.

If, perchance, Billy didn't run into anybody in the first joint, he'd just eat one plate of food, set the empty plate on the bar, and wander off to the next watering hole where the whole process would start anew.

He fancied himself quite the horseplayer, but there was never a more died-in-the-wool chalk player that ever walked the earth. He wouldn't even think of betting on a horse whose odds were longer than even money. And then, he'd bet 'show', meaning that his horse could come in first, second or third and he'd be a winner.

He'd walk around like the cock of the walk, announcing he'd bet a hundred on somebody like Secretariat. What he didn't say was that he'd bet Secretariat to show. That was like betting on the sun coming up tomorrow morning. Secretariat would go off at something like one-to-five, meaning that if you bet five bucks on him to win and he did win, you'd walk off with your five and a buck from the track. Wow. Betting Secretariat to show in that race would have earned you fifty cents for your five.

Billy's hundred to show would net him ten bucks. Double wow. Man, though to hear Billy tell it, he had scoped the Racing Form (known in those days as the 'Telly', or Morning Telegraph) from stem to stern, using his ultra-secret race-doping methodology that combined the horses' number of starts, money won, positions at the eighth-pole in each race, wind speed and direction and phase of the moon. Dude, it was Secretariat, fer chrissakes. The goddam pari-mutuel show ticket had more souvenir value than the ten bucks he won.

Billy bought my old window-mounted air conditioner and I took it over to his apartment in a cab the morning of July 4, 1976. The day of the big bicentennial. The real news of that day, however, was that the Israelis had rescued their hijacked countrymen in one of the slickest military operations ever attempted, the raid on Entebbe.

Idi Amin's goons had hijacked a plane and were holding scores of hostages at the Entebbe airport in Uganda, thousands of miles deep in Africa. Under commander Uri Dan, Yanni Netanyahu (Benjamin's brother) led the world's most elite troops under the radar all the way in, killed all the bad guys and had gotten every single hostage out and free. Netanyahu was the only good guy killed, if I remember correctly. It mesmerized the world, along with me and Billy Ruben and his new air conditioner. Man, did the questions fly that morning.

He and I had nothing to do to celebrate the bicentennial and no one to do it with, so we went down to 264, made our way up onto the roof and watched the Parade of Tall Ships sail up the Hudson, drinking warm beer for most of the afternoon. Truth be told, I didn't mind hanging out with Billy. We could commiserate about the lowly Republicans and how they were run by big business and the fact that they had a conspiracy to take over the country. Now that I think of it, we might have been right.

The last time I saw Billy Ruben he was sitting in one of those vest-pocket parks on East 54th Street, just east of Madison. I saw him, he didn't see me. I didn't go up to him because it had been years and I didn't want to deal with all the questions. Too bad. I wish now I would have.

I wonder if he's still alive.

****

One time my grandfather, Newt, was staying with Jeanne and Dale on West 48th Street. He was making dinner for Iz and I have no idea why he did what he did, but this was a beaut. He seemed to be warming an unopened can of Franco-American Spaghetti in a pan full of water on the stove. Maybe he thought the pan was too grungy to actually put the spaghetti into or something. Anyway, he forgot it was on the stove and the water started boiling. He and Iz were watching television or something when BOOM!, the can exploded. There was spaghetti plastered everywhere, the walls, the ceiling, the cupboards, refrigerator, floor – everywhere. He could curse with the best of them and this time the air turned a very surly blue. He spent the next couple of hours cleaning everything he could reach, which did not include the ceiling. The ceiling remained a piece of food art until they moved, three or four years later.

I never saw so many roaches in my life as were in that apartment. Jeanne and Dale did their best to try and keep them under control, but it was a continual losing battle. About once a week, they'd get a couple of cans of roach spray and attack the place with a vengeance. As the roaches ran out of their myriad hiding places, Jeanne would run around sucking them up with a vacuum cleaner. Once the battle was over, Dale would tear down to the street with the vacuum cleaner bag and drop it into the nearest trash can. Yuck.

I was visiting them one New Year's Eve, had to be the year 1965 turned to 1966 or '66 to '67. There was a little liquor store on the next block, on 47th Street. Dale and I walked over to purchase some hooch. Even though I was only 14 or 15, they'd let me drink dry vermouth on the rocks. I didn't know any better and thought it was great. As we walked into the store, there were three young New Year's Eve merrymakers arguing with the proprietor. Something about proof of age or something, like it ever mattered in that little dump, especially on New Year's Eve.

Anyway, Dale decided to ride in on his white horse and said, "Don't worry, Mr. Proprietor, I'm buying whatever it is they want and I'm certainly old enough." As the guy shrugged, the three guys whirled around in amazement of their good luck.

I couldn't believe my eyes. It was Snover!

Tom Snover! From home! From Liverpool High School! Snover played first trumpet in our junior high school band and I played first trombone. He and I got into a heap of trouble one day when our band was invited to play at another of the schools in our area and Snover and I fucked around through the whole thing, throwing spitballs back and forth at each other. We played our parts really well, we just fucked around too much. It bonded us for life.

And there, in a phone booth-sized, hole-in-the-wall liquor store on West 47th Street in New York Goddam City, was Snover in all his drunken glory. He'd talked his folks into letting him go to New York for New Year's. They must have been comatose for allowing that.

"Jimmy", he said once he finally focused on me and realized we were both in New York City, not Liverpool, "what the hell are you doing here? Do you come down with us? I don't remember you on the ride down here."

"No, you idiot. I'm here visiting my uncle and aunt."

"Hey! Why don't you come with us?"

And get arrested? Or rolled? "Uh, Nah. You guys go on ahead. I'll catch up with you just before midnight. Where are you gonna be?"

"Times Square!"

"Good. Why don't I meet you guys in Times Square about a quarter to twelve?"

"Alright! Check out what we're wearing so you'll be able to recognize us."

"Got it. Jeans and brown jackets. Don't worry, I'll find you." Right. Save me a good spot among your million or so new best friends. And hold your breath 'til I get there.

"Great. And, thanks again, mister."

"Happy New Year", said Dale.

Talk about a small world.

A year or two later, Jeanne and Dale moved into a brand new twenty story apartment building at 52nd and Eighth, 888 Eighth Avenue.

Things were looking up at Real Fountains.

SIX

Dale had a big idea.

Most racetracks had a big pond or lake in the infield. What better place to build a huge fountain?

He actually designed and sold one to Suffolk Downs Racetrack outside of Revere, Massachusetts, a suburb of Boston. Suffolk Downs was a fairly decent track, but certainly a step down from the New York tracks, like Aqueduct, Belmont or Saratoga. It was kind of on the level of Rockingham Park in Nashua, New Hampshire or Narragansett Park in Narragansett, Rhode Island.

He got the go-ahead to install it in the early Spring, when the racing was still in Florida for the Winter. My mom and Jean and I met them there during our Easter break and I was of the age where I could actually be of assistance. Damn.

It was really strange being the only people in this huge racing establishment that, during the racing season, would hold 20,000 people on a good day. We scoped out the entire complex, opening any and every door we could find. We didn't find any hidden treasures or anything, but it made for some fun afternoons.

When the adults located me during one of our recon missions, I was enlisted to help carry stuff from the parking lot to the pond. Mostly, I had to carry these long lengths of copper pipe and the trek was about a half-mile in each direction, having to walk from the pond, across the racing surface, through the grandstand, past the entrance and into the only parking lot that wasn't locked. And back again.

And it was cold. Somewhere in the low- to mid-40s. I didn't have any gloves and, it being Easter vacation and Spring and all, I was sporting a snazzy new windbreaker. I might as well have been buck naked. I was frozen. And those forty degree copper pipes turned my hands to cold stone in no time. Miserable.

But there was a saving grace. We had access to the tote board, that big board in the middle of the infield that displayed the current odds during races. The numbers were displayed by electric light bulbs that threw off a ton of heat, especially if the number read "8", when most of the bulbs were lit. Dale found a tester's panel inside the tote board and set all the numbers to "8". I'd make a trip that took maybe twenty minutes and warmed up in front of the 8s for ten minutes. Problem somewhat solved.

Dale needed a couple of extra adult hands on board besides him, Bubniak and half of me. His brother Paul had his magazine crew scorching some town in New England and sent over a couple of guys, including some doofus named Danny. Danny was so dim he couldn't have gotten a job as one of the bulbs on the tote board. He reminded me of Goober, that guy on the old Andy Griffith Show.

Danny was elected to do something with the equipment out in the pond. Dale had him don full rubber waders, the kind that have suspenders that go over your shoulders to hold them up. The front of them went up chest high. Danny looked quite proud of them.

The afternoon was wearing on when Danny came running in to our headquarters in the grandstand, screaming and cursing and moving funny.

"Danny! What's wrong?!?" Everybody figured he'd electrocuted himself or something. It was something we'd been expecting.

"Quick! Help me get these goddam things off!"

Maybe Danny had encountered a piranha or snapping turtle or something out in the pond.

As the waders came off, about thirty gallons of 40 degree water slopped onto the floor. "What the hell happened?"

"I dropped my wrench in the water and bent down to pick it up. All this water rushed in. Christ, I can't even find my dick!"

Danny, the dim fucking bulb.

A few summers later, Real Fountains hit the big time as far as racetrack fountains: Aqueduct. The Big A. Top of the heap. Arguably the best, most popular racetrack in the world.

I've been in the money room at Aqueduct. Years earlier, a guy named Tommy Trotter was racing secretary and he was kind of friends with our family. His father, Tobe, had been a jockey's agent back in the dim, dark past, when my Uncle Johnny had been one of the nation's up-and-coming young riders. Tobe represented Uncle Johnny for a while and he was friends with Newt, my grandfather. That is, until Tobe went fishing in the Everglades one day and was never heard from again. Everybody figured a gator got him.

One Saturday when the family was at Aqueduct, we ran into Tommy. He asked me if I'd like to see the money room. Sure.

He took me into the area behind the pari-mutuel windows, which was plenty cool in and of itself. He led me into the middle where there was this steel spiral staircase, standing all by itself in the center of the room.

As we were ascending the stairs, I looked up and saw the stairs ended at a big box suspended from the ceiling. It had a door and no windows. Standing at the top of the stairs, in front of the door, was a guy with a tommy gun, a machine gun. He knew Trotter, waved us on by and unlocked the door. Inside the door was another guy with a machine gun. The room was nothing but shelves lining both sides of the room. The shelves were packed with piles of cash. A room full of cash.

I asked Tommy how much money was in there. "Oh, about 30 million", he said. Thirty million bucks. In cash. All bills. In something like 1964. No wonder they had guys with machine guns.

That was pretty cool.

The job at Aqueduct was a big one. The huge fountain in the lake in the infield would have a sixty-foot diameter outside spray ring and a thirty-foot inside ring. The jets had aerators built into them so the water shooting out of them looked very full-bodied, if you will.

Turned on, it looked like a huge, living wedding cake, with a big single jet in the middle soaring a good seventy-five feet in the air. It was outstanding in the fountain world.

Being older, I think I was eighteen, I was a big part of the whole set-up.

We set the thing up during the month of August, when New York racing spends its summer vacation at idyllic Saratoga Racetrack in upstate New York.

I drove back and forth from Manhattan to Queens every day for a three or four weeks in one of my all-time dream cars, Dale's 1960 white Caddy convertible. It was at least three blocks long and fins that were eight or ten feet high. Or so it seemed. And, Dale had had an air conditioner put in so you could cruise with the top down AND the air on. Put the top down on that baby, crank up the air and the radio with Tommy James and the Shondells doing "Crimson and Clover" or Marvin Gaye asking the outrageously philosophical musical question "What's Goin' On?" and you were smokin'!

The Caddy had had some hard miles put on it though, somewhere north of a hundred thousand of them. By that summer, things were starting to go a little sour with it once in a while.

For example, you had to put the top up and down by hand and, with a car that size, it was like erecting and tearing down the big top of a three-ring circus. That's because the top had a leak somewhere in one of its hydraulic lines. It wasn't putting the top up and down that was the real problem. It was the fumes from the leaking hydraulic fluid. Whatever was in that fluid gave it a scent that was somewhere between flowery and oily.

It's hard to explain. But after inhaling it for an hour or so in Long Island Expressway traffic, the fumes started making me sleepy every time I drove the goddam thing. Ninety degrees, eighty percent humidity, sun beating down, doing a snappy thirty mph on the LIE and pretty soon I was dreaming I was driving. Lucky I didn't kill somebody.

Also, the Caddy had developed a nasty habit of overheating. Which meant I had to not only turn the air conditioner off, I had to turn the heat on full blast to bleed off the heat from the engine. So, ninety degrees, eighty percent humidity, a snappy thirty, breathing toxic hydraulic fluid and the heat going full blast – sometimes not even Tommy James and Marvin could help.

I told Dale it might be a good idea to get the hydraulic lines looked at. He thought that would cost a fortune and had a better idea. Good idea for him; shitty for me. We figured out the fumes were escaping up through the boot in the back, the area behind the rear seat that had a black canvas covering. The canvas had been torn for years.

"You know", said Dale, "if we sew up that hole in the boot, the hydraulic smell won't leak into the car. Just sew 'er up and she'll be good as new."

"Fine. Great idea. Where should we take it?"

"Take it, hell. We'll just sew it up ourselves." Which meant I would be the one doing the sewing.

Okay, fine.

We kept the car in a garage in the building next to 264. I went to the hardware at 38th and 8th – Scheman and Grant, run by little old Moe Scheman, who was two or three inches under five feet tall and looked like the little scientist guy on the Mighty Manfred cartoons, oversized glasses and all. I got a big needle and some pink twine-type stuff that Moe pawned off on me, telling me it'd work just fine.

Into the garage and up I went to the car which was parked on the third floor in this dark, airless – except for automobile exhaust – cavern of a room, crawled over some shit-ass old Chevy and into the back seat of the Caddy. The top was up and I couldn't see a damned thing. It was also at least one hundred and forty degrees in the back of that car.

I started sewing by sense of touch, which is kind of painful considering the thing you have to touch is the business end of a three inch needle. After about an hour, I had sewn about a five inch portion of what was a six foot tear in the fabric. My clothes were wet with sweat and sticking to me all over. And two of my fingers were bleeding from trying to find the goddam needle in the dark. This is fucking impossible, I thought.

I went next door and upstairs to the office.

"This is fucking impossible", I said, dripping sweat all over the orange and yellow shag carpet in the office.

Dale laughed like hell. "No, it isn't. Come on, I'll help you."

Fine, I thought, this'll show him. He won't stand for trying to sew that thing for five minutes. I'll be driving to the nearest convertible top repair shop within the half hour. Maybe I'll catch "Crimson and Clover".

Up we went. "OK", he said, handing the needle and pink twine back to me after I'd tried to pawn it off on him. "Hell, look – you're almost done."

What.

Dale's 'help' consisted of sitting in the front seat, whistling, and asking me every two minutes, "How you coming?"

Just fine, asshole.

He finally decided to swing into high gear with his assistance. Every ten minutes he'd start the car and blast the air conditioner for me so I wouldn't pass out from the heat. What he didn't take into consideration was the fact that every time he turned the car on, the hydraulic leak would start, the fumes would hit me directly in the face and it was all I could do to stay awake. I finished sewing a couple of hours later, thoroughly dehydrated and stoned out of my gourd on primo hydraulic fluid.

Nice idea but it didn't work. The next day I started out for Aqueduct and slipped into dreamland before I hit the Elmhurst Tanks.

We had a couple of gasoline-powered generators out at the site. Part of my job was to make sure there was always enough gas for them.

"Hey, Dale", I offered, "why don't we get four or five 55-gallon drums delivered?"

"Nah, we'll do it ourselves." Meaning, of course, I would do it myself. "Go to Scheman's and get a few gas cans and stop at a filling station on your way out." Fine. I was thrilled with this idea because it would afford me the opportunity of schlepping gas cans back and forth between the site and filling stations every other day for the next three weeks.

I told Scheman I needed five or six gas cans. He said, "Sure. What're you gonna do? Help 'em burn down Harlem?" Scheman was a prince.

I arrived at Aqueduct with a trunk full of gasoline but, natch, had to park behind the grandstand. I took a hand truck and ended up stacking five, full, five-gallon gas cans on top of each other. How the hell was I going to get this hand truck across the racing surface? I certainly wasn't going to walk back and forth ten times carrying them one at a time – I'd have to log a good four or five miles! The pond was a good half-mile from the car.

I found an Aqueduct guy and told him my problem. Lo and behold, he was actually a guy who could help. He told me I could take the hand truck through the tunnel that ran beneath the finish line out to the tote board. I had no idea such a thing ever existed. Sure, he said, how do you think we get the electricity out there? And other various and sundry items?

How cool!

That little idea worked great, except I had to go down five or six steps to enter the tunnel and up five or six steps to exit it. The tunnel was pretty wide, about six to eight feet. All the electrical cables ran along one of the walls. The tunnel was concrete and was nice and cool inside.

I didn't have to schlep gas quite as often as I'd feared, maybe only half a dozen times. I got into a little routine and it wasn't so bad. I only had one problem during this little exercise and it turned out to be a real pain in the ass.

Patty Walker, my sometimes girlfriend from Liverpool, was attending Pratt Institute in Brooklyn and spent all Summer there. I was scheduled to go out to pound brews or something with her and some of her friends one evening. Great, thought I, I'll schlep the gas in the late afternoon and head down the Belt Parkway to the Gowanus and over the Kosciusko Bridge and, owing to traffic and hoping I wouldn't pass out from the fumes, would get there around six or so.

I had bought a pair of white jeans. Not beige, white. Bright white. I'd break those babies in tonight. So, there I was, a hand truck loaded with gas, about to make my way through the tunnel to the site, make a quick drop-off and zoom – outta there. Maybe I'd get laid.

Somehow, going down the six stairs into the tunnel, the goddam load of gas cans shifted. I adroitly recovered the load in time, but the top can's screw top wasn't screwed on tight enough. The jarring caused it to open and a plume of unleaded rose into the air. As it always seems to do in moments like that, time slipped into slow motion. The plume came in my direction. I mouthed a slow-motion "No-o-o-o!" and the plume ended its journey on my leg, starting at the pocket and running down as far as my calf.

I had gasoline from my pocket to my crotch to my knee and beyond. It felt cold. Right!, I thought with false hope, because it's gasoline, it'll dry in no time. All will be well. Damned fool. It dried in no time, all right. It dried before I got to the end of the tunnel. It dried, however, a bright orange-yellow.

I finished my task and made my way back to the Caddy, with one bright white pant leg and one bright orange-yellow pant leg. Smelling like a filling station.

Sure made a hit with Patty's friends. When I walked in, they looked at me thinking I'd pissed my pants. Then I sat down and smelled like a gas station. I'm sure they thought I was some degenerate gas jockey who'd pissed himself on the way to the bar. I didn't even try to explain. I kept my eye on everybody's matches and cigarettes all night, though. Didn't get laid, either.

It was a great ride back to midtown, though. The scent of leaking hydraulic fluid and regular unleaded combined in such a way with the beer and the heater going full blast on a hot summer night had sent me into gales of hysterical laughter all the way up the Westside Highway from Chambers Street to the garage.

I had a notion to take the pants to the office, into the fiberglass room and dunk them in some acetone. Then I remembered my sister's shirt. I threw the pants away.

There were a couple of other goofy things I found myself involved in with the installation of the big fountain in the pond.

For one thing, a bunch of swans – check that, a gaggle of swans, I believe – lived at the pond and they had had a group of young 'uns not too long before we started. I think young swans are called signets. The mama and papa swans, mostly the mama swans, weren't used to having a bunch of humans screwing around in their pond. They were quite territorial. Actually, they were very territorial.

Have you ever had a thirty- or forty-pound swan running at you, full speed (which is fast!), neck straight out, pissed, and ready to take a big chunk out of your ass? We all did.

Most of the time, the swans would lie peaceably in wait until a couple of guys were carrying long pipes between them or otherwise had their hands full of something heavy and unwieldy. Just as the guys would think they had passed the danger point and the swans were letting them pass unaccosted, here they'd come. A swan bite in the ass is quite a painful thing, to which all the guys would attest.

The little swan/human racetrack infield pond drama was becoming quite disruptive to the installation process. Somebody had to act as a swan screen to keep them off the installers' asses. Me. I was the youngest and I wasn't sure if that meant Dale thought I was the most fearless or that I was the most expendable.

I spent several afternoons facing down angry swans, which was no mean feat. Sometimes they fell for my bravado and sometimes they didn't. I changed tactics on them constantly to keep them off guard.

Sometimes I'd run in a decoy direction away from the guys carrying stuff. Swans only run so long and so far – they don't want to get too far from the nest, so this wasn't overly taxing. Sometimes I attacked them back – a game of chicken with a fowl of a different stripe. This tactic was unnerving, probably for the swan, but I know it was for me. One would charge and I'd charge right back at her, screaming obscenities and flailing my arms like an idiot. Usually the swan backed off. A couple of times, though, we ended up on a collision course until I veered off at the last possible second. Each time, I got bit in the ass. Not the best part of the plan, but I had to mix it up.

I set an Aqueduct Racetrack record of sorts during this whole process.

I was the only person ever to have run across the finish line on the main track at the largest racetrack in the world in my underwear. In the middle of the afternoon. That record might still stand to this day. For a lot of reasons, I hope it does.

Bubniak and the others doing the installation always wore waders while they were in the pond. One afternoon, after having delivered my gas cans and transitioning on to my job as swan wrangler, Bubniak needed one more set of hands to hold some pipe while he welded it.

I, of course, was wader-less. "Take off pants. Nobody here", said John.

So I took off my pants, shirt, shoes and socks and waded in, clad only in a snazzy pair of Jockey briefs. God, wading into that pond was gross. The bottom was covered in the shit – guano? – of various aquatic and semi-aquatic birds: swans, geese, ducks, seagulls, terns and any other bird that thought of the pond as its own private shithole. The muck squished between my toes. Hey – anything went for an up-and-coming fountain tycoon, though, right?

About an hour later we were finished and I was wandering around waiting for the hot August sun and whatever breeze there was to dry my underwear while I was wearing them. I found myself up along the main track rail and was hit with a brainstorm. Maybe it was a brainfart.

"Hey, John! Watch this!" And I climbed under the rail, trotted maybe fifty yards up the track and turned for the finish line, running as fast as I could. I crossed under the finish line, looking for all the world like Roger Bannister breaking the four-minute mile. I turned to the grandstand and waved to the hundreds of thousands of imaginary admirers. Imagine my surprise when I heard the sound of several hands clapping and voices raised in honor of my achievement. A few of the Aqueduct workers had been goofing off in full view of my little escapade and were just showing their appreciation of a completely foolish waste of time.

SEVEN

The whole Aqueduct deal went sour, real sour.

It cost Real Fountains, of which now I was a real part, albeit a part time part, a ton of dough.

Dale had been given the go-ahead to build the big fountain by somebody real high up in the New York Racing Association, could've even been Tommy Trotter. The problem was, the NYRA administration changed sometime over that Summer.

The new guy or new guys coming in did what all new guys coming in do: "Freeze everything! Don't spend a nickel! I'm in charge here now and I want to know everything about everything and everybody before I make a single momentous decision! Where the hell are we getting our toilet paper and how much is it costing us? I wanna know and I wanna know now!" That type of corporate horseshit.

The big fountain fell somewhere between the cracks. There was a lot of back and forth correspondence authorizing us to buy the materials and install the thing. What I don't think existed was an actual purchase order, though Dale and Jeanne had been assured all along that they had a verbal go-ahead.

The fountain was even shown on nationwide television as part of the opening sequence in one of the major televised races early that September. We were hanging out at The Garden on 163rd Avenue in Jamaica, Queens, when the opening credits were shown on the television in The Garden's bar. There, right in the middle of the screen, with some sponsor's logo superimposed over it, was THE FOUNTAIN. Man, were we proud. And rightly so. It was terrific. The announcers even commented on the beautiful new fountain in the pond in the infield.

The incoming NYRA goons told us to go pound sand – they never officially ordered it and weren't going pay for it. Tough shit. Shoulda had a signed purchase order. Now get outta here.

We claimed that Aqueduct and the NYRA benefited monetarily for showing the fountain on TV. If they didn't really want it, why did they feature it on one of their major telecasts? Needless to say, the NYRA sent in their army of suits. And their asshole lawyers. And their deep pockets (that we helped line, goddammit). They were able to postpone this hearing and that hearing and filed this motion and that motion until hell wouldn't have 'em.

Real Fountains, Inc. and Jeanne and Dale didn't have the money to be able to compete with their corporate Chinese water torture terrorism. We eventually let it drop. Maybe we saw a couple of grand out of the whole deal but it didn't begin to cover our costs. As I write this, thirty-six years after the fact, let it be known that the New York Attorney General's office is investigating the entire NYRA and its upper management for little things like fraud and grand larceny. Two executives were just indicted the other day for cheating on the jockeys' scales. It's not the same people who were there way back then, but it's the very same culture.

Karma, as they say, is a motherfucker.

The Garden on 163rd Avenue in Jamaica was right up the street from Jamaica Ave. that had an el (elevated subway track) running over it.

The Garden was Real Fountains' home away from home for quite a while. Why we would pile into the Caddy and drive way the hell out to Queens never made much sense to me, but we did it anyway. I guess they poured good drinks, bought their fair share of rounds and would kindly extend the necessary credit while, at the same time, cashing checks on funds not yet covered by real money.

The Garden was run by Nick the Greek, Jr. Nick the Greek, Sr. was kind of old and very seldom around. Nick, Jr. was a real nice guy with an easy smile and a friendly demeanor. Served good food, too. He put raisins in this sauce that he used to cover this one chicken dish I ordered all the time.

The head bartender looked just like Mr. Clean. Exactly. We called him Mr. Clean. I remember he thought my mom was the most beautiful woman he'd ever seen and threatened to run away with her. She wasn't having any part of it, but I'll admit to having sweaty-palm thoughts about introducing Mr. Clean as my stepfather.

There was an old lady who hung out there. Her name was Hildy and she had glasses that made her eyeballs look about three inches in diameter. She was the original New York Mets fan. Really. She had a free set of box seats right behind the Mets' dugout, considered guys like Casey Stengel and Ed Kranepol and Gil Hodges personal friends and was interviewed on most Mets' telecasts during their early days. She knew more about baseball – especially the Mets and the National League – than anybody. She couldn't walk very well and kind of waddled slowly about.

She kept inviting me to go with her to a Mets' game, but I always put her off because I was afraid she'd die on me or something, right there in the middle of a seventh inning Mets rally. Or maybe it was looking at those three inch eyes that freaked me out. I don't know, but now I wish I'd have done it.

I especially didn't want to go with her that year, 1969. That was the year the Mets were good enough to win the World Series, but it was nip and tuck all summer long. I feared her heart would give out during the stretch that September. It didn't. As Tug said, "Ya gotta believe!"

One night we stopped at The Garden before heading up to Bristol, Rhode Island to visit Dale's brother Paul, the magazine crew guy. Dale got a call from Paul who told us he was sending some guy to meet us at The Garden to ride up to Bristol with us. He'd be there within the hour. Fine.

What Paul had neglected to tell Dale until just before he hung up was that the guy was an illegal alien, named Dominic, from Guatemala or somewhere who was being chased by the cops for kiting checks or something. He worked for Paul and Paul was kindhearted toward the downtrodden.

We had a carful of fountain stuff, me, Dale, Jeanne and their two cats, Ming and Susie. It was pretty crowded, even for the Caddy. Besides, we didn't want some guy who was on the lam and who didn't speak

English sitting in our midst for the three-hour drive. So, when Dominic showed up, we made him ride in the boot. Dale had finally relented to have the hydraulic leak fixed or the fluid had completely run out, I can't remember which, but the odor was pretty much gone.

Ol' Dominic never said a word, just crawled into the boot and fell asleep. With my past history with the boot, I was sure he'd died somewhere between New Haven and Providence. He made it, though. Must've had some pretty spaced-out dreams, though, because I still noticed an olfactory residue of the hydraulic fluid.

At the time, Paul was living on a boat he'd bought. It wasn't a boat, really, it was a huge fucking yacht. One hundred feet from stem to stern at the waterline. A hundred and five feet at the main deck level. It was built in 1920 and was a little scruffy around the edges but Paul was gradually taking care of that. It was so big, and Paul knew so little about boats from rowboat-sized on up, that he had to hire a captain every time he wanted it moved, which wasn't very often. Right now, it was docked in Bristol, Rhode Island.

We also referred to Paul as PL, for Paul Leroy. PL was a tall, slim, brooding guy who was Dale's older brother by three years. And, as one whose magazine crews were known for scorching the earth they passed over, he was half nuts. He used to be fully nuts, but had contracted diabetes and that had slowed him down considerably.

Back in the old days, PL had a pretty violent streak in him. He would routinely kick the living shit out of people who may or may not have been expecting it. He was always pretty boozed up back in those days. I'd seen him shaving in the morning with a razor in one hand and a bottle of Johnny Walker Black in the other.

Back in the day, PL never tied his shoes. The reason being they would be easier to take off and use as weapons in a bar fight or something. He'd whip off a shoe and beat guys with the heel. A dirty trick, but highly effective.

One time PL was standing at a bar minding his own business, according to him. Seems there was a guy standing next to him – sort of standing next to him. The guy had one good leg and one that was missing from the knee down. Used crutches, naturally. Supposedly the guy was becoming a little obnoxious to PL's way of thinking. PL politely asked him to hold it down and let everybody enjoy their drinks.

The guy told PL to go fuck himself. Without a word, PL kicked the guy's crutches out from under him, grabbed one in one hand and one of his untied shoes in the other and beat the guy unconscious in about fifteen seconds. An ambulance was called. The bartender asked PL why he had beaten a guy who had only one leg so mercilessly. He shrugged and said a cripple with only one leg ought to learn how to keep his fucking mouth shut.

PL lived in West Memphis, Arkansas when he wasn't on the road with a crew. He had a pretty good-sized farm and raised Santa Gratudis and Charolay bulls. We called him The Arkansas Cattle Baron.

The reason Paul got the boat is he figured it would be cheaper to keep his crew on it than in motels all the time. Picture that. A yacht basin in Bristol, Rhode Island, full of some of the fanciest and most expensive watercraft on the eastern seaboard, owned by old money and captains of industry. And the largest craft – the one everybody had to pass on the way down the main gangplank – was brimming with a couple dozen drunken misfits. And PL, walking around like Captain Fucking Queeg. It was beautiful. PL only had the boat a year or two. The idea of saving money on motels was offset by the inability to move from city to city as magazine crews do, especially those cities and towns that weren't along the coast. He should've thought of that.

He didn't sell the boat or anything. PL's yachtsmanship came to a much more ignominious and much more highly publicized end than that.

At some point, he'd had the boat moved to the south shore of Long Island. He'd moved a number of times during that period of time, but usually only fifty miles or so and was racking up expensive captain's charges each time. PL was tight as the bark on a tree. The boat was docked in Lido Beach and he wanted to move fifteen or so miles east, to Long Beach.

He figured, what the hell. How hard can it be? We'll back the goddam thing out, go out a mile or so, keeping the land in sight, turn the baby to the right and look for the Long Beach marina. Take less than an hour. So that's what they did. They, being a couple of his half-assed lieutenants and him.

Early one morning they backed the goddam thing out, went out a mile or so, had the land in sight, turned the baby to the right and a massive fog bank rolled in. In minutes they couldn't see a thing. Not fifty yards.

Now, of course, PL had no navigational systems on board, not ones that he knew how to use anyway. He got all balled up as to which direction they were moving in, didn't know if they were going forward or backwards because his diabetes had flared up and he went almost catatonic. They were all afraid they were heading straight out to sea, next stop the Azores or something.

Did PL cut the engines and drop the anchor? Hell, no. Just kept going around in what he thought were circles, waiting for the fog to lift. He had taken an insulin shot and was starting to come around.

All of a sudden, wham! The hundred-foot boat shuddered for one second and came to a complete dead stop, with its bow firmly imbedded in something they couldn't see. Everybody on board was certain they'd hit something out at sea and they were going to pull a Titanic and they'd all drown and nobody'd ever find them, PL not having filed any sort of report with the harbor master or naval authorities.

They had a little fiberglass dinghy on board and PL swung into action by ordering one of his guys to throw it overboard, jump into it and try to determine the damage. Over went the dinghy. Over went the guy into the dinghy. But it was a cheap shit dinghy and the guy went straight through the bottom of it. Only he stopped going through it at his armpits.

"Hey!", he yelled. "I'm standing on something!"

What he was standing on was sand. The beach, basically. PL had run the boat aground on a sand bar about a hundred yards from the beach. Not Long Beach or Lido Beach, but some beach on the Queens/Nassau County border. And it was high tide. The boat was firmly imbedded in the sand and the tide was beginning to go out. The whole motley crew abandoned ship. Guess they had to. They weren't going anywhere. As the tide transitioned from high to low the boat, being high and dry, simply tipped over and lay on its side, like a dead marine creature.

While all this was happening, the fog had lifted and a crowd had been drawn, including a photographer from the New York Times. The next morning, there's was ol' PL's boat, laying on its side, high and dry, right on Page One, below the fold.

People being what they are, they began scavenging the boat almost immediately. PL told of standing there on the beach, looking forlornly at the boat, mentally tallying his loss (natch, he'd had no insurance). Some guy came running from the direction of the boat, arms loaded down with stuff, yelling to PL, "Hey – you better hurry up and get while the gettin's good. Everything'll be gone in no time!"

PL and his crew went back to staying in motels.

EIGHT

I had gone to college for three years at C.W. Post College in Old Brookville, Long Island.

The reason I'd gone there was because it was across the road from Peter Moorehead's farm.

Dale and Jeanne had a couple of mediocre racehorses and a fairly nice brood mare named Nita Dee. Nita Dee was in foal at Peter Moorehead's and one of my jobs was to look in on Nita Dee once or twice a week to see how she was progressing.

Horses have always been the love of my life so this part of the job was the best. The very best.

Not to mention the fact the Peter Moorehead always had a refrigerator stocked with the nastiest alcoholic beverage ever known to man, ginger-flavored currant wine. It was the goofiest thing you ever tasted but went down like soda pop, so you'd get hammered in a heartbeat. Which is exactly what we'd do with regularity.

Peter and I had an almost standing date a couple of times a week, early in the afternoon.

I'd spend an hour or so in the pasture to make sure Nita Dee was okay. That was the best two hours of my week. Then, Peter and I would get hammered.

He was always bitching about the college kids from across the road getting all fucked up and coming over and bothering his horses. "The sonsabitches keep spookin' my mares!"

The combination of Peter Morehead's horses and the fact that there was a large group of kids my age getting all fucked up and carousing were the factors that persuaded me to enroll there. Unfortunately, Peter Morehead retired about ten months later, so I was left with kids my age getting all fucked up and carousing.

I had tried to persuade Dale to sell me the Caddy for months, hydraulic leak and all, but to no avail. So I ended up with a 1961 VW convertible that I got from a friend of the family for a hundred and fifty bucks.

As I was in school full time and an up-and-coming fountain tycoon part time, I would supplement my non-existent income by delivering fountains on the side. Cruising the New York metropolitan area with a fifty-inch diameter fiberglass bowl tied upside down on my torn canvas roof was my stock in trade. A good gust of wind, however, would lift the bug and me right off the pavement. Steering was an adventure sometimes.

Boy, did that thing burn oil! Because there was no real heater in a VW, the defroster and what cabin heat there was were generated by the heat from the engine simply passing through rubber hoses to the inside of the car. Because The Vicious Volks burned so much oil, the air coming in from the engine was laden with it, causing my windshield to have a constant oil slick on the inside of it. I lived with it, though.

I dropped the car off at a gas station one day to have the oil changed and when I went to pick it up, the guy said, "That'll be five bucks." Five bucks! I thought that was the deal of a lifetime. When I asked him why it was so inexpensive, the guy said, "This piece of shit isn't worth an oil change. It was almost empty so I put in three quarts. That'll be five bucks."

The Vicious Volks came to an ignominious, though unpublicized, end as well. I was driving across campus in a rainstorm one night and came to a stop sign at the end of a parking lot. There was a minor 'thump!' somewhere below me but I didn't pay it any attention and cruised through the stop sign, made a left and started up a little knoll between some dorms. At the top of the knoll was another stop sign, but this one had a crosswalk attached to it so I had to stop.

Or tried to stop. The 'thump!' had been my brake cable snapping so my foot went right to the floor when I stepped on the brake. Luckily, the people in the crosswalk saw me coming with what they perceived as no intention of stopping on my part. Lucky, because I didn't have a horn and the emergency brake didn't work, either. I sailed through the crosswalk, barely missing three jocks and a hippie.

At the crosswalk, the knoll started down on the other side and about a quarter mile ahead were the main gates that opened onto Northern Boulevard, a major four-lane thoroughfare.

I had to think and do something fast or there'd be trouble with a capital "T" in about ten seconds. Although the speedometer didn't work, either, I figured I was doing eight to ten miles an hour. I downshifted into first, but the Volks didn't have synchromesh, so the engine stalled and I was simply coasting.

There was a pretty high curb on my left that surrounded a lawn behind a dorm that dropped away in about a hundred yards into a parking lot filled with cars. I steered directly at the curb, hoping it'd stop the little Volks. Nope. Hit it and hopped right over it. Now I was heading down the lawn toward the parking lot and had one hope left: a young but sturdy-looking sapling standing sentry a little to the right.

I opened the door in case that last little trick didn't work and I had to bail before going headfirst into a bunch of parked cars and steered straight for the little tree. The little tree saved my sorry ass and stopped the car dead. Worked like a charm.

I started laughing. What a sight for someone looking out a dorm window: Here's a car, engine not running, in a rainstorm, veering directly for a head-on collision with a tree. I left the car there. Next morning it had an "illegally parked" sticker glued to the windshield. No shit, Sherlock. You had to hand it to our crack campus police, they were certainly astute. I ended up having to go to some on-campus kangaroo court and getting fined ten bucks. I thought of it as adding injury to insult. It was a wash, though, because I sold the car to some guy for ten bucks. He wanted to use the body for a dune buggy. I don't think he ever did, though, because the corpse of the Vicious Volks sat in the adjacent parking lot for the rest of the school year.

For some reason or other, at the end of my third year at C.W. Post, my fourth year of college 'in toto', I received a letter from the administration inviting me not to return when classes resumed in the fall. I guess they decided to downsize or something. Couldn't have been the fact that I hadn't been to more than ten percent of my classes the past couple of years or anything. I figured, hell, I'm paying for this. What skin is it off their asses if I don't show up?

Maybe it had to do with the fact that the Vietnam War was in full swing and I was blessed with a 4-F deferment, meaning women and children first. Maybe it had to do with the fact that some guys were busting their asses to stay in school to keep their 2-S classification. If they weren't in school, with a so-and-so grade point average, they became 1-A, meaning they'd probably come home in a box within the year. Fuck 'em, I was paying good money for the opportunity to hone my party skills, was current in my payments, and the administration had no right to do what it did.

Or maybe it was the fact that I was the first one in the dean's window when we took over the school after Kent State back in '70.

Either way, I was done, finito, at C.W. Fucking Post.

That's when I became a full time up-and-coming fountain tycoon.

NINE

I moved into Manhattan and found a studio apartment on 50th Street between Ninth and Tenth for a hundred and twenty bucks a month. Interestingly enough, my cousin Iz was living in a drug rehab clinic right next door, though she was never allowed to leave the house to see me. She 'graduated' about six months later and moved into a place in the same building as Jeanne and Dale.

When I moved in I had no furniture, naturally. I went to the Salvation Army place in the neighborhood and got a green couch that folded down into a small bed if I ever had company, a black naugahyde rocking chair and a single mattress. I was in clover.

I bought a twelve-inch black and white TV and had Little Joe cover two big cable spools in black fiberglass, one to serve as a coffee table and one to serve as a TV stand. My sister gave me a red inflatable chair for Christmas and that worked a little bit. The part that served as the back and arms got a hole in it so it became more or less an objet d'art. My mom gave me a pole lamp that same Christmas and that worked fine.

We had an old air conditioner at 264 and Bubniak and a couple of guys put it in my window. It was probably built in 1954 and weighed in the neighborhood of four hundred pounds. If I positioned my chair directly in front of it, it worked like a charm.

My triumphal entrance into adulthood in Manhattan coincided with the Houbigant Fiasco.

Houbigant Perfumes, or whatever the company was called, had bought three *thousand* counter-top fountains to be used as displays in department stores across the country. The stores would add a little Houbigant perfume to the water and that'd smell the place up with their perfume fragrance. The thought was that women would go wild and buy thousands of gallons of the stuff.

The fountains had little fifteen-inch aluminum bowls and the water would cascade down over eight little plastic discs. They looked cute.

Dale and Jeanne had priced them carefully and the whole order, being our largest ever, would be nice and profitable.

Dale and Bubniak devised a pretty good assembly line – we were always devising assembly lines – and John had gotten hold of a whole crew of guys from Poland. It really worked like clockwork. We were turning out about a hundred units a day and shipping them over to Houbigant's distribution warehouse in Moonachie, New Jersey.

About a week after we shipped the last batch, we got a frantic phone call from our contact at Houbigant. It seems the little fountains were splashing water and perfume all over department store counters across the United States and the store managers were pissed.

Oops.

Here was the problem in a nutshell: The eight discs, piled on top of each other, meant the water was cascading from too great a height. We had a rule of thumb in the fountain business: whatever the diameter of the bowl was, that was the maximum height you could go with the water. If the bowl had a fifteen-inch diameter, the water couldn't go any higher that fifteen inches. Or else you'd get splash outside the bowl.

Dale had been pretty vehement in pointing this out when working with the Houbigant people in designing the fountain. But they wanted as much height as possible, the better to be seen amongst all the rest of the shit on department store counters. And they said it wouldn't be a problem and they were paying for it so make it eight discs. The eight discs measured a height of about seventeen inches, two over the limit according to the rule of thumb.

Luckily, only a few hundred fountains had been shipped from Moonachie, so the problem was caught before it became a complete disaster.

Our suggestion was to make the discs only five high. You'd still have plenty of height to be seen over the countertop shit and they wouldn't splash. We could turn them out in no time and the parts could be shipped to the fountains already in the field and our guys could go to

Moonachie, open the boxes containing the fountains and replace the disc element on all fountains remaining to be shipped.

Great, said they. Only make it three discs, not five. What? You wanted eight so they'd be seen. Then we suggested five and they'd still work fine. Now you only want three? What gives? Seems their corporate assholes snapped shut when the complaints started coming in and they got gun shy. My guess is that whoever was in charge of the project for Houbigant figured it'd be his neck on the line if they had any more problems and he'd rather be safe than sorry. Whatever.

John and I and several of the Polish guys spent the next couple of weeks shuttling back and forth to Moonachie.

The Houbigant folks set us up in a big empty room in their warehouse and, naturally, we set up an assembly line. We'd set out rows of the individually-cartoned fountains and one of us, armed with a box-cutter, would go down the rows slicing the tape open; another guy would follow right behind to remove the packing 'collar' around the top of the fountain; the next guy would unscrew the offending disc element and drop it into a pushcart; the next guy would take a new element from his pushcart and screw it into place. Once all that was done, we'd start at the head of the line and reassemble the packing collars, re-tape the boxes, with the last guy stacking the boxes on a big dolly.

It was a pretty smooth operation, really. But BOR-ING! I mean, we had to retrofit something like twenty-five or twenty-six hundred of the goddam things. How anybody could spend thirty years on an assembly line is completely beyond me. What price money?!?

TEN

As the newly-installed National Sales Manager –what a crock of shit, I was making minimum wage plus time-and-a-half – it was my job to set up and oversee the showroom and the direct mail operation.

Our office "suite" consisted of the "office", the "showroom" and the "back room".

The "office" was the room off the elevator hall where Jeanne had her desk, Dale had his easy chair base of operations, a couch, a coffee table, a small fountain on a pedestal and one of our statue fountains standing in the corner. God, those statue fountains were hideous. They were Grecian or Roman babes pouring water out of a gourd into a shell which overflowed into a larger shell. And they were "antique white and gold" – the cheesiest color in the world. Italian Restaurants loved them.

We had a map of the United States on one wall with pushpins, ostensibly to demonstrate our vast array of dealers and distributors. The pushpins fell off and disappeared within the first couple of weeks and, of course, weren't replaced at any point over the next nine years.

The entire building was concrete on the inside, so Dale had Bubniak cover the walls with cheap-ass sheets of wood-grain painted fiberboard paneling, like the kind people put in the basements of their homes back in the '60s to turn a cellar into a "rec room". Dale went nuts with that paneling over the years, throughout the building.

As I pointed out, the concrete floor was covered in orange and yellow semi-shag wall-to-wall carpeting that had the traffic pattern worn into it within the first month.

As my status as up-and-coming fountain tycoon gradually elevated to straight-up fountain tycoon, I used the couch as my sometimes-base-of-operations, but it always pissed Jeanne off if I wasn't actually looking busy and it's hard to look busy sitting on a couch.

The "showroom" was a room in a the back of the building, behind the office and through the "back room". It was truly dramatic. Honest.

We had painted the walls black and blacked out the windows. Oh – those were the only windows in our whole office. Neither the office nor the back room had windows, so I often didn't really know what the weather was from eight in the morning 'til six at night. We had seven or eight fountains in there, everything from our smallest 24-inch diameter fountain – the Mark III - up to our eight-foot diameter "Eight Foot Extravaganza". When you walked into that deathly quiet black room and hit the "on" switch, all hell broke loose.

Water to the ceiling, bright colored lights, a sound like Niagara Falls – it used to blow people away. Just let me get a potential customer past the office into that showroom and I had 'em dead to rights.

One day, the elevator bell rang and in walked Art Fleming. Yes – *that* Art Fleming. Who the hell is Art Fleming?, you're asking yourself. Well, he was none other than the host of *Jeopardy!*, that's who. Long before there was an Alex Trebek there was an Art Fleming. I was properly impressed.

"That's a beautiful fountain", said Art.

"No, Art, you're supposed to say, 'Is that a beautiful fountain?' – you know, in the form of a question." Boy, was I on!

He smiled politely like he probably did a hundred times a day. He ended up buying one of our fiberglass waterfalls – The Olympia.

"Discriminating choice, Art", I opined. I had it delivered to his apartment the next day.

Speaking of The Olympia, another celebrity of sorts also came in to the showroom and bought one – Mrs. Don King. In swept this very nice, very well-dressed woman with an entourage of what looked like two or three heavyweights-in-training. She fell in love with The Olympia. "Discriminating choice, Mrs. King", I opined. Had it delivered to her and Don's apartment the next day. It would have been cool if Don had been with her, but he was off attending to some scam somewhere.

The "back room" was really my purview, or at least that was where I had my honest-to-goodness base of operations. I had an old grey steel desk that I placed jauntily on an angle in the corner, facing the doorway to "the office". It wasn't so much that I had any operations to survey, but it was always good to be facing the door as we were on the second floor of a building a hundred steps off Eighth Avenue and, quite often, some rather disreputable characters would suddenly appear. Most of these disreputable characters were junkies that would steal a red-hot stove.

Our filing cabinets, such as they were, were in the back room. Invoices and unpaid bills and shipping documents and other paperwork were basically stacked in piles on top of the cabinets and once every year or so, we'd have a crash filing party, Jeanne and I, mostly because Dale had spilled a cup of coffee or something on one of the piles, causing him to notice the piles for the first time in the last fifty-some-odd weeks.

Also, the back room was the home of our direct mail operation which, in all honesty, was no slouch. Our daily goal was 20,000 brochures mailed out a day. We usually made it or came damned close. That's where the envelopes with the pre-paid checks came from, the ones Dale loved to open and strew about his armchair base of operations.

We did a lot of advertising in those business-oriented "bingo card" mailings, the kind where you get an envelope of forty or fifty individual self-addressed advertising cards. All you had to do to get more information on the product was to fill out your name, company, and address and drop it in the mail. We advertised in things like "Modern Restaurants" and "Modern Nursing Home" and "Institutions". When the cards came in, we'd send them a complete catalog and add them to our mailing list.

We kept our mailing lists on what was then a new-fangled thing called "Cheshire", a Xerox brainchild. Each Cheshire card held one name and you put a stack of them through the label machine and heat-sensitive gummed labels would come out. We boasted that we had a quarter of a million names and we probably did.

Because Dale insisted we do as much in-house as humanly possible, we did our own printing. Check that, I did our own printing. We had three printing presses in the back room, two small multilith presses and a huge Addressograph-Multigraph 1870 With A Two-Color Head. I became a printing fool.

The big press could print "two-up", meaning an 11-by-22 sheet of paper that, when cut in half, would be two 8-1/2 x11s. Natch, we had a paper-cutter, too, that was specially designed so you couldn't cut off a finger or anything.

Not only could the big press print two-up, it could also print two colors at the same time. To print in color, you need to put down four colors of ink: yellow, red, blue and black. In the printing business, blue is called cyan, but we were in the fountain business so we called it blue. I'd print yellow and red on the first pass, wait 'til the ink dried, and run it back through putting down the blue and black inks.

I became a wizard – no shit. I could get the ink to lay down perfectly uniformly, the right amount of water on the rollers and the registration virtually dot-on-dot. Dale would check out my work with a jeweler's loupe and say, "Goddam it, Jim, this is the best printing I've ever seen." I don't know if he meant it – couldn't have – but we both knew he was just trying to keep me motivated.

I'd be running two printing presses at the same time – the big 1870 With the Two-Color Head and a little '1250', with envelopes rolling through at the rate of five thousand an hour.

The only problem was that with the presses running, you couldn't hear a goddam thing. Neither Jeanne nor Dale could talk on the phone in the office – it sounded to the person on the other end like they were in the engine room of a tugboat or something. So Dale had Bubniak put up a big sound-proof door between the office and the back room. Naturally, the office side was paneled.

We had a big, used collating machine that had bins you'd fill with the various pages you wanted in the catalogs to be mailed. I became a wizard at that, too. I became a collating fool.

Once the catalogs were collated, they had to be stapled with two staples in each. Early on, we used a contraption that Bubniak had fashioned consisting of two regular office staplers held together with a piece of brass pipe and a large electromagnet. A foot pedal caused the electromagnet to engage, bringing the brass pipe down onto the two staplers at the same time, thus stapling the entire brochure in one fell swoop. It worked pretty well when the staplers didn't jam, which happened only every two minutes or so.

Later on, we actually bought an Official Electric Stapler, though that stuck in Dale's craw for a month.

The finished brochures were then run through the postage machine. We had a bulk mailing permit but we had to take the business part of the postage machine to the post office, hand the postal worker a check for however much you wanted in postage and they'd use these little tools to reset the machine. It was all very official. God forbid somebody'd try to cheat the post office by printing postage marks that couldn't be used on anything but envelopes.

Everybody – I mean everybody – had to go get that damned machine filled once in a while. Me, the people I had working under me, Bubniak, non-English speaking guys from Poland, various and sundry hangers-on – everybody but Jeanne and Dale. Actually, it often wasn't so bad. At least it gave you a chance to breathe fresh air and, in the winter, see the sunshine sometime between Sunday afternoon and Saturday morning.

Once the postage was put on the brochures, we had to tie them in bundles, put them in these big canvas bags provided by the post office and deliver them to the bulk mail window (loading dock, actually) at the post office. Now, that was a job you didn't really want. Having to lift six or eight hundred-pound bags of mail onto a dolly, wait for the freight elevator, jockey the dolly through rush hour foot and vehicle traffic and lift them onto the dock at the post office. Usually four or five postal employees stood around watching you flirt with a hernia. That job sucked.

I'd get the mail all ready to go and would go off to find John so he could get one of his guys to go. He'd collar a guy and say, "Hootsh, pon. Nah poachta!" "Hurry, mister. Post office!" The guy would never move fast enough for John and he half scream, "Hootsh! Hootsh!" and then chastise him in Polish, though I seldom heard 'kuravamotch' or 'skuravissin' during one of those chastisements so I guess he wasn't really mad.

We had a little Polish guy one time, Piotrowski. Looked like a bird. Even though he was one of John's smallest guys at the time, I think he used him because Piotrowski was smart and never fucked up a mission. Piotrowski's wife was able to come to America with him. How, I don't know. But she worked with us for a while, too. She was called Piotrowska, the "a" being the feminine form of Piotrowski. She was real pretty and had a quiet elegance about her. What she was doing with that little sparrow of a Piotrowski was beyond me. I figured she was probably an Eastern Bloc spy using him as her cover. The only thing is, she could have been a little more liberal with her underarm deodorant.

Piotrowski tried to say "post office", but it came out "poach-toppee". He was resourceful enough to stick his head in the back room every day around 4:30 and ask me, "Poachtoppee?"

"Yes, poach-toppee."

I still refer to the U.S. Postal Service as poach-toppee.

ELEVEN

Virtually every night – four or five nights a week for me – and *every* night for Jeanne and Dale, we'd meet up at Gallagher's on 52nd between Broadway and Eighth. Gallagher's is a world-famous steakhouse and has been forever. The keep their meat aging in a huge refrigerator with a glass window so everyone who enters can see it.

Their matchbooks said – maybe even still say - "Join the Regulars at Gallagher's". We were the regulars. Along with a core of probably 25-30 others who were in every weekday night and a lot of them on the weekends.

It was an incredible scene. An incredible drinking scene.

The "regulars" included publishers, lawyers, corporate executives, writers, columnists, cops, bookmakers, girlfriends, bimbos, restaurateurs, retirees, stagehands, musicians, actors, people "between jobs", hangers-on and fountain tycoons, among others. It was an eclectic group, to say the least. An eclectic group that had a collective hollow leg.

The bar is the dominating feature you notice when you walk in. It's a huge oval affair and takes up the lion's share of the large front room. It's to your right as you enter. There are a few small tables along the left wall in that room and the place opens out from there. Along that left wall, in addition to a few small tables, were two booths, generally reserved for celebrities.

One of the great things about Gallagher's, if one was inclined to imbibe, was that for every drink or two you bought, the bartenders bought one. Sometimes it was even better than that – sometimes you didn't even get a bill. This was encouraged by the management as the group of regulars spent a fortune there anyway and it made the joint a real scene.

One of my favorite bartenders was Nick Mellis, a short Greek guy that was built like a fireplug and who always had a complete poker face, which was hilarious considering some of the antics he'd witness. He had a great open smile, but that came out only occasionally. Usually, most people would consider him to have a dour countenance.

One night, the late comedian, Paul Lynde (remember *Hollywood Squares*?) was sitting by himself at the bar, pretty early in the evening, but drunk as a skunk. I guess he was kind of intrigued by Nick's expressionless facial expression so he embarked on his own little "Bet I Can Make You Laugh" game. He peppered Nick with a litany of one-liners – I sat there laughing like hell – it was Paul Lynde, fer chrissakes, *doing Paul Lynde*. Nick never cracked.

Nick would wander around, pouring drinks and acting generally busy and every time he walked in front of him, Lynde would fire a zinger in his direction. Nothing. This went on for the better part of forty-five minutes, the one-liners flying and Nick pushing fresh drinks in Paul's direction. Still nothing.

Finally, Lynde, totally exasperated, blurted out to Nick, "What the fuck is wrong with you, you old walrus?!? Don't you fucking understand English?" Nick roared. He *was* an old walrus.

Bernard Brill was one of the most intriguing people I've ever known. Everybody loved Bernard. And it was Bernard, not Bernie. Christ, he wasn't a Bernie. Bernard looked like Ben Franklin, sort of. He had the Ben Franklin hair style and an ever-wise look about him. Bernard smoked a pipe that was always spewing hot ash into the air and ruining his suits. He always had his main meal at lunchtime so he could drink all night without having to worry about ruining a good drunk with food.

Bernard owned and published a bunch of magazines, the best known being *Official Detective, Modern Detective* and that cheap shit knock-off *Mad Magazine* called *Cracked*. He also owned a chain of Manhattan hosiery stores. He had a lot of money and lived in a big apartment at Seventh Avenue and Christopher Street in the Village, with his wife, Ruth.

Bernard loved women. Loved them. He was always on the make, but the way a gentleman would do it. I don't know how often he scored, probably not very often, but he sure played the game like a champ. He was officially gallant. So women loved Bernard, too.

Especially this goofy bimbo from Jersey, Susan. Another one who was crazy as a shithouse rat. Susan had been Bernard's mistress for probably thirty years and I'm sure Ruth knew all about it. Susan sure knew all about Ruth. Hell, much to Bernard's consternation, both women would be in Gallagher's on the same night at the same bar, but on opposite sides of it. Bernard would deftly cruise back and forth in his gallant manner and the place never once exploded, no thanks to any of us who were coyly, but clumsily, egging it on.

Susan was married to some rich guy in one of the upscale New Jersey towns, like Ridgewood or something. Incredibly, Bernard had somehow arranged the marriage or something very close to it.

One Friday night I got there early, around six. The only person I knew sitting at the bar was that crazy bitch Susan. That bummed me out no end, but I had no choice but to sit on the stool next to hers. I was sober as a judge, but Susan was obviously three sheets to the wind. As she always did, she sat there bitching about Bernard and how badly he treated her, blah, blah, blah. I was nodding as if I was listening and actually gave a shit, but wasn't paying attention to her in the least.

She seemed to get kind of excited in her reverie, because I noticed out of the corner of my eye that she seemed to be flailing around pretty good on that bar stool, arms waving in the air and rocking and rolling on the stool. All of a sudden, she and the stool rocked back on two legs. I grabbed for her to try to keep her from going straight over on her back and landing in the middle of a tableful of diners four feet behind her. She grabbed for me like somebody falling off a building and down she went, though missing the table by scant inches.

There she was, lying on her back, legs in the air, skirt up around her waist (you didn't really want to look), screaming.

What really bothered me is that, in grabbing for me, she got hold of my wristwatch, broke the goddam watchband and the watch and band went flying somewhere halfway across the room. Okay, I'd find it in a minute. In the meantime, I felt I should do something to rectify the mess at my feet, so I reached down and helped Susan to her feet.

And she started screaming at me.

"Why did you push me over?!? Why on earth would you do that?!? What the hell is the matter with you?!? Somebody – HELP!"

Uh.

George, the maître d', had seen what had happened and said, quietly in my ear, "Jimmy, don't worry about it. It ain't the first time that's happened and it won't be the last. I'll take it from here." He bowed and scraped for her and motioned for one of the female waiters to help Susan into the ladies' room to get herself together. Off they went.

As Susan was coming out of the ladies room, as refreshed as she could be given that she couldn't walk in a straight line, in swept Bernard.

"Bernie! (she was the only one that ever called him Bernie) *Bernie!* That horrible young man (pointing at me), just pushed me off a stool!"

Bernard just gave me an all-knowing grin and asked, "Did you get a good look up her skirt?"

A lot of celebrities ate in the booths along that one wall. They were pretty much left alone, except for the occasional out-of-town tourist who didn't know any better. Even when one those yokels would stand in front of their table, gushing and pleading for an autograph, they were always quite gracious.

One night we were hanging out and there was a commotion at the front door. A scrum of bodies and a hail of flash bulbs. The maître d's, George and Michel, made for the door, began separating the celeb's party from the paparazzi and out popped Elizabeth Taylor. The place went silent and every head in the joint turned to look at her. She and her party were quickly seated in one of the booths. I was hanging out at the end of the bar and she sat about fifteen feet to my left, smiling sweetly and full of grace. I swear her eyes were the color of irises. I've never seen eyes that were somewhere between blue and lavender. Incredible.

Naturally, all the regulars knew enough to ignore her and leave her alone, but several other diners approached her table during her meal. I figured her goons sitting at the next table would nip that in the bud, but Miss Taylor received each of the fans in turn, smiled warmly at each of them and actually had a short two or three minute conversation with each. What a nice person. That knocked me out.

Speaking of being knocked out, one night I very nearly knocked out Richard Burton. It's just a coincidence that I'm mentioning Elizabeth Taylor and Richard Burton so close to each other, but they had long been divorced and there were probably two or three years between incidents.

He was sitting at one of the corner booths and, being a bon vivant and man-about-town in my own right, I only glanced in his direction once in a while. I was standing at the bar somewhat near him and had to go to the men's room. I finally decided that, rather taking the shortest, most direct route to my destination and going by his table as everybody else did, I'd take the long way, around the bar. Being a fountain tycoon, these are the type of decisions one was faced with.

Off I went.

The men's room attendant, Larry, was standing outside the door, but that wasn't unusual. It's what he did when the men's room was empty. I said, "Hey, Larry" and pushed the swinging door inward with an exaggerated little flourish.

Bang!

Oops.

Somebody seemed to be in the process of exiting the men's room at that very moment and I'd smashed him with the door.

It was Richard Burton.

He looked at me as though he thought he was about to be rubbed out.

I simply said, "Oh, sorry", and we did our best to dodge each other as we passed through the doorway. The thought raced through my mind that I should explain that I was really trying to leave him alone and not act like some asshole from West Buttfuck and took the long way around so it wouldn't seem that way and all but that probably would have made me look to him like I was either from West Buttfuck or a guy who really was trying to rub him out.

I went from fountain tycoon to major jamoke in one flourish of the men's room door. Bette Midler sat in one of the corner booths one night with some people. I noticed one of those people waving to me. What the hell? Oh, God, I thought – maybe I look gay and they want me to be in her chorus line or something.

Hold on – it's *Wuz!* What the hell was Wuzzy doing sitting at Bette Midler's table? Sitting next to her, no less? Wuz and I had been in the Theater Arts department at C.W. Fucking Post and worked on several shows together. I was one of the stoned-out lighting guys and Wuz worked in production.

Wuz came over and told me he'd scored a gig working on Bette's production team. According to him, he had a pretty good gig. I didn't doubt it, he was sitting right next to her.

He was traveling the country, staying in the best hotels, flying first class, making good money – all was more than cool.

"Me? Why, Wuz, I'm a fountain tycoon."

"A fountain tycoon, huh? Well. Good to see you, Jim."

He went right back to the table, obviously unimpressed with my fountain tycoondom. I'd always figured the sonofabitch was gay.

We were sitting at one of the corner booths one night. We weren't celebrities, it was just a slow night. In walked Jaclyn Smith and that doofus she was married to for a while – the blonde male bimbo – Dennis somebody – he was in a bunch of made-for-tv movies. They sat right next to us.

I guess it was a slow night for them, too, because we all actually got into a couple of real nice conversations. Dale and Dennis Whatsisname started talking about boats or something and I had a nice talk with Jaclyn. I don't have the faintest idea what we talked about, but she was animated and seemed interested. I hope to fuck I wasn't talking about fountains or something.

What I really wanted to say was, "You're one of the most beautiful women I've ever seen and I'll gladly walk into the kitchen and have the chef cut off my right arm with a meat cleaver if you'll run away with me forever." But I didn't. I probably talked about fountains. Shit.

She still looks damned good and I read where she dumped that doofus shortly after she and I met. I'd like to think her titillating conversation with me stuck with her and it was one of those romantic tragedies that she just could never find me again.

TWELVE

Sometime in the mid-70s we changed the name from Real Fountains, Inc. to General Fountain Corp.

Dale was enamored of big corporations. And, dammit, we were a big corporation, too. General Motors, General Electric, General Dynamics, General Fountain Corp. Top of the corporate heap. Interchangeable.

We didn't make a big splash of it or anything, just changed the name on all the printed propaganda. Man, I had those presses 'ka-thump, ka-thump'-ing for a good month.

Hey – we were pretty big, though, for what we did. We touted ourselves as the "world's largest manufacturer of self-contained water display fountains, submersible pumps and underwater lighting". Which wasn't really true if you took each of those elements individually, but as a conglomeration, just maybe. Who the hell would ever take the time or energy to try to prove us wrong, though?

Later, we would become the "world's largest manufacturer of self-contained water display fountains, submersible pumps, underwater lighting, electric wheelchairs and cloisonné picture frames", but I'm getting ahead of myself.

We were really hitting our stride. Business was good. We were growing and making money.

One of the reasons we were making money is that Dale always tried desperately not to pay his bills.

Oh, we'd pay the guys we needed to. The companies whose products or services we absolutely couldn't do without. The fiberglass people, the electric motor people, the light bulb manufacturers, those types. But anybody else was in for some aggravating shit. Actually, nobody got paid when they should have. It would take a final cut-off of shipments before we'd pay a bill, but at least we paid it.

It would go like this:

We'd have a bill for motors or something that was in the neighborhood of 120 or 150 days old. Months. We'd be running short of motors. Jeanne would call and order more motors.

We'd get a call back telling us they weren't shipping them until they were paid. The bastards.

Dale would call his buddy, the president of the company or some guy real high up, and tell him to go ahead and ship, we were sending a check out today. Promise.

OK, fine, just make sure the check goes out.

Done. Just make sure the motors go out.

Done.

"Jeanne, how much do we owe them?"

"About nine thousand dollars."

"Okay, send them a check for three thousand and postdate it two weeks from now." We'd get the motors and they'd get partial payment. Fair is fair.

If we bought one thing on a one-time basis, the poor bastards never got paid.

We always bought it on credit and if they wanted our credit references or anything, Dale just had them call the vice-president of our bank, Jim Lucey, old "hole-in-the-head".

That'd impress 'em.

If they did call, and that happened very seldom, Lucey would vouch for us uphill and down.

We'd get in whatever it is we'd ordered and went on with our lives.

We'd get a bill. A month or two later, we'd get a "friendly reminder". A month or two later, we'd get a "past due" notice. Another month and we'd get a "final notice". Then the phone calls would start.

Ring.

"Hello, General Fountains."

"Dale Hodge, please."

"May I tell him who's calling?"

"Joe Jaboni from the We Just Got Chumped Widget Company."

"One moment, please."

Put him on hold. Wait ten seconds.

"I'm sorry, Mr. Hodge is out of the office. Would you like to leave a message?"

"Yes, please. Would you be kind enough to tell him we have an outstanding invoice that is approximately six months old and we'd like to clear it up. Oh, and please ask him to call me."

"Certainly. Here, let me get your number." No pen. No paper. No intention of writing anything down.

"It's 555-555-5555."

"Okay – let me make sure I've got that. It's 555-555-5555, right?"

"Yes, that's it. When do you think I can expect a call?"

"Oh, probably first thing in the morning." How's never? Is never okay with you?

"That would be great. Thank you very much. 'Bye".

"Good-bye." Dipshit. Hope it doesn't mean his job.

Four days later…..

Ring.

"General Fountains."

"Dale Hodge, please."

"May I tell him who's calling?"

"Joe Jaboni from We Just Got Chumped."

"One minute, please." On hold. Ten seconds.

"I'm sorry, Mr. Hodge is out of the office. May I take a message?"

"I left a message for him last Wednesday and never heard back." And you never will.

"I'm terribly sorry, he's been in and out a lot lately."

"Who am I speaking to?"

"Bill Leith." I never used my own name on those calls. I had a number of 'em: Bill Leith. Harry Hyatt. Al Gonzalez.

"Do you have anything to do with accounts payable?"

"No, sir, I don't. But I'd be glad to give Mr. Hodge the message."

"When will he be in?"

"Probably on Monday. He's out of town."

"Well, just make sure he gets the message, OK? We have a bill that's over six months old."

"Sure will." It'll have fucking hair on it before you ever get paid, pal.

A week or so would go by before the next call. He'd ask for Dale. Not here. He'd ask for Bill Leith. Not here. Who's this? Harry Hyatt.

This went on all the fucking time. See, none of these bills were ever large enough to get sued over. Oh, they'd get turned over to a collection agency and the whole phone thing would start all over. Finally, the collection agency gave it back to We Just Got Chumped because it was costing them more to chase down the money than they'd ever make on it. We Just Got Chumped would turn it over to collection agency number two and the whole song and dance would continue until We Just Got Chumped wrote it off as a bad debt.

Worked like a charm.

We actually had a guy named Bill Leith who worked for us for about six weeks. I had gone to C.W. Fucking Post with him and we were friends, not close friends, but we got along. He was a pretty good bookkeeper and we needed some books kept. He'd sit there at the adding machine and I'd notice him sweating when it wasn't really warm. I asked him if he was alright and he said he'd sweat when he got nervous. Seems our books made him pretty nervous. He was sweating most of the time.

The idea of my using his name as an alias came to me one day when one of those calls came in and it was just him and me in the office. The person looking for money asked who he was speaking to and I was looking at Leith, so I just said "Bill Leith".

Leith got all pissed at my having used his name like that and I told him not to worry, the guy on the phone was from Ohio and I guaranteed him the guy wouldn't come looking for him. Leith still didn't like it and I think I noticed some extra sweat oozing from his brow.

I think it was just because it bugged Leith that I started using his name. That, and because it came trippingly off the tongue.

The thing that sent him over the edge was when he answered the phone one day and a guy asked for Bill Leith.

"Speaking."

Uh-oh.

"When I talked to you last week you promised a check would be sent *that* night and there's still no sign of it! Blah! Blah! Blah!" Leith got his asshole royally reamed.

He left shortly after that. I asked him why he was leaving – he wasn't working too hard, was getting paid pretty good (hah!), was able to set his own hours. Didn't get much better than all that.

"'Cause you bastards are nuts!"

He left, sweating. Haven't seen him since.

I've been known to still use his name on occasion.

THIRTEEN

About that time, I moved from the West 50th Street apartment.

Jeanne and Dale had been friends with this older couple, Andy and Barbara (aka Barb) for a few years and I knew them. Andy was a pretty cool old Italian guy and Barb was a pretty mouthy old Italian lady.

Andy got sick and died.

They had a pre-war rent-controlled apartment on the northwest corner of 51st and Eighth.

If I recall, it was a walk-up but the apartment was on the second floor. After Andy died, Barb wanted to go live at a house they owned up in Ulster County or someplace. She had a bunch of middle-aged, never-married women friends up there that she really liked.

Jeanne and Dale and I believed they were all, as Ellen De Generes puts it, Lebanese. I think maybe Barb may have been Lebanese, too, even having been married to Andy all those years.

No matter.

I worked out a deal with her to sublet her apartment. She told the landlord I was her nephew. She became known as Auntie Barb.

It was a great apartment, or it could've been a great apartment. It had a sunken living room, big dining area, a bath-and-a-half, a big bedroom and good-sized kitchen. Real estate like that didn't come around too often, especially at the rent-controlled rate of $195 a month.

It could have been a great apartment if I had had a lot of money and it was really mine and I could have furnished it myself. But that wasn't the case and luckily, I guess, I rented Auntie Barb's apartment furnished. Like a complete asshole, I actually put my cheap shit Salvation Army stuff in storage.

I was now a 23-year-old single guy living in the greatest city in the world in an apartment that had been furnished by an old Italian couple. It was furnished in mid-nineteen-fifties Italian. There was gild and gold leaf everywhere. A couple of the living room chairs and the couch were covered in lovely clear plastic slip covers. Everything had washed-out rose-colored flowers on it. Every square inch had a knick-knack on it. Man, I couldn't wait to pick up a chick and wisk her off to that baby.

There was a white Spanish Conquistador statue that stood guard at the top of the sunken living room. I know the Conquistador was somewhat incongruous with the Italian motif, but maybe they were trying to branch out and go a little more Mediterranean. I called him Con and patted his helmet for luck when I walked by.

I swear the sonofabitch was alive. At least a dozen times when I came home drunk he gave me a mean cross-body block that sent us both crashing to the floor, the bastard.

The place just totally freaked me out. There was too much stuff in that apartment just waiting to get trashed. And, no shit, I just couldn't bring a girl back there. There was no way I could have explained the whole situation before she bolted.

About the best I did was to persuade one of the waitresses at Howard Johnson's around the corner to come up after her shift. I kind of knew her anyway and she was a few years older so I didn't put much hope into my chances. The whole idea made me want to cry. We ended up sitting on the couch with the clear plastic slip cover and watching George Romero's "Night of the Living Dead". It was the night of the living dead alright.

After a year or so of this dismal existence, I'd had enough. Auntie Barb had probably had enough too, having noticed a dearth of knick-knacks and the fact that Con's sword had broken off in his hand.

I found a place in a renovated building on West 46th Street, between Ninth and Tenth.

It was in Hell's Kitchen. In all, I lived in Hell's Kitchen for nine years and really liked the neighborhood a lot. It was very racially and ethnically mixed, with the majority of inhabitants being either people of Irish descent that had been there for generations or of Puerto Rican descent who had been there anywhere from a day-and-a-half to twenty years. I'll admit it was a tough-looking neighborhood but I never had a lick of trouble all the while I lived there, in the Seventies when New York was at its most rough-and tumble.

The place on 46th between Ninth and Tenth was on the second floor. It was one big (not really) room, with windows overlooking the street at one end and a half-baked kitchenette at the other. One wall was all brick, though, and that was cool, I guess. Even though it had been newly renovated, the floor sloped in about three directions.

During this period, all of Hell's Kitchen was crawling with hookers.

It was the age of the pimpmobile. There was a place on 50th called Small's. The pimpmobiles, in all their glory, would line both sides of the block in no parking zones. The cops didn't really give a shit.

Except for one – Lieutenant Gallagher, not to be confused with Gallagher's Steak House, though that's where he often hung out. Lieutenant Gallagher was one of the higher-ups at the Midtown North precinct house on West 54th Street. He hated pimps and he hated their pimpmobiles.

He had a trick.

He'd just send out four or five NYPD wreckers to put the pimpmobiles on the hook and have them towed straight out to the crusher in Queens. No ticket. No questions asked. Just block-long, tricked-out pimpmobiles in all their glory reduced to shit in about an hour.

He got away with it by requiring the pimps to show him their IRS records from the prior year demonstrating they had really earned enough money, legally, to purchase those fine luxury automobiles. Never happened. Boy, he killed a slew of pimpmobiles, Lieutenant Gallagher did. I always kind of grudgingly liked him and he always called me "kid".

He also had a trick for the hookers. He knew damned well that if he arrested them, they'd be out on their pimps' bail before dawn and would be back on the street before noon.

His trick was to have them rousted and put into a police van. The van would then drive the girls out to Riverhead or Montauk at the very eastern point of Long Island, about a hundred and twenty miles from Manhattan. The cops made the girls get out. And the van would drive back to Manhattan, empty. That'd mean the girls would have to get back into town somehow, which usually meant calling their pimps, collect, and they'd have to drive 240 miles to get their property back so they could get back to work.

Ol' Gallagher spent a lot of time thoroughly pissing off those in the illicit sex trades.

Speaking of pimps, I had a pretty good customer who was a pimp. His name was Mose. He wasn't a big-time pimp and didn't have a pimpmobile. He ran a massage parlor up on Eighth Ave. between 48th and 49th Streets.

He came into the office half a dozen times, always bought a Mark III fountain, a 24-inch diameter black fiberglass job with a single spray ring and a bright white light in the middle. You could change the color of the light by purchasing "color disks" in either red, blue, green or amber. The fountains cost $195 each, plus the color disks, which retailed for $7.50 each. I always made a point of throwing in all four colors and rounding the total to $200, thereby saving Mose a handsome twenty-five bucks.

He usually wore black leather pants, a black leather jacket with a white rabbit fur collar, and a black leather pimp hat with a feather in it. You could smell the leather from a dozen feet away. Real cheap shit, but he sure looked like he was pimpin'.

He would pay half down, a hundred bucks, always in beaten up twenties, natch. He'd pay the balance when I delivered it to the massage parlor and set it up, which consisted of pouring a bucket of water into it and plugging it in.

This was my kind of delivery.

I'd walk into the place and be stopped by some goon at the door. He'd be the one to whom one would say, "I would like a massage, my good man." Or at least that's how I figured it.

But I was there on business. I'd say, rather coolly, "I'm looking for Mose."

"Who's lookin' for him?"

"Tell him 'Jim' – and tell him I have what he ordered." Man, was I the real deal, or what? "Wait a minute." And off he'd go.

A minute or two later, Mose would breeze out into the stark waiting room.

"Jimmy – my main man! Right this way, m'man."

The sorry-looking bastards sitting in the plastic chairs waiting for a stroke-job looked at me with a combination of hatred and envy, but I was in.

As I was setting up the fountain, the girls - the ones who weren't otherwise occupied – would crowd around in various states of undress and ooh and aah over their new decorative display unit. It usually took me a helluva lot longer to set up one of those babies in that place than it did in some red and gold flock-walled goombah restaurant in Middle Village, Queens, I'll tell you that.

I was always hoping Mose would tip me by saying, "Jimmy, my man – great job! Just take your pick and have a good time." Never happened. He'd fish out an old wrinkled fiver and flash it at me as though it would impress both the girls and me.

Christ.

My block, 46th between Ninth and Tenth, was, except for Eighth Ave., ground zero for hookers. The Eighth Avenue hookers were trolling mostly for pedestrian guys while the girls on my block's specialty was guys in cars.

The Lincoln Tunnel dumped you into Manhattan at either 40th Street or 42nd Street. 40th Street ran eastbound and 42nd Street ran east and west. Guys from Jersey could easily come through the tunnel, take either of those streets and jump on Tenth Avenue going northbound either four or six blocks, depending on which exit to the tunnel they used. They could hang a quick right on 46th, which went eastbound and, voila! Hookers!

I'd sometimes sit looking out my second floor window and watch the action. Often, there'd be eight to ten hookers standing on the curb or in the gutter on either side of the street and the cars would cruise slowly past. I'd usually see the same cars go up the street two or three times, the guys narrowing their options each time they went around the block.

We aren't talking about the crème de la crème when it came to these hookers. It was pretty much the last stop on the John chain. Most, but not all, of them were female, but even if they took off their clothes and stood buck naked in the street, you wouldn't necessarily want to look. A couple of them lived in my building and were pretty pleasant. We'd exchange greetings if we met in the entryway or on the stairs.

"Hi." Me.

"Hi."

"How's business?"

"Sucks."

How was I supposed to take that?

I even got kind of friendly with a skinny black girl who lived in the building across the street. We'd run into each other in the Puerto Rican bodega on the ground floor of her building. I'd probably be buying beer and cookies and she'd probably be buying cookies and beer. She was a sweet girl. Hard, but sweet. We had a number of conversations about everything from the weather to the cops to the Yankees. All the while, I kept wondering what would happen if I, you know, asked her. I didn't but I did live rather vicariously through those meetings for a while.

The people who ran the bodega were the hardest working people in New York. It was family-run, with a thirty-ish mom and dad and a couple of little kids always running around. When I left the house at 7:30 in the morning, they were open. When I stumbled in at 10:30 or 11 at night, they were open. Seven days a week. I don't know how the hell they did it.

One day I was paying for my beer and cookies and they both asked me to look at a twenty dollar bill.

"Is this real? Is this good?"

It was the worst looking counterfeit I'd ever seen. Looked like it had been copied on a mimeograph machine. Some asshole'd passed it to them figuring they wouldn't know any better.

They didn't.

"No, it's a fake."

"What's a 'fake'?" I think they knew by the looks on their faces.

"No good."

"What we do?" Tape it to your forehead.

"I don't know, unless you can give it to somebody in a pile of change. But be careful, most hundred-dollar bills around here are fake, too."

"Take it to police?"

"No. They'd only laugh at you and make you feel worse."

Every couple of months afterward I'd inquire as to whether they'd gotten any more 'fakes'.

"No, we very careful now." The offending piece of paper was yellowing, taped to the back of the cash register.

Although 46th between Ninth and Tenth was hooker haven and Eighth Avenue was, too, 46th between Eighth and Ninth was one of the coolest blocks in the city. It was and still is called "Restaurant Row". There must be eighteen or twenty good restaurants on that block and they did a bang-up business because of the location, with its proximity to the Theater District and all the parking lots on the block. The block was all restaurants on the ground floor of walk-up apartment buildings and parking lots.

I really wanted to live on that block.

FOURTEEN

One of the world's great characters hung around 264 every once in a while.

His name was William Perez Acuna and he was originally from Argentina. Actually, he had fourteen or fifteen names between William and Acuna, but only used one around us heathens.

In Spanish, naturally, Acuna is pronounced "ah-coon-yah", but again, to us heathens, it was "ah-coon-ah".

Acuna was probably in his sixties, but looked and acted quite a bit younger. I knew him from the time I was twelve until I was thirty and the sonofabitch hadn't changed an iota. He was pretty tall and fancied himself one of those Latino movie stars: jet black, slicked back hair, dark brown eyes, an aquiline nose and a pencil-thin mustache. He always dressed in a suit, tie, and white shirt with cufflinks. Clear nail polish when he was flush.

Real dapper.

I had his number early-on though, when I was about twelve.

I was hanging around the office, probably being a pain-in-the-ass kid who was underfoot, when Dale said to Acuna, "Acuna, why don't you take Jim and get him some lunch?

Here's twenty." Great. Twenty sounded like a good lunch was in the offing.

Off I went with Acuna.

To Tad's Fucking Steakhouse. Tad's Steakhouses were a cheap shit chain of restaurants that boasted "Char-Broiled Steak, Baked Potato, Vegetable and Fresh Green Salad" – all for $2.99. Even in the early '60s, this was a deal that was too good to be true. The steak was tiny and like shoe leather, the baked potato was cold in the middle, the vegetables were Green Giant and the salad wasn't much either.

I know Acuna pocketed the fourteen bucks in change.

I don't know how Jeanne and Dale and Acuna hooked up but supposedly, at some point in the late '50s, he'd pulled off quite a swindle.

It was in the early days of credit cards, maybe only Diners Club was around at that point.

He'd gotten his hands on one or more and had gone and bought something like twenty or thirty-thousand dollars worth of airline tickets with them. That was a lot of money back then. I guess he had a stack of tickets a few inches high. No names on the tickets, just tickets.

In those days, airline tickets could be turned back to the airlines and they'd give you the refund in cash. Acuna would fly to some city and turn back a bunch of tickets and live on the cash. When he got tired of that city, he'd go somewhere else and do the same thing. Over and over. From what I'd heard, this went on for two or three years, over several continents.

Seems neither the Diners Club nor the airline people had gotten paid for any of Acuna's journeys and were somewhat pissed. They sicked the authorities on him and they were chasing him down with all kinds of horrible potential charges because of all the state and country borders he'd crossed. They almost nailed him in Honolulu, but he skipped, gave up the rest of the scam and basically disappeared.

Later, when I knew him, Acuna would show up in New York one day after two or three years in God knows where and would stay for a year or two, then disappear, then show up and hang around again for a year or so then disappear again. He never said, but I was always thinking the authorities hadn't given up completely and things were heating up so he'd go hide 'til the heat was off.

He never had a nickel, but man, he always looked the part.

He was always starting newspapers when he was in New York. Little, bullshit weekly or monthly Latino rags that came out maybe once, then folded. They never had any real news, but always featured plenty of neighborhood restaurant reviews. There'd be a picture taken inside the place, with the owner and maybe his family smiling proudly. For some reason, Acuna was always in the group shot.

Here's how that worked: Acuna would tell the guy that he'd write a very favorable review of the place and throw in a picture. It was essentially an ad. But, instead of taking cash he knew the guy wouldn't part with, Acuna would take it out in trade. You know, a couple of meals to be able to know enough to write the review, then a dozen or so to cover the price of the newspaper space. Acuna would have several places from which to choose to dine, would have a cheapie issue printed to show the restaurant owners the reviews and pictures and that things were progressing nicely. When a few months went by and no newspaper hit the streets and he ran out of excuses, he simply stopped showing up.

Worked like a charm.

It obviously took a lot of work, though.

He'd finally had enough of working very hard and, on his forays into New York City, worked for us – for me – at General Fountain Corp.

We wouldn't let him anywhere near the phone or customers or anybody else. We had enough work selling and building fountains and pumps and lights and ducking creditors without having to deal with trying to clean up a potential Acuna scam.

He spent all of his time collating and stapling brochures. And running off at the mouth.

He was funny as hell and we had a great time back there in the back room, making up stories and telling lies when the goddam presses weren't running full steam and we could hear ourselves think.

Acuna couldn't drink for shit, though.

We all tried to keep him from picking one up, but it was pretty hard when everybody was pounding them down and he sat there looking like he'd just lost his best friend.

Trouble was, give Acuna three drinks and he went nuts. His eyes would glaze over, he'd start giggling like an idiot and would go off on tangents none of us could follow. Then he'd stand up, shoot his cuffs, and announce he was off to see one of his girlfriends. We couldn't imagine any woman in her right mind who'd want to put up with that, but off he'd go.

He'd show up the next day and I'd inquire as to his evening.

"Oh, Jeemie, it was syuperb. A leetle wine, a leetle food, a leetle love. Eet ees what life ees all about, eh?"

Yeah, right. A little wine, a little food and a little love with Acuna. God.

I always figured he'd made a foray up Eighth Avenue. On foot.

"So, Acuna. How do you feel this morning?"

"Ah, Jeemie. I dun fill like ehdreenking today. Heh, heh, heh."

I'd light up a cigarette. "Want one?" He usually smoked Chesterfield Kings.

"Oh, no, Jeemie. I dun fill like ehsmoking today, either. Ha! Ha! Ha!"

One time, we made the mistake of letting him come into Gallagher's with us. We'd been there a little while and the crowd of regulars were there in full force and there was a lot of noise and general bedlam.

At some point, I looked over and saw Acuna talking to a couple of good looking women sitting alone at one of the tables along the wall, adjacent to the bar. This couldn't be good. They were trying to have dinner and Acuna was standing there over them, gesturing grandly and talking a mile a minute. The two people at the next table seemed to have been caught up in the conversation as well. I went back to talking to whomever I was talking to and kind of ignored it.

A few minutes later, George the maître d', walked over to me and spoke quietly in my ear. He was always speaking quietly in people's ears.

"Jimmy, you know your friend over there?"

Uh-oh.

"Yeah."

"You know he's been buying drinks for both tables and himself and putting them on Dale's bill? Now, those ladies are trying to leave to get to the theater and he's offered to walk them over there and they told me he's making them nervous."

Perfect. Vintage Acuna.

I walked over to him and told him he'd better leave well enough alone and get the fuck out before Dale asked for his check and saw an additional fifty or sixty bucks on it, courtesy of one Mr. William Perez Acuna. Problem solved.

He finally disappeared one day in the late '70s and we never heard from him again. Even after two or three years. He's probably dead somewhere.

FIFTEEN

Dale had a brother, Jack, that still lived in Marion, Indiana.

Jack was another piece of work.

He'd made it big. Really. He had a farm with half a million egg-laying chickens and had his own trucking company, Jack Hodge Transport. He was, at one time, the largest Kenworth fleet owner in the country.

He hauled for big outfits like Kroger. Kroger was especially fond of him because his drivers would go through any striking picket line. He'd have two or three tractor-trailers full of stuff and they'd just go through the line of picketers, nose to tail. Often, the picketers would pour nails and tacks all over the ground and a lot of truckers didn't want to deal with a number of flat tires. Didn't matter to Jack, though. He'd let his guys drive right up to the loading dock on eighteen rims. He knew Kroger'd pay for the damage and he was getting paid real good dough to deliver.

Every few months, Jack would come to New York for a few days. When he did, he'd have some eighteen or nineteen year-old bimbette with him. There was a different one every time. We'd all go out drinking and eating and carousing and Jack would order the bimbette around at will.

"Go to the corner and get us tomorrow's Telegraph."

"But, Ja-a-ack", she'd drawl in that semi-southern, mid-Indiana accent, "Ah've never been to New York before and ah don't have the faintest ahdea how to do that."

"Just go out through the door and make a left. Or a right. Or ask somebody. Just go do it and don't take long, alright? We gotta make our picks for tomorrow."

She'd pout a little, stamp her foot and off she'd go.

Jack'd look after her as she walked away and say something like, "Whaddya think of my new little filly, huh?"

Nice, Jack. Does her mother know she's out for the evening? Or the week?

Jack never brought his wife, Gladys. Gladys was a wonderful woman with a heart of gold. She used to say that as long as he got home safely, it was okay with her. After all, what was she going to do or say?

One time I asked him why he never brought Gladys. "Shee-it, Jim! You never bring the main mare! The main mare's gotta stay home and watch things."

Jack had four boys, JD, Billy, Mark and Little Alan, in that order, age wise.

Jack had a couple of Thoroughbred stallions and people would send the mares (the real kind) to him for breeding purposes. During the breeding ceremony, it always fell to the youngest to "guide the honker". That is, to make sure the stallion didn't miss his target. I remember Little Alan whining one morning, "Dad, do I *have* to guide the honker today?"

Broke me up.

JD was a serious young man who obviously wanted to take over the business. Mark was a normal kid who played on the Marion High School basketball team in the kind of games that draw four or five thousand people. Basketball is big in Indiana.

Billy was a complete fuck-up. He was my favorite.

He was about nineteen years old when he came to New York the first time. He arrived with a bandage the size of a boxing glove on his left hand and drunk out of his mind. Those two circumstances were explained by a truck transmission falling and nearly slicing his hand off and the fact that he spent the entire flight from Indianapolis to New York screaming "Cocktails!" so loudly and so often the flight attendants told him to shut the fuck up or they'd have cops waiting at the gate to arrest him.

Dale and Jeanne and I drove out to Marion one Thanksgiving. We stayed at the only overnight accommodations in town, the lovely Holiday Inn.

Thanksgiving morning, we drove out to Jack's. Billy asked me if I wanted to take a ride – wink, wink – and he'd show me around town – wink, wink. Sure.

We took off in his new Lincoln Continental Mark IV. Jack had bought five of them, one for himself and one for each boy, even though two of them weren't old enough to drive. Billy pulled out a joint the size of a twenty-dollar Cuban and we proceeded to smoke the whole thing while driving through the countryside.

In Indiana, all the roads are f-l-a-t and s-t-r-a-I-g-h-t and they all l-o-o-k a-l-i-k-e. I thought I was in an unending movie loop. Anyway, we drove around for a little while and went back to the farm.

Billy said let's go into one of the henhouses, there's something he wanted me to see. We walked into the longest building I'd ever seen. It was full of chickens. And it was absolutely silent in there. I asked him how many chickens were in there and he said about two hundred thousand. Christ.

He said, "See how quiet it is in here?" Yep.

"Watch this."

He flicked on the main lights and the place exploded in a cacophony that rivaled any rock concert I'd ever been to in terms of decibels. Then he flicked the lights off.

Absolute silence. On. Cacophony. Off. Silence.

Seems the chickens think it's nighttime when the lights are off and daytime when they're on. Chickens aren't too smart but I guess they're quite talkative during daylight hours.

Every day they'd get four or five chicken dying from "blowouts" – chickens laying eggs that were too large for their birth canals or whatever they have. Ouch.

According to Billy, a good egg-laying chicken lays two eggs every eighteen hours. As they get older, and it's only a matter of months, the time between laying their eggs gets longer and longer. Once a chicken lays an egg only every twenty-four hours, they cost more than they produce.

That's when they'd be shipped off to Campbell's Soup. Of course, they'd buy and sell chickens in lots of twenty-five to forty thousand, so it there'd be truckloads coming and going. Jack said Campbell's then sold the feet to China.

I also learned how to tell a Grade A egg from a non-Grade A egg and I won't bore you with the details. Suffice it to say, though, of the dozen eggs in your Grade A carton, probably four or five won't be, but you won't know the difference.

Jack and Dale caught up with us and Jack said the four of us were going out to see his plane. Jack had his own Piper Something-or-Other that he'd fly around the Midwest calling on various customers and what not.

Off we went, Billy and I still stoned out of our gourds.

We got to the little airstrip and Dale and Billy got in the back and I sat in the co-pilot's seat next to Jack. Off we went.

We were just flying around and Jack said, "Watch this." Up we went. Straight up. Until the fucking engine died. I almost shit myself.

Down we fell, Jack laughing like hell. He pushed a button or something and the engine started up again and we were okay. "How'd you like that stall?"

"Great." I wanted to cry.

Next thing I knew, he sat back, crossed his arms and said, "OK, Jimbo, fly the plane."

"What?"

"The plane. Fly the plane."

God, how I wished I hadn't smoked that dope.

There was a steering yoke in front of me, just like the one in front of Jack. He said, "Grab hold. Pull back and we go up. Push in and we go down. Left is left and right is right."

I did. And, dammit, it was fun. Before long, I was pulling back slightly and turning to the left, doing a mean banking maneuver. Sailing all over flat ol' Indiana in a bright blue sky and having a ball. I felt like Sky King.

"Christ! Watch out for that plane!"

Plane? What plane? What fucking airplane? Where?

"Over there."

It was a few miles away but almost at the same altitude as we were. You don't see wings when you're at the same altitude. Just a little tube going through space.

"See, in a small plane like this, you have to kind of go up and down all the time so you can see if anybody else is near you."

Point taken.

Jack took over and again said, "Watch."

We flew for a couple of minutes and a voice came over the radio telling us that we were approaching restricted airspace and please turn away. Jack just sat there, humming. A few seconds later, the voice came on again and said the same thing, only this time with a little more urgency behind it.

Hum-de-dum.

"Piper, you have now entered restricted United States Air Force airspace. You are now subject to apprehension and disbursal by U.S. Military Jet aircraft."

Disbursal?

Jack banked away. "I just like to see if they're on their toes. 'Specially on Thanksgiving. I figured they'd all be half-drunk or something. That makes me feel better."

Yeah. Me, too.

We finally landed safely and went back to Jack and Gladys' for Thanksgiving Dinner. Just as everybody was about to sit down to a huge feast, Jack put out his hand and opened it. There was a button or something in it.

"See this? It's one of the buttons off the co-pilot's seat. After we landed, ol' Jimbo went into the men's room. When he left, I went in after him. Looked down in the bottom of the toilet and found this. Looked familiar so I went back to the plane and sure enough. Ol' Jimbo'd got so scared he sucked this button clear off the seat."

Nice, Jack. Now can we say grace?

The next day, off we went to see Dale's aunt and uncle, Ruby and Everett and his cousin, Roy Gene, and his girlfriend, whose name doesn't matter here and mattered probably just a little more to Roy Gene.

Everybody referred to Uncle Everett as Hoghair, because he'd always had a brush cut. He was a pretty straight-laced guy, but would get into it every once in a while. Every time he did, though, it caused a little ruckus in the family, especially with Aunt Ruby.

A few months earlier, it seems ol' Hoghair got to hanging out with Jack and his son, JD and a few of Jack's drivers. They were at the Elks' Club, drinking and playing punchboard. Like most places, it's illegal to really gamble in Indiana, but punchboards were real close to it. I can't remember exactly how it works, but there are a series of numbers written on a blackboard or something and you bought a punchboard from the bartender. You punched X number of holes in the card and if some of the numbers revealed on your card matched the ones on the blackboard, you won cash, the amount depending on the number of matches. Playing punchboard was like eating peanuts when you were sitting at the bar – addictive.

Anyway, Jack and JD and all the guys would kind of rotate in and out of the Elks as they were going about their day, but ol' Hoghair held the fort down from mid-afternoon until mid-evening, bending his elbow and playing punchboard. He was tight as the bark on a tree, so he must've been cleaning up on the punchboard. Natch, he was plastered.

It got kind of late and Ruby called Jack's house to see if anybody knew where Hoghair was. Jack said he thought so and would have him brought home. He sent JD back to the Elks to retrieve him. JD said he was in such bad shape he couldn't get out of the chair he was sitting on. JD was a pretty big guy, so he picked up Hoghair, held him on his hip and got him to the car.

Upon arriving at Hoghair and Ruby's, he rang the bell, Hoghair under one arm and on his hip. Ruby answered. JD: "Hi, Aunt Ruby. What do you want me to do with Hoghair?"

"Just set him down in front of the door." Bang.

Hoghair woke up around dawn, cold as hell and with a face that looked like the reverse image of the cocoa mat that said "Home Sweet Home".

When Hoghair went off, he went off big time. And Aunt Ruby would be pissed for days.

Cousin Roy Gene was a real piece of work. If I remember correctly, he raised popcorn. And he fancied himself quite the swordsman with the ladies. His demeanor was that of a pot-bellied, forty-five year-old Indiana hick trying to act like Elvis did in his twenties.

One night he was out in the country, parked on the side of a very dark road in his brand new Cadillac with some bimbo and things were getting hot and heavy. Now, a lot of the roads in Indiana are completely deserted at night, hence the reason Roy Gene and the bimbo were parked there. Pitch black.

In the middle of the bumping and grinding, Roy Gene sort of noticed some headlights coming up behind them, maybe a mile or two away. Didn't give it much thought at the time. Probably some farmer coming home from a bingo game. Pretty soon, though, those headlights came up right behind Roy Gene's Caddy and sat there for a few seconds, maybe twenty-five feet away.

All of a sudden, he heard the other car's engine gun and the tires squeal.

BAM!

The car ran directly into the back of the Caddy.

"Jesus Kee-rist!"

The car backed up. The engine gunned again, tires squealed again and…..

BAM!

"What the fuck?!?"

The car backed off and rolled up parallel to the Caddy. He recognized the car as his other car – a year-old Lincoln, now with a nearly-totaled front end to complement the nearly-totaled rear end on the new Caddy.

The automatic window slid down and his wife yelled to him, "What's that do for your old hard-on, buddy?" And drove away into the night.

Alright, Roy Gene!

SIXTEEN

Because we never knew if Acuna would ever re-appear – and because he was slow as shit anyway because he never shut up – we would sometimes hire somebody to work in the back room to help get the mailings out.

We hired my friend Beaver's sister, Allison, once and she was there three or four months. Beaver's real name was Steven, but no one ever called him that. He looked exactly like Beaver Cleaver and probably had since he was a kid. He had a terrific girlfriend named Leslie and I couldn't figure that one out for the life of me.

My feeling was that Beav was like a big, loyal mongrel dog who would happily do anything Leslie asked. I tried, time and again, to surreptitiously steal Leslie away, but I think she knew she had too good a thing going with Beav to chuck it for somebody who wouldn't ask "how high?" when she said "jump". Damn, we could've made some beautiful music together, though.

So, on occasion, I made music with Beaver's sister, Allison. It was like taking candy from a baby, which she wasn't – honest. She was around twenty. And it'd only happen when I was drunk. All I had to do was try and snap my fingers, lousy as that sounds.

One night, Jeanne and Dale and I had Allison accompany us on our rounds. Started at Gallagher's and before we'd been there an hour, I noticed Allison's eyes were kind of looking in two different directions at the same time. We left Gallagher's and headed to Howard Johnson's at 51st and Eighth.

Believe it or not, in the early 70s, the bar at Howard Johnson's was packed every night. They had a happy hour and would bring out those little pieces of diced sausage and white and yellow cheese, along with Swedish meatballs and those Little Smokie hot dogs in some god-awful catsup-based sauce. Naturally, Billy Ruben loved the place. They poured real stiff drinks and you'd have six or seven and when you asked for the check, it'd read, $4.50. No shit. See, the bartenders would double-charge the tourists so ours got paid for. We tipped the guys real well, though. Worked like a charm. For us.

There was one bartender, in particular, Danny, who would be almost brazen about it. Even if the place weren't crowded and there were only eight or ten people in the joint, the same thing would go on. I guess the tourists figured everything was just expensive in New York. After all, here they were, all the way from West Buttfuck and were sitting in a sophisticated cocktail lounge in the greatest city in the world!

Rubes.

There were always rumors that the Howard Johnson corporation would send spotters into their places, to make sure the shareholders were holding their own and not getting ripped off. At least everybody, including the bartenders, thought they were rumors.

I was sitting in there one night, by myself, having a few and shooting the shit with Danny.

Billy Ruben had left when the Little Smokies ran out. I snuck a look at my check riding in front of me on the bar and saw something like $1.60. Smirk.

I looked over and saw Danny deep in conversation with some guy in a suit and tie, but didn't think anything of it. Next thing I knew, Danny was taking his apron off and walking away. Funny time for him to be going off duty – he didn't even ask me to settle up when his shift changed. Didn't even say goodnight.

I asked one of the waitresses – the Night of the Living Dead one – "Hey, what's up with Danny?"

"Gone. Fired."

"Just like that?"

"Just like that. You see the guy in the suit he was talking to? He's a Howard Johnson's spotter and had been watching Danny for over an hour. For one thing, he saw you've had four or five drinks and your check never left the bar. Bang. Gone."

"Oh."

For a minute there, I felt a little responsible. Got over it, though. Paid my $1.60, left a buck on the bar for the new guy and split.

By the way, that was the Howard Johnson's where Angela Davis was caught.

Jeanne and Dale and Allison and I made our way there from Gallagher's and Allison was just barely hanging on. As a matter of fact, Dale and I determined we couldn't take her in there with us. No bartender would serve a party with someone in her condition in tow. So we had her stand out front in full view of the window so we could keep an eye on her.

There were a couple of awning poles and we kind of propped Allison up against one of them and had her hold onto it with both hands. She bobbed and weaved a little, but never went down and never let go of the pole.

When Jeanne and Dale and I would go out to lunch, we'd leave Allison at the front desk so she could answer the phone. One day she asked me, "Who are these guys Bill Leith and Harry Hyatt?" Never mind, Allison, they're just not here, but take a message for them anyway.

I guess she'd get bored, because she'd write herself these weird-ass notes, then tear them up and throw them in the waste basket. The reason I know this is that one day when we got back to the office, Jeanne found one of the notes that hadn't been torn up, just tossed on the floor in the general direction of the basket.

She looked at it to make sure it wasn't something important – or, she was just being nosy – and said in a stage whisper (Allison was around the corner in the back room.), "Hey, look at this."

I won't go into all the details, but it was obvious that she had some self-esteem issues along with a few sexual hang-ups (don't look at me!). The note began, "Dear Cream Cheese....."

Yeesh.

From that point onward, we referred to her amongst ourselves as Dumb Old Allison.

She left sometime soon after that.

There was an old harpy that would come into Gallagher's every once in a while and Jeanne always had a soft spot for old harpies. I can't remember her name but she lived in the Ansonia, up on Broadway around 74th or 75th Street. At one point, when she was half a century younger, I guess she'd been an okay artist. She still worked at it but it was pretty obvious the old hand-eye coordination had slipped a bit. Either that, or at one time there had been a market for art that looked like it had been done by a third-grader.

She had a grand-niece from Colorado that was coming to live with her. Her name was Andrea. According to the old lady, Andrea was 22 years old, tall and blonde – "a beautiful girl".

Twenty-two? Tall? Blonde? Beautiful? From Colorado? Must be one of those ski-bum chicks that had completely acted up too much and her folks were sending her to the old lady to calm her down a little. Yes!

I should have known better, coming from a goddam eighty year-old third grade painter.

Andrea was twenty-two, alright. And blonde, except at the roots. And tall, if you think five-six is tall. And weighed in around 175. And, the word "vapid" comes to mind. Or, dumb as a box of rocks.

Christ.

She came to work for us, thanks to Jeanne's soft spot for harpies.

She was an okay worker. Not great. Not bad. So that was good.

Acuna was still around and I couldn't tell if he wanted to put his Argentine moves on her or not. I don't think he could, either. That would have been a pair to draw to.

Andrea was always – I mean *always* – trying to lose weight. The only problem is that she had absolutely no self-control.

She'd pack herself a lunch at home and bring it in. Not bad. Small tuna sandwich, a few carrot and celery slices and an apple. She'd eat it at her desk and go back to work. Around 2:30, 3 o'clock she'd head downstairs.

She'd come back with three packages of Ring-Dings and a chocolate milk shake from Chock Full o' Nuts. And inhale them.

"Oh, I just needed a little snack."

"Oh."

We had a doctor's-type scale there in the back room. Dale was always on it. "Maybe I'll cut back on the bread and butter." Never mind the quart of scotch.

Andrea put many more miles on that scale that Dale did, though. Like eleven or twelve times a day, which worked out to almost one time every half-hour.

She'd walk in in the morning and hop on the scale. Drink a cup of coffee and jump on the scale. Go on a four-block mission and get back and get on the scale. Ride the elevator to the twelfth floor, ride it back and get on the scale. I think she was just a little pre-occupied with her weight, though it really never changed.

The worst one, though, was when she went to the bathroom and came back in and got on the scale. She had to walk past everybody in each direction. And, it was obvious to everybody in the joint that she went into the ladies' room, took a dump, and checked to see if that dump had lost her any weight. Shame? What shame?

She was a far cry from the ski-bunny I had first envisioned. A real far cry.

The Polish guys were in love with her, though. It was probably a combination of forced celibacy caused by living in a room with five other guys in Greenpoint, Brooklyn, and the fact that, in Poland, I guess they liked 'em stout. The extra weight will get 'em through the nine-month Polish Winter or something.

The lecherous bastards would jump at the chance to talk to her. Only they couldn't. They didn't know a word of English. Andrea, in her shining wisdom though, thought that if she...spoke...English...very...slowly...they...would...understand...her.

It's a well-known fact that if you speak English very slowly, everyone in the world will understand it. The Polish guys didn't care, though. She'd be speaking slowly and they'd yammer back and forth to each other, laughing. I didn't know the Polish language either, but I sure knew what they were saying.

Believe it or not, one Friday she told me she was going over to their apartment in Greenpoint with them for dinner. Off they all trekked around six o'clock, the Polish guys giggling and yammering and Andrea...trying...to...talk...slowly...to...them. I don't know what really happened over there in Brooklyn that night and I don't wanna know.

On Monday, she told me they had been perfect gentlemen and they'd eaten a nice meal.

Probably bologna on Wonder Bread. I asked her what they'd all talked about and she said, "Oh, nothing much."

No shit.

Al Gonzalez, the real Albert Gonzalez, worked for us, too. Al was terrific. Really terrific. Worked hard. Smart. Funny. We had a great time there in the old back room.

Al could collate, staple, stuff, run stuff through the meter, tie, bundle, fill the bags and deliver the bags like nobody's business. He was always moving.

We all really liked Al.

We'd listen to Newsradio 88 or 1010 WINS all day long and one-up each other on fictitious back-stories on the news items. It sounds stupid when I read it, too, but trust me, we had a good time doing it.

We'd also bet on snowstorms. Whenever we'd hear a weather report calling for, say four inches of snow overnight, one of us would blurt out, "Odds on inches!" The other guy would have to say whether he thought we'd get four inches or not and lay odds on whether or not it would happen. Usual bet was a buck. It was the only thing that made a fucking snowstorm in New York City any fun.

Al couldn't quite get with the program of ducking creditors. Couldn't lie for shit. He was tricky, too, the bastard.

If Al was on phone duty, it'd ring and he'd say, "General Fountains."

"Dale Hodge, please."

"Who may I ask is calling?"

"Joe Jaboni from We Just Got Chumped."

"Hold on, please." He'd put him on hold.

"Jim. Jim!" I'd be around the corner in the back room.

"What?"

"It's for you."

"Who is it?"

"I dunno. Said he's a friend of yours. Seems like he knows you."

"OK. Hello?"

Al would laugh like hell and I'd have to have Harry Hyatt or Bill Leith deal with that asshole Jaboni.

SEVENTEEN

There was another goofball who hung around for a few months. Johnny Vance. He wanted to be called John Vance, because that sounded a little more sophisticated or something, but he was Johnny Vance.

He was one of PL's stooges and PL had placed a running ad the Daily News for impressionable young lambs that would be led to the slaughter. You know, "Travel! See the U.S.A. and get paid. Good Money. Free transportation. Call Mr. Vance (212)XXXXXXX".

Mister Vance.

Like I said, Vance was a stooge of the first order. Who else but a stooge would stay in some cheap-ass hotel for months, having to beg PL on a daily basis for food and walking-around money? And sit around and wait for the phone to ring?

Dale had let him use one of our rollover numbers, one of the ones we never gave out.

Vance would show up every morning and sit at one of the old steel desks in the back room. He always wore a shiny suit and a tie from Tie City, the place you could get three for five bucks. And carried a fucking briefcase! Now, what in hell would Vance need a briefcase for? To carry that day's copy of the News? Al and I used to speculate what was in that briefcase that he never opened. Pornography? Shakespearean quattros? His only change of underwear and socks? The other two ties from Tie City?

He never did any work, just sat reading newspapers and running up Dale's phone bill by spending hour after hour talking to PL or six or seven of his other goons. Vance was always on the goddam phone. His visage was always one of import. Whatever he was talking about sure was important. If you tried to get his attention to send him for coffee or something, he'd scowl and wave you away, like you might overhear state secrets or something. Right.

"Vance! Hang up the goddam phone and go down to Joe's and get us some coffee.

Now!"

"Uh – I'll have to call you back. Something just came up."

That's right, Johnny, something just came up. A mission for two blacks and a regular. We got most of our coffee from Joe's on the corner. We bought one of those automatic drip coffeemakers one time, but the roaches decided it made a better motel for them than a coffeemaker for us.

Joe's was one of the classic little holes-in-the-wall that you can only find in New York. Coffee. Bagels. Donuts. Egg creams. Scrambled eggs. That sort of thing. Joe was an old guy at the time and must've had foot problems. No wonder, what with standing up for twelve hours a day, five days a week for fifty years. He had those funny soft-soled shoes that had the ties rather rakishly at an angle at the side of your foot. The other guys who worked in there must have been with him from Day One, too. Real nice old guys.

A guy named Utah used to live in the basement under Joe's. Six or seven stairs ran from between the sidewalk and the building to a door down below. I mention that for a reason. Utah was really a street drunk, probably originally from Utah or why would he have gotten that name?

He had no real voice left, sort of like a constant raspy stage whisper. And he tended to wear the same clothes for months on end. Utah was generally a total mess.

Every so often, he'd clean himself up for a few days and would work for Joe taking out the garbage and sweeping the sidewalk – that sort of thing. When he was sober, he was a real nice guy who could actually carry on an intelligent conversation. Boy, but was that seldom, though.

Most often, he would stand there drunkenly panhandling. If he wasn't too far gone, his panhandling was a thing to behold.

We were kitty-corner from the Port Authority Bus Terminal and every weekday morning and late afternoon, a couple hundred thousand people would pass through it. I mean throngs of people would traipse up 40th Street and all the other streets surrounding the Port Authority to go about their mundane existence of ride bus, walk, work, walk, ride bus.

Utah would stand there, right in the middle of the pedestrian traffic pattern, so as to make a complete pain-in-the-ass of himself, and beg. Naturally, everybody totally ignored him, head down and moving. He'd get off some terrific one-liners and putdowns in the direction of certain people as they passed.

To a fat lady: "Hey, blimp-o. Where'd you learn to walk like that? A duck?" Or, "Hey, fat lady, isn't it time to sing?"

"Hey, hot-shot! Nice suit. I hear that style's coming back."

Granted, they weren't hilarious, but you had to consider the source.

Sometimes, he'd stand most of the way down the stairway in the sidewalk and scream and yell. To the uninitiated, it appeared that a drunken head was sitting on the sidewalk, throwing insults.

Vance wouldn't ever have any of the kids answering the ads come up to the office. I suspect Dale drew the line there. A few of them made it as far as the hallway by the elevators, though. Not that they didn't seem like nice kids or anything, just suffice it to say that it was doubtful whether Mr. and Mrs. America would invite them into their houses to hear the virtues of the Ladies' Home Journal or Sports Illustrated.

Vance usually met the interviewees at a coffee shop somewhere. That's probably why he was always sweating the walking around money from PL. He was probably somewhat embarrassed – yep, even Vance - that he might have to scam the kid out of paying for the coffees.

If a kid actually got hired, it was Vance's job to get him or her to whatever city PL and the crew were in.

PL would send Vance half-a-dozen prepaid Greyhound or Trailways tickets (maybe that's what was in the briefcase!). Natch, he wouldn't trust Vance with the money to go out and buy the tickets himself. Vance would tell the kid to go home and pack and meet him at the Port Authority at a specified time in a specified place. Vance would then put the kid on the bus and off he or she would go, with visions of luxurious nationwide travel dancing in his or her head.

Next stop, York, Pennsylvania.

Here's the kicker – PL would charge the kid for the bus ticket. The kid would show up in York. PL had a goon pick him up and take him out to dinner. PL would charge the kid for dinner. By the time the kid got to the motel, he already owed PL sixty or seventy bucks, but he didn't know it.

PL would say, "Kid, you need some new clothes. Gotta look good, you know. Earl, here's a couple hundred. Take the kid out and get him some new duds." Off they'd go. Of course, when they got back, the two bills were history and the kid had a sackful of new shitty-looking stuff from Kmart or something.

Unbeknownst to the kid, he was now into PL for two-seventy.

Until the kid started bringing in some real money, PL would charge him for his share of the motel room – still unbeknownst to the kid. Maybe another hundred-and-a-half over the next two weeks. Plus, PL would hand him some "walking-around" money.

By the time the kid's first paycheck rolled around, he'd be informed that he owed the company – PL – somewhere north of five hundred bucks.

The kid would get scared or pissed or something and start a minor ruckus. PL would say, "Kid – you have over five hundred dollars of my money. You can either start working it off or you can walk out without giving it back. Of course, if you walk out, I'll call the cops right now and have your ass thrown in jail. Mr. Vance told you how this worked before you ever took this job so don't try and tell me you didn't know anything about it."

Sure, Vance told him. You just know he did.

Worked like a charm.

How quickly the kid worked it off depended on how good a salesman he was. If he worked hard and toed the line and PL took a liking to him, it'd be gone in no time. If he was a fuck-up and PL didn't like him, it was probably just this side of indentured servitude.

We were visiting PL one time. Why, I don't know. But we were.

I walked out of my room in the morning to find an ambulance in the parking lot down in front of one of the other rooms. There was a little commotion by the door so I ambled on over to see what was up.

The attendants were leaving the motel room with a young woman strapped into a wheelchair which they proceeded to load into the back of the ambulance. She didn't seem sick or injured, just really pissed off and screaming obscenities. A meth overdose, perhaps? In jumped the attendants and off they went.

PL was walking my way.

"What's up with the girl?", I asked him.

"Ah – she didn't want to go to work today. Told me she had a stomach ache. Third fucking stomach ache this week. Figured she oughta have it checked out, you know?"

That was another of PL's tricks.

He'd get one of these people that just didn't want to work and would try everything to pull the wool over his eyes so he or she could sit around and watch television and bullshit all day.

After two or three of those "sick" excuses, PL would simply call an ambulance and have them taken to the hospital to get thoroughly check out. There was never anything wrong with them, but they came back with a whopper of a hospital and ambulance bill.

Of course, PL would pay it and it'd be added to the person's PL debt.

They wouldn't get sick again for a long, long time and, lo and behold, would become a selling demon.

PL certainly had a way of motivating people. A regular Jack Welch.

EIGHTEEN

My fountain tycoon-dom was about to take a turn for the better.

We decided it'd be a good idea to begin having a booth at various trade shows that were conducive to selling fountains. Hotel shows, restaurant shows, display shows, home shows – that sort of thing.

The shows would be my bailiwick.

I thought it was great because I'd get to go to other cities like real businesspeople, stay in hotels, eat at nice restaurants and not have to run that goddam press and be Harry Hyatt or Bill Leith for a few days.

By the way, that gave ol' Al an honest-to-God excuse when somebody called for one of them. "I'm sorry, Mr. Hyatt is in Chicago this week attending a trade convention." Even sounded legit to the guy from We Just Got Chumped.

We thought we should get our feet wet close to home the first time so we signed up for a booth at the annual International Hotel and Motel Association's show – the Hotel Show - at the Coliseum right there in New York.

We decided on a 10-foot by 20-foot booth and would feature our piece-de-resistance, the "Satellite Fountain". It was a very cool fountain and we called it that because it looked like Sputnik when the fountain wasn't on. When the fountain was on, the water kind of gave the impression of a dandelion just before it goes to seed. When you can blow on it and the stuff sails away on the wind. Boy, that looks lousy on paper, but it was pretty. It could probably be better described as a ball of water. There are a couple of massive ones on Sixth Avenue that we copied. Maybe they're still there.

The fountain really caught peoples' attention because it sounded like Niagara Falls and, with clear white lights under it, the water sparkled to beat the band.

We also had our fifty-inch "Rainbow" and 36-inch "Mark IV", both of which had the obligatory "eleven dramatic color changes and three water pattern changes a minute" feature. A couple of smaller 24-inch "Mark III"s, an "Olympia" fiberglass waterfall and a six-gallon cocktail fountain, inspiringly called the "6G".

By the way, there are no such things as "champagne fountains". See, the bubbles in the champagne cause too much air to pass through the submersible pump and nothing will come out. Besides, who the hell would want champagne splashing around anyway? It'd be flatter'n a pail of piss in thirty seconds.

We always used a lot of artificial greenery in and around the fountains. Plastic. Couldn't use silk or any other cloth-like material because the water would wreak havoc with anything but plastic.

When we got the contract for the Hotel Show, we discovered that everything but the "personalized hand-lettered" sign for the back of the booth and the drape it hung on was a la carte and cost a fortune to rent. You wanted electric? Extra. A carpet? Extra. A table? A table drape? A chair (of which you could choose several models) or couch? A wastebasket? Everything was extra.

I was sitting there on the couch, in my office base of operations, going over this stuff with Dale and Jeanne.

"Gee, this stuff is a little pricey, but I guess we should do it, huh?", I opined.

"Hell, I don't want to pay through the nose to rent that stuff. We'll go out and buy all the materials you need and you can set it up here at the Coliseum, then take it with you to all the shows."

"Oh. Okay."

Damn, I kind of thought I'd be able to order all that shit for each of the shows, ship the fountains right to the booth, fly into the city, waltz into the convention center, get one of the workers to put a few buckets of water in the fountains, turn 'em on, adjust 'em, and break for the hotel and the attendant cocktail lounge without working up a sweat.

This was sounding very different.

It was.

I went out and bought three heavy-duty folding tables, three large black pieces of cloth to use as table drapes, a ten-by-ten carpet and a few other incidentals.

I asked what kind of a chair they thought I should buy.

Jeanne: "Chair? What do you need a chair for? You'll be busy selling fountains and, besides, if you're sitting down, people will think you don't care about what you're doing."

"Uh, right." That's okay, I don't mind standing on a concrete floor with a half-inch piece of cheap shit carpet underfoot from nine in the morning until six at night, three or four days in a row. "We don't need a chair." Maybe I could steal one from another booth.

For that first show up at the Coliseum, I enlisted Bubniak and a couple of the Polish guys to help me get the stuff up the street and get set up.

It went pretty smoothly because we didn't have to use the loading dock, just carried the stuff in through the door. The Polish guys had never seen anything like the Coliseum or what was being set up inside it.

The poor bastards who'd had their stuff shipped in sometimes had to wait six or seven hours for it to be delivered to their booths. Maybe there was something to this do-it-yourself shit after all.

Ah, the unions.

Every guy who worked at the Coliseum – and at every convention center in a city of fifteen people or more – was a member of one union or another. Teamsters, electrical workers, plumbers, police, firemen, food workers – everybody.

And that meant you had to pay hourly union rates to use them. In our case, just to get a simple electrical line to our booth would cost us two hours at sixty dollars an hour. A hundred and twenty bucks to get a guy to bring out an extension cord and plug it in.

Ah, but there was always a way around the unions.

I always thanked my lucky stars for that very first union guy I ran into at the Coliseum.

He said, "Sure, go sign up to have your electric cord brought in. It'll run you one-twenty and it'll be in before nine tonight. Or, just give me twenty bucks and I'll have it done in five minutes."

Every union guy in every city works the same scam. Chicago. Boston. Houston. Washington. Myrtle Beach. Dayton, Ohio (Dayton, Ohio?!? Yep. Dayton, Ohio).

Go into the convention center in any city and toss around twenties like they're hot potatoes and you're done in no time.

I wondered if the chancellor of the exchequer of the union or whatever he's called ever asks why the union doesn't make more money off these shows. Probably not. He's probably just pissed he can't get in on the scam.

The Hotel Show at the Coliseum was quite a success and I was treated like an official fountain tycoon each night when I got to Gallagher's after the show closed. The folks at the bar, the bartenders, waiters, maître d's, Larry the men's room guy, even Honey the hat check girl – everybody wanted to know how I did that day. I even eclipsed Dale as fountain tycoon there for a couple of days.

Not only that, I made some pretty good money. Remember, if somebody came into the showroom and I made a sale, I got five percent. Anything I sold at the shows got me ten percent. I'd make a couple of hundred bucks a day at some of these shows, especially the Hotel Show. Hell, a couple of times I had to have people wait in line to place their orders. It was like Joe's on the corner, but instead of chocolate egg creams, they were fountains.

My booth made a lot of noise, It sounded like an afternoon storm in the Amazonian Rain Forest. And it always brought the same stupid comments from people walking by:

"Whoa, Sally. Listen to that. Hey, Pal, I'll bet you make a lot of trips to the men's room, huh? Ha-ha-ha!"

No, dude, I just piss in the cocktail fountain whenever the urge hits me. Wanna try it out?

The Hotel Show worked out pretty well for us.

That was in November. We decided to try out the New England Restaurant Show the following April.

By this time, we had another car we had gotten from Dale's father, Roy. It was a '67 Pontiac Catalina, another boat. But it ran well and we decided that I'd load it up and drive it to Boston. Actually, Dale and Jeanne had decided that. My days of flying around the country ended before they began.

It was loaded up alright. I didn't take The Satellite, that would've been an impossibility. But everything else went, though. I looked like Jed Fucking Clampett tooling north on the New England Thruway. The ass-end of the Catalina cleared the road by about six inches.

The thing that made me nervous is that I had the three tables tied to the roof. Because the Catalina was a coupe, it didn't have any window frames to tie the rope onto. When you put down the front and back windows, you had nothing but air for about six feet. So, we had to run the rope all the way around the roof, horizontally. That meant I had ropes in front of my forehead and behind the back of my head. I was afraid I'd hit a bump and strangle myself.

Not only that, but when I got up around sixty, the wind caught up under the tables and lifted them up a couple of inches. We hadn't tightened the goddam ropes quite tight enough. So, there I was, tables banging over my head, ropes flapping around my head, never having driven to Boston before and cursing myself for being a fountain tycoon.

When I got there several hours later, I was content in knowing that at least I'd be able to carry all the stuff in and set it up myself and not have to wait by some loading dock 'til the cows came home.

As I pulled into the convention center, whatever it was called, it started to sprinkle. Okay, fine, a little sprinkle. Nothing to get my shorts in an uproar over.

"Where can I park to unload this stuff?", to some attendant in a slicker.

"Up in the parking lot in the back. Up the ramp."

"Thanks."

"No problem."

Man, I hated it then when people said, "No problem" and I still hate it today. Of course it was no problem for him to spurt out twelve fucking syllables, sitting there on his goddam stool. A simple "you're welcome" wouldn't do? Asshole.

Up the ramp, looking for a parking place nearest an entrance. I was rolling now.

I found one a good quarter of a mile away. The parking lot was also used by people who worked in the area and there must have been a thousand cars on the lot.

A fifty-inch "Rainbow" fountain only weighs about forty-five or fifty pounds. Made it in the entrance, found my booth space and thought, OK, we're getting there now.

Then I started unloading in earnest.

I had four boxes of brochures, each weighing about sixty pounds. I had a "Mark IV" – a mere thirty. Two "Mark IIIs" at ten apiece. An "Olympia" rock waterfall at about seventy-five.

A box of cables, buckets, tools, stapler, business cards and other stuff, weighing in at an unwieldy twenty-five or thirty. The cheap-ass carpet at about fifty (though I could throw it over my shoulder with the ends dragging on the ground). And three goddam tables at fifty each. In all, about 600 pounds of stuff.

At a quarter mile each trip with the stuff and a quarter mile back to the car, empty-handed, I made twelve round trips of a half-mile each, or six miles, total.

Oh, right – the rain started coming down in buckets approximately halfway through round trip number four. I was drenched to the skin and my arms were falling off.

I hated my life. I hated being a fucking fountain tycoon. I hated everything.

I finally got everything together and the show went just fine and I sold a whole bunch of stuff and about ten in the morning of the last day I began to think of the load-in process and my stomach started to ache. It would take hours and I'd probably die of a heart attack in some parking lot in Boston, with old "no problem" sitting on his stool picking his nose. I found the bar (every restaurant show had a bar) and had three quick Bloody Marys.

I called the office to check in.

"General Fountains." Al.

"Al, Jim. Can I talk to Dale?"

"Nah. He's out."

"Out? Where?"

"I dunno. Said he was going to meet Harry Hyatt and Bill Leith."

"Just put him on the phone, asshole."

Dale was happy with the results of the show and he must have gotten some advance money in the business reply mail, because he told me to go ahead and sell my demonstrator models for whatever I could get for them. Just bring back the tables and carpet and any leftover brochures and whatnot.

Hooray!

And the sun was shining! And, I'd found a parking spot only an eighth of a mile away! And I figured I'd made a good seven-hundred and fifty bucks on the show!

Man, I loved my life! I loved being a fountain tycoon! I loved everything!

NINETEEN

Dale announced he had decided to write a book.

On Henry Ford.

What.

Yep. He was Dale's hero and Dale thought the world needed another book on Henry Ford. He'd read a dozen of them and thought he now knew enough about him to write a book.

Dale, if you've read a dozen of them, and there are probably dozens more you haven't read, what is there that you can share with the world that hasn't already been shared? In other words, what's your unique selling point?

Oh, that doesn't matter. People will always buy a book on Henry Ford.

What.

He called Bill Ruben for advice on how to research the book. Billy told him to go to the New York Public Library, get a slew of reference books on Henry Ford and the Ford Motor Company and a whole litany of other things that started to make Dale's eyes glaze over.

See, that's what Billy Ruben did. Research. Never got around to writing anything, but he surely knew how to do research. Ruben offered to come to the office to talk the thing over with Dale. Dale was bored with the conversation by now so he said okay, come on over.

Before Billy could start discussing the finer points of research, he had to have two or three hot dogs from the microwave and a couple of scotches. Man, Billy had it down to a science.

Finally, he said, "Well, Dale, ready to go to the library?"

Billy could be so dense. Dale had never seen the inside of a library and he had no intention of doing so now.

"Bill, here's what you do. You and Jim go to the library and check out some of those reference books on Henry Ford and bring them back here."

"But Dale, you can't check out reference books from the library. They have to stay there. You can only take them to a table and read them."

"Jim, take Bill and go get the books."

Ruben: "But, Dale, you can't take those books out! We'd have to steal them. We could get arrested or something!"

Off we went. It was only a five- or six-block walk. Up the stairs, past the lions and in the front door.

"OK, Billy, lead on."

"Oh, I don't like this. I don't like this at all."

Fortunately, it was March and everyone was still wearing winter coats. It wouldn't be a problem.

Forty-five minutes or so later, we had several Henry Ford reference books in our possession. Now to get them out.

"Here, Bill. Slide a couple of these bad boys down the front of your pants. And button your coat." He did it and I did it, too.

"Now, let's just walk on out."

And we did.

"Don't worry, Bill. We'll bring them back when he's done."

Right.

Actually, Dale did want the books returned. But not before having Billy stand there and Xerox every single page of every single book. Didn't bother Ruben, not one little bit. It took him three days, in which time he'd downed a dozen or more hot dogs, gotten taken to lunch once or twice and hopped on the Gallagher's Express at the end of each day.

He was in clover.

When he was done he announced he would return the books. Fine. He tucked them blatantly under his arm. I said, "Whoa, Bill. I thought we'd get in trouble if we took those books out. Aren't you gonna sneak them back in?"

"Nah, I'll just tell them I'd come across them on a bus, saw that they were property of the New York Public Library and am returning them to their rightful place. I'll be a hero!" Bill Ruben, Library Hero.

Dale never wrote the book. Oh, he plagiarized each of the books, lifting entire paragraphs from each and stitching them into three or four chapters, but that's as far as it went.

Too bad. Maybe the world needed a single book on Henry Ford that was an amalgam of six or seven books people had wasted their time writing on their own. We'll never know.

It was around this time that I moved one block east on West 46th Street, onto Restaurant Row. 326 West 46th Street, just west of Eighth Avenue. Second floor rear in a four floor walk-up. Studio. Two-twenty-five a month.

I liked that little place. It had two big windows in the back and there were several large trees back there.

Still had the same furniture with the exception of the blow-up chair. I can't believe I paid a few hundred bucks to keep it in storage when it'd cost me less than a hundred to buy it from the Salvation Army.

As I said, there were a lot of great restaurants on the block, including Barbetta, Broadway Joe, Joe Allen's and a number of other ones that I can't remember.

My favorite was Joe Allen's, a pretty famous place that had its fair share of celebrities, mostly Broadway types. It was really a glorified burger joint and, as such, had great burgers. Poured a good drink, too. But it was little expensive for me.

So I found Jimmy Ray's, right around the corner on Eighth Ave. between 45th and 46th. Jimmy Ray's was also a Broadway-type hangout, but for chorus line kids and other out-of-work actors.

On the nights I wasn't at Gallagher's, I behaved myself. I'd watch TV, have two or three beers, maybe a bowl of weed, and around nine o'clock would head down to Jimmy Ray's. I was in there probably three nights a week. I always took whatever book I was reading and spent an hour and a half or so reading over dinner by myself.

I almost always had the same thing: two extra-dry Beefeater martinis, straight up with a twist (they were nice and big and ice cold), a cheeseburger, rare, with raw onion, and french fries. All that and my book and I was in hog heaven.

Jimmy Ray's was a fairly small place with maybe fifteen tables, tops. To make it look larger, the entire back wall of the room was one big mirror.

More than once, somebody sitting at one of the back tables, with his or her back to the mirror, obviously wasn't paying attention and thought that the room went on farther back. It could be an honest mistake, especially if one were imbibing. He or she would get up, ostensibly to go to the rest room they assumed was at the back of the place, and WHAM! – face first into the mirror. Nice surprise, huh?

I'd often stop to talk to Father Bruce on the way home.

Father Bruce Ritter was a pretty famous guy who ran the church next door to my building. He'd made his name and the name of his organization (which I can't remember) helping hundreds of young runaways and gotten a lot of media attention, though he was very unassuming. We'd shoot the shit about the neighborhood, how the hookers had taken over Eighth Avenue and how it was all he could do to keep up with all the runaways over the past couple of years. Seemed like a real honest citizen and always had his broom out sweeping the sidewalk in front of the church at night. I think the broom was just a prop so he didn't just have to stand there, trying to keep the peace.

I think I remember him getting into some kind of trouble a number of years later. I think he was accused of boinking some young kids, but who knows. He surely helped thousands of more kids than he'd boinked, that's for sure so, on balance, his karma must be pretty good.

I didn't really know anybody in my building and that's the norm for Manhattan. I did have an interesting character who lived in the other apartment on my floor, though. Obviously, a hooker, but that was also the norm in Hell's Kitchen during the 70s. What wasn't immediately obvious was that the hooker was a transvestite.

We'd passed in the entryway a few times and I'd kind of thought, hmm, not bad, at least she's not fat. Looked pretty good, actually. Then one morning, I left for work around 7:30 and ran into this person again. Ouch.

My floormate had very obviously had quite a night and there was very little vestige of keeping up the female persona. Let's just say five o'clock stubble and a cockeyed wig can wreak havoc with the aura, OK?

While I was living there, Joe Allen's expanded. They built out into what had been the back yard – had probably doubled the size of the place. And, fortunately for me and indirectly for them, they had put a clear roof over the new addition. They would always write the day's specials on a blackboard posted on the wall. Now, with the new addition, the blackboard was put up on their back wall. This enabled me to see what special offerings were available and I could make a decision whether to run downstairs or still go around the corner to Jimmy Ray's. Whenever it was homemade chicken pot pie, Joe Allen's was my destination.

I liked living on Restaurant Row because it was a little more in the mainstream than Whore-ty Sixth between Ninth and Tenth. It was right in between the office and Gallagher's, only about a ten minute walk from each and only a little over a block to Tin Pan Alley and the theater district.

In the winter, the walk to the office was mostly underground. I could walk down into the subway at 44th and Eighth and walk all the way to the corner by Joe's. It was a pretty interesting walk, too. There were a number of newsstands and a few pretty nasty retail clothing stores, though it gave me something to look at.

The walk on the west side of the Eighth Ave. subway took you right under the Port Authority bus station and there were always thousands of people to gawk upon.

There was a little coffee shop just before I exited at 40th Street and I always got one on the way to work. The two or three people who worked there knew me by name. One time I thought how weird it was that I was known by name by these underground cave dwellers.

One time, I walked down into the subway at 44th Street and there were cops and yellow tape all over the place, particularly over by this bank of coin-operated lockers. Gaggles of cops weren't unusual in the subway, especially in the winter. They'd be indoors, warm, and could always justify just hanging out.

"But, Sarge, we heard there was a gang of pickpockets on the loose down there and we spent the shift attempting to apprehend the alleged perpetrators." Uh-huh. Those aren't doughnut crumbs on that overhanging gut of yours, are they, O'Malley?

Anyway, a tighter band of New York's Finest was hanging out around right in front of the lockers. There were three garbage bags laying on the floor that seemed to be the center of attention.

Being a New Yorker, I asked one of the cops, "Hey, what's in the bags?"

"Body parts." Pointing to the largest one, "That one there's the head."

"Oh. Man or woman?"

"What's it to you? Move along."

Right.

****

Dale's father, Roy, had this Norwegian girlfriend, Bettina, that he'd had for a decade or two.

His wife, Harriet, was one of the most beautiful, most sophisticated, funny, happy people I've ever known. She lived in Bal Harbour and lived a very nice life semi-carousing with some real money people and seemed to be quite satisfied. She knew all about Bettina and that she lived with Roy in King of Prussia, but couldn't understand it for the life of her, nor could anyone else.

Harriet was originally from Minneapolis and had been one of the three singing Albee Sisters who had been popular in the '40s. They were like the McGuire Sisters, I guess, just came along before they could make it big on television with Lawrence Welk or somebody.

Harriet was a pisser. As a kid, she was a helluva pool player. Once, in a competition when she was in her early twenties, she ran four racks of balls in rotation. I mean she was good.

She also had the unique distinction of once having won a beauty contest in the morning and a funny face competition in the afternoon of the same day. Harriet knew Hubert Humphrey pretty well and she and Roy had been front and center at LBJ's inaugural.

Even in her 60s, 70s and 80s, Harriet could turn heads.

Bettina, on the other hand….

Well, again, back in the magazine business when Roy was sending Europeans around selling for him, he was honing his marketing even more. He finally settled on having a crew of talk, blonde, Scandinavian beauties. Nothing wrong with that. Absolutely nothing. He had six or seven knockouts. They all looked like Elke Summer. Even Bettina. And, instead of knocking on doors, Roy had them calling exclusively on doctors' and dentists' offices. Now that was brilliant. Why he didn't make more money at that is beyond me.

Maybe Bettina was the exception to the Scandinavian rule or perhaps she proved it, but her looks started falling apart in her late thirties and went pretty rapidly downhill from there. Maybe it was just Bettina or maybe most Scandinavian women start falling apart at that age, having to do with growing up in frigid darkness half their formative years. I don't know.

Roy and Bettina had opened up a wig store, The Wig Cottage, down outside of Philadelphia. Most of his clientele were women who were undergoing chemo or were elderly and getting tired of the female version of the comb-over. The business was always close to the edge, but I think they eked by. Roy didn't want to make any kind of a profit, because the IRS was *still* on his ass and he'd had enough of forwarding his checks on to them.

I remember he sold "Skin Wig of Elura" and "Eva Gabor" brands, with ol' Eva's smiling kisser in a bunch of wigs that were best suited to Halloween. Or on a charter bus to Atlantic City.

He thought our direct mail operation was a "good idea". Roy never, ever handed out compliments and "good idea" meant he thought it was brilliant and wished he'd thought of it. He started sending out brochures.

Roy fancied himself quite the *artiste* and would sit there in his ascot laying out his brochures. When finished, I'd have plates made and the brochures would be printed by none other than yours truly, the Multilith Maven.

Roy's layouts sucked big time. As with so many self-proclaimed retail *artistes*, he tried to get every conceivable product squeezed into every possible centimeter of white space. Naturally, every price had a line through it and the sale price printed in another color. Oh, good idea, Roy, now I'll having to run the fucking thing through twice. Wanna try a third color? His runs were too small for the 1870 Addressograph-Multigraph With the Two-Color Head.

Know what his tagline was? "Younger than Springtime....Are We".

Just like that – "Younger that Springtime period period period period Are We".

He agonized for half an hour over the number of periods between "Springtime" and "Are". Too many? Too few?

Roy: "Jim, ask the folks in the office what they think."

 What they think of what, Roy?"

"How many dots – periods – should we have between 'Springtime' and 'Are'?"

"Really?"

"Yes, goddamit, I want it to be right!"

"Oh. Okay."

Dale heard that and broke for the elevator. Jeanne's fingers started flying on the adding machine.

Are we having fun yet?

"Hey, Al. What do you think, two periods, three periods, or four?", pointing out the three variations.

"What?"

"Should there be two, three or four periods, goddam it. Don't overthink it."

Every time Al rolled his eyes he made me laugh. He rolled his eyes a lot. This time, too.

"OK, fuckface, that's a 'four', right?"

"Whatever you say, Jim."

On to Acuna.

That stupid bastard actually took it seriously. "Jeemie, let me talk to a-Roy about this. I have some ideas."

No!

Too late.

Roy hated Acuna. Didn't even acknowledge his presence, which could be a little disconcerting at times. Around the corner he went.

Ten seconds.....

"Jim!" Roy.

Around the corner.

"Yeah, Roy."

"I didn't ask for a goddam dissertation from this guy on how to lay out a goddam brochure. Didn't you just ask him the question?"

"Uh, yeah, Roy. Hey, Acuna, I think I hear your stapler calling you."

Ol' Acuna's eye twitched, which it did whenever he got nervous. A perfect stone face except for that twitching eye. Off he flounced back into the back room.

"Roy, I think four periods look good. Kind of spreads out the message on the page, know what I mean?" Get this over in a hurry.

"Good. That's what I thought, too. Let's go with four."

"Right."

I was savvy enough not to mention that the phrase, "Younger than Springtime....Are We" was the most asinine thing I'd ever heard.

Bettina, who had been sitting there prattling on to Jeanne who would nod every once in a while, said, "Hey! What you talking about?" Bettina was always about thirty seconds behind the rest of the world.

Dale never got involved with Roy's brochures. He was footing the bill for the whole thing and I think it pissed him off.

Roy and Bettina had this little terrier, Chumley, who barked incessantly all the time he was there. They kept his leash tied to a chair in the office and Tiger, the cat, would sit there staring at him, just out of his reach.

Bark. Bark. Bark.

Roy: "Chumley!"

Bark. Bark. Bark.

Bettina: "Chumley!"

This went on for a couple of hours.

Poor Chumley. He was really saying, "Somebody save me from these people! Help!"

Then Tige would sneak around on him and bite him on the ass.

Poor dog.

TWENTY

Business was booming along pretty well and Dale decided I needed something better than a '67 Catalina if I was going to be driving to more shows, especially the Restaurant Show in Chicago, the granddaddy of them all.

He called his old buddy, Ray Worden, out in Marion. Ray worked at a Ford dealership and had been in the business his whole life.

He'd worked for Dale way back when Dale had had the Dodge dealership. He was Dale's sales manager.

Everybody called Ray the "Round Man". I think it was because he was kind of short and kind of chubby. Kind of round. The Round Man.

The Round Man had been on the Indianapolis. Right. That Indianapolis. The one that had been on a super-secret mission carrying the Bomb toward the end of World War II, had been on radio silence and had been hit by a Japanese torpedo thousands of miles from nowhere in the middle of the Pacific.

Something like fourteen hundred guys had gone into the water and three or four days later, when the rescuers finally showed up, something like only three hundred still lived. The sharks had gotten the rest. If you want the details in earnest, Quint talks about it in "Jaws".

Round Man was one of the survivors. And he never, ever talked about it. I know. I asked him one night. The smile he'd been wearing disappeared. He just shook his head, as in "don't ask". I looked him in the eye. Shook his head again. Said nothing. 'Nuff said.

Once, back when he was working for Dale at the Dodge dealership, he was certain his wife was having an affair while he was at work. For about a week and a half, Round Man would announce that he was going to lunch, which he never did.

Dale found out he was going home and hiding under the bed, waiting for his wife and her supposed paramour to indulge in an afternoon delight. He'd lay under that bed for two or three hours. Along about three o'clock, he'd figure it wasn't on for today and make his way back to the office. Like I said, this went on for ten days or so, every day. By the way, his wife wasn't having an affair, it was just Round Man being paranoid.

Not that Round Man didn't have a thing or two going for him on the side. Dale found out about it, too. One girlfriend called about the same time every mid-morning. Dale thought it might be fun for all the guys in the showroom and shop to hear one of their little lovey-dovey phone conversations. So, he answered the phone one morning and it was the girlfriend.

"May I speak with Mr. Ray Worden, please?"

"Certainly, just a minute." He put her on hold, but put it on 'speaker' and put the dealer-wide loud speaker microphone in front of the phone. Round Man didn't quite realize that. As he was talking on the phone in his office, ostensibly having a nice private little coochie-coochie talk with his girlfriend, it was broadcast throughout the entire dealership.

When Round Man hung up and walked out of his office, he received a rousing ovation by the salesmen, parts guys, mechanics, secretaries – everybody. As you can imagine, he was just thrilled.

We decided to get a Ford van, but a fancy one, one semi-customized at the factory. We also decided to meet Round Man halfway between New York and Marion, at my Aunt Betty's house in Collins Center, NY, a little crossroads adjacent to Lake Erie about halfway between Buffalo and Erie, Pennsylvania.

Aunt Betty is Jeanne's and my mom's younger sister and has lived in Western New York her entire life. She's made her living owning and servicing vending machines at small tavern and saloons in the area and to go with her on her "route" was always quite an experience. The purpose of her "route" was to replenish the vending machines and collect the coins. She can roll quarters, dimes and nickels faster than any human on earth.

Until about the fourth stop.

At every stop, she knew almost everybody in the joint and, even though she started on her route in the late morning, the drinking had already begun. So, that meant five or six drinks at each stop on the route. She was always astute enough to hit her biggest moneymakers early in the day, when her mind was still fresh.

Our plan was for Round Man to drive the van to Aunt Betty's and we'd trade him the old Catalina, not that it was worth anything, but we had to have a way to get to Collins Center and he needed a way to get back to Marion.

Whenever I went anywhere with Jeanne and Dale, we never left for anywhere with any sort of advance plan. I never knew when we were going to leave, always hoping for an early start so as to get to our destination at a reasonable hour. Never happened. We always seemed to leave around seven in the evening, no matter how long a drive lay ahead. This time was no different.

We got going, like a herd of turtles, around seven-thirty on Friday evening, somewhere around seven-and-a-half hours later than I was hoping for, but I wasn't driving. That put us into Collins Center around three in the morning. Thrilled my Aunt Betty no end.

Round Man had gotten there at a reasonable hour early in the evening and, not really knowing Aunt Betty, had hit the hay early. He got up when we arrived. Natch, after a long ride, we had to wash the trail dust out of our throats, but Aunt Betty only had half a bottle of vodka and a big honkin' bottle of Amaretto. Jeanne and Dale hit the hay around five in the morning, but it was starting to get light, so I was getting my second wind. Round Man and I sat there nursing that jug of Amaretto until the rest of the house roused itself around ten.

Around noon, Dale wanted to try out the new van, so he and I and Jeanne and the Round Man piled in.

It was a pretty cool vehicle. Nice thick grey carpeting everywhere, walls included. It had captains' chairs up front that could swivel all the way around. It was silver in color, with orange and purple and yellow paint rakishly going front back to front and a porthole window on each side. Not bad for a van. I had been expecting one of those white Econoline jobs that was steel inside and out. It would sure as hell beat cruising in the Catalina with the tables bouncing up and down on the roof.

As was kind of our custom, we cruised around to several roadhouses and taverns, each one containing Aunt Betty's cigarette machines, jukeboxes and coin-operated pool tables, a bunch of neon beer signs, and cheap drinks.

We hit this one joint on a hilltop outside of Gowanda, the largest nearby town. Gowanda's claim to fame was that it had what used to be called an insane asylum and a big leather tannery. Aunt Betty and my cousins used to live there before chucking the big city and moving to Collins Center.

When we walked into the tavern, who should spin around unsteadily on his barstool but my Uncle Austin. Uncle Austin used to be married to Aunt Betty and was the father of my cousins. My grandmother lived with the family until she died and she hated Uncle Austin. She referred to him as "Oz" or "The Oz" or "The Wiz" as in "The Wizard of". He was a complete mess and had been for years.

He used to be a chiropractor, probably the only one in town. When we were kids, he always insisted upon giving each of us "an adjustment", which we always felt we needed as much as we needed a head in our collective hole.

We'd each have to stand there, me, my sister Jean, and probably Iz, and take our turns. I'd be first. Or last. He'd lay me down on this chiropractor's table, on my stomach. Really, all he did was crack my neck, which is the worst thing in the world. Or so it seemed then. He'd grab ahold of my head and I knew what was coming.

"Just relax, Jimmy." No. You're going to break my neck.

"So, Jimmy". Here it came. "How was school this year?"

"Fine." CRACK!

Bastard.

"How were your grades?"

No-o-o-o!

"OK." CRACK!

I always thought he was going to break my neck because he was always half in the bag when he did it.

After one of those CRACKs, I envisioned myself unable to move and numb all over and hearing, "Oops."

Didn't happen, though, thank God.

Aunt Betty had finally divorced him somewhere along the line and I guess his neck-cracking business went to hell, too.

He had a big round head.

I worked at a pool hall as a kid and the guy who owned it was named Angelo Tucci. The fellow that owned the service station next door was Pat Oriend and Pat had a big round head, too. Whenever he walked in, Angelo would say to him, "Pat, if I had your head full of nickels, I'd be a rich man."

If I had Uncle Austin's head full of nickels, I'd be a rich man, too.

To go with the big round head, Uncle Austin had a big round face, too, made even worse with his advanced alcoholism. Were one to lay a nickname on him, probably "Mars Face" would do. Big and round and red.

Ol' Oz was sitting there drinking away, downing pickled egg after pickled egg from the big jar on the bar. Well, he downed a lot of each egg, but a good portion of each found itself stuck to various pieces of real estate on the Mars-scape. Or on his shirt or in his lap. It was lovely. Just fucking lovely.

He was grinning like an idiot. At least I think he was grinning. By this point, his eyes were just slits in the Mars-scape and his mouth was either frozen in a smile or grimace, it was hard to tell which.

"Hey, kids! Great to see you! What a surprise. Here, have a drink on me." Looks like you have several on you already, Oz. They go nicely with the egg bits that missed your mouth.

"OK." We engaged in small talk for a few minutes, downing a few watered-down eighty-five-cent rotguts.

"Hey", said the Oz. "I have something in my car that I think is going to be the next big thing. You folks can probably sell millions of them. I'll show it to you, but don't forget, I get a cut out of everything you sell."

This should be good. Of all the gin mills in all the world, we just happen to walk in on the 'next big thing', compliments of The Wiz, in all his stupored glory.

We all trooped out to the dirt parking lot to The Wiz' beaten up old Bonneville station wagon and he rummaged around in the back seat for a minute before turning around and putting this thing on his big round head.

It was a mini-umbrella with a head band that held it in place on his head. The panels of the umbrella were multi-colored, as in blue, yellow, red, green and white. There stood the Oz, mini-umbrella firmly affixed to his head, smiling like a demented Buddha.

Then came the topper. "Watch this", he said, reaching up and turning on a switch attached to the umbrella. At that moment, a tiny fan, smack in the top of the middle of the mini-umbrella, began to whirl diligently.

It was a mini-umbrella, specially designed to keep the sun off one's head, replete with a mini-fan in the top to keep one's head cool. I surmised it wasn't to be used in the rain, as the hole in the top where the fan resided measured about four inches in diameter. One doesn't keep one's head dry in a rainstorm with a four-inch hole in the center of one's umbrella.

"Ta-da." Oz.

This was just too fucking surreal. Standing in the middle of a dirt parking lot of some no name tavern on a hill outside of Gowanda,

New York, looking at my beyond-polluted Uncle Austin – the Oz, The Wiz – standing there with a multi-colored umbrella planted firmly on his big round head, the fan in it whirring away, and him grinning goofily with pieces of hard-boiled pickled eggs still sticking to his Mars Face.

God, was I proud.

We told him what a good idea it was and that we'd get back with him first of the week.

We hopped in the van, looking for all the world like the Keystone Kops, and I looked out the back window at Oz standing there, umbrella on his head and all, in a cloud of dust, waving at us.

His body finally caught up with his mind and they buried him a few months later.

At least we had a new van.

TWENTY-ONE

My first trip in the van was to the National Restaurant Show in Chicago the next Spring.

Bubniak and the boys got me all loaded up and early one Monday morning I pulled away from 264 West 40th Street with everybody, including Dale and Jeanne, Acuna, Al, and probably even Utah, waving me off like I was in a Conestoga bound for California.

Through the Lincoln Tunnel to Route 80 West, through the Delaware Water Gap, across six hours of Pennsylvania, cruising along just nicely, thank you.

Outside of Cleveland, the goddamdest thunderstorm hit. I couldn't see a thing. Lightning was incessant and thunder sounded like mine explosions. Great, I thought, there's obviously a tornado in the area and I'm gonna get killed on some goofball interstate outside of Cleveland Fucking Ohio. Beautiful.

Because I was in a van I had this fantasy I was in a truck. I noticed all the big rigs tucked in with about eight feet separating them, still doing about fifty. Well, I guess us truckers know how to do it. I joined the line. I could almost reach out and touch the back of the trailer ahead of me and just kept my eyes glued to his taillights. Went along like this for about forty-five minutes when the weather began to clear.

I pulled out from behind the truck I'd been following, gave him three toots on the horn and flashed my lights at him as I passed. We were truckers. We were buddies.

I bet he wondered what that doofus in the van was all about, honking like an idiot and flashing his lights.

Ah, the life of a long distance driver. I think I even began singing, "Convoy" about that time. Maybe I was just glad to still be alive.

I spent the night in a Holiday Inn outside of Toledo. Only about three hours to go in the morning and I'd be in Chicago.

I made it without incident, but I had to drive through Gary, Indiana. The sky was red. Not from a beautiful sunrise, but from shit that was belching into the atmosphere. I didn't know how people lived or worked there. It was a toxic waste site – at least the air looked and smelled toxic. Jesus.

I made it to McCormick Place, one of the largest buildings I'd ever seen in my life. And even though I was driving a fancy new van, I still had to unload the way I always did – by carrying stuff through parking lots, up ramps, through checkpoints, down fifteen miles of exhibitors' aisles and to my ten-by-ten booth.

Some of the exhibits were actual buildings brought in and assembled specifically for the show. Those companies must have spent hundreds of thousands of dollars on these shows, had armies of guys driving high-lows, laying cables, erecting light trusses, bringing in custom-made furniture – real elaborate productions.

And there I was, with a shit-ass carpet, three folding tables, a bunch of cardboard boxes and some things that looked to the uninitiated like flying saucers and a rock or two. But I had learned and learned well. I was well-armed with a stack of tens and I got guys to do shit for me like I was a caliph or something. Done in no time.

I figured Dale's "we'll do it ourselves" indicated that I certainly had leeway in ascertaining what the word "do" meant.

The show went great, I sold a ton of stuff, including the demonstrator models off the floor. I saw a little bit of Chicago, driving back and forth from the hotel, and was really satisfied. Dale and Jeanne sounded thrilled, too.

One small thing, though – at a restaurant show, an awful lot of exhibitors cook food and hand out samples all day long. A lot of that food is deep-fried. There is nothing quite like walking into a place that smells like hot three-day-old grease warming up at 7:30 in the morning – especially with a wee bit of a hangover and three hours' sleep.

At the end of the show, I packed up my stuff in a flash and got it loaded in no time. Once the demonstrator models were gone, it was basically the shit-ass carpet and tables, along with a box or two. I had also found a good place to park that morning, adjacent to the nearest doorway. I was getting to be a trade show wiz, in addition to being a fountain tycoon.

I headed out around six in the evening and made it to Elkhart, Indiana, before I'd had enough and needed a place to stay for the night. Elkhart, Indiana is the world capital of the recreational vehicles and travel trailers. Nearly every manufacturer is headquartered there and the city thrives on that industry.

What I hadn't known driving into town to hunt down a motel was that Elkhart was having its annual buyers' week or some such thing. The town was jammed with RV and trailer dealers from around the country. The Holiday Inn was full. So was the Ramada Inn. And the Hilton. And the Sheraton. And every other place with a name you've heard of. I finally found some goofball-looking place – it could've been Bob's Motel, for all I remember. Or, at the time, cared.

"Do you have any vacancy?"

"Let me see…….Yes, sir, we have one room open. The only thing is, it has a water bed."

A water bed. In Bob's End-of-the-Road Motel in Elkhart Fucking Indiana.

Perfect.

"Sounds good to me."

I'd never slept on a water bed before, but I thought I'd remembered hearing or reading that the thing was supposed to be pretty much filled with water. Either I hadn't gotten my information straight or Bob was trying to save on water, because when I lay down on the bed I felt like I was being swallowed whole by The Blob. I found that if I lay there on my back with my arms and legs straight out, I didn't sink quite so deeply into The Blob and fell asleep looking like I was trying to make "snow angels".

I finally rolled into New York, unscathed, about nine o'clock the next night.

Ah, business travel.

I put plenty of miles on that van over the next few years, including to and from Chicago another four or five times.

I drove to a show in Myrtle Beach late one February. I thought this would be outrageous, leaving the nasty old grey New York City winter behind and walking up and down the Strand in the evenings. Rained the whole goddam time, with temperatures in the forties. Also blew out the universal joint getting there and had to have it replaced.

I went to a show in Dayton, Ohio and don't think I sold squat. The only thing I remember about the thing was this strange-looking thing that hung suspended from the ceiling in the lobby of the convention center. It looked like a hundred-foot-long snake. Well, I thought, maybe this is the home of the world's largest snake or something.

It wasn't. Seems the Wright Brothers were from Dayton and, even though Kitty Hawk, South Carolina is a long ways from Dayton, the city fathers thought it'd be a fitting tribute to the boys to have an exhibition of the length of the Wright Brothers' first flight. That was it. Good idea. Totally fucked-up execution.

I was at a regional restaurant show held at the Capitol Hilton in Washington, D.C. Business-wise, that one sucked, too. But, as one is wont to do at these trade shows, I got pretty friendly with an old barker named Harold who had the booth adjacent to mine. That didn't help my business, either.

Harold sold some sort of Cuisinart-type thing that chopped, sliced, diced, skinned, pureed, mashed, and liquefied anything you could think of to put in it. He gave hourly demonstrations, the kind with a mirror over his head so the crowd could really see what he was doing and that he wasn't trying to scam them somehow.

He had a microphone around his neck and had about a fifteen minute spiel that was a beauty to behold. I must have heard it fifty or sixty times and every time he did it, it was exactly the same each time.

Same words, same timing, same accents, same everything. But each time it sounded like he was doing it off the cuff. The guy was good, but the spiel finally drove me completely nuts and really put a crimp in my business because who wanted to see fountains when a free sample of pureed shit was just around the corner?

He was big on vegetables. They were colorful, easy to work with, easy to clean up and, if you threw a bunch of 'em in together and pureed the hell out of them and poured it into little paper cups, it tasted okay anyway.

He had this one line about people not getting enough vegetables. He'd say, "The way people eat today, they're not constipated, they're (slapping his stomach with both hands) consti*pasted*!" With lines like that, he had 'em right where he wanted them.

Made me want to come up with my own barker line….."Don't piss often enough? Get a fountain!"

Dale and Jeanne and I figured we'd do really well at the Texas Regional Restaurant Show. Big state, lots of restaurants, aching to be cosmopolitan – all that. So I went to it. In Houston. Because it was so far from New York, we actually decided to have me fly down. You know, just like the big guys. Ship the stuff. Fly the kid.

It was held at some massive hotel that had the biggest swimming pools I've ever seen. I kind of expected that, considering the size of the hotel.

What I hadn't considered is the fact that The Shriners were having their annual convention at the hotel at the same time the restaurant show was there. Shriners, all decked out in their natty fezzes. The higher up in the organization they were, the more doodads they had hanging on the ol' fez. And they seemed to wear them all the time. They even had the silly little cars in the hotel. And it seemed to be one big traveling drinking party, from one room to another, from one floor to another.

The goofy bastards had a good time, though.

Me, I wasn't so happy. The show attendance sucked royally. Dead. Nada.

The saving grace, however, was that the Laredo/Ciudad-Juarez Tourist Bureau had a booth right next to mine and they were pouring margaritas out of pitchers.

I had two of our small cocktail fountains on display at my booth. The model was the Elegance Cocktail Fountain (dynamically referred to as the ECF) and it held about a gallon of liquid. We actually used the basic Houbigant perfume fountain platform with a few extra parts added to make it a cocktail fountain. They came in either the Elegant Gold or Silver Satin Finish, also known as anodized aluminum.

I got together with the Laredo/Ciudad-Juarez folks and they put their margaritas in my fountains. Our adjoining booths became the hit of the show, not with any outside potential customers, but with all the exhibitors. We were all half in the bag for three days and had a ball.

I ended up selling fifteen or twenty little ECFs to exhibitors, not that those sales were worth a damn – surely didn't pay for the show – but those little babies were certainly profitable to make and ship.

Speaking of the sales not paying for the show, it was not only the first show I ever flew to, it was also the last.

TWENTY-TWO

We also used to hang out at Jilly's, at 52nd and Eighth.

Jilly's was pretty famous because it was supposedly one of Frank Sinatra's hangouts. It was owned by Sinatra's close friend and sometimes bodyguard, Jilly Rizzo. Had Frank's photos all over the place. It had a pretty good little bar business but their food business was pretty lean. Either way, I couldn't see how they ever had enough business to pay the rent.

The restrooms at Jilly's were down a steep, narrow set of stairs, with hand railings on both sides. Having been a gymnast in high school and knowing a little about the parallel bars, I could jump halfway down the stairs, grab onto the railings and swing myself to the bottom of the stairs. In other words, negotiate a set of about thirty stairs without ever touching a stair. Wow, huh?

I'd generally do this when visiting the little boys' room, and one night I decided to reveal my maneuver to whomever was in our little group.

"I can make it from the top step to the bottom without ever touching a stair."

Blank stares.

"No, really. I can go from that top step over there and make it all the way to the bottom without ever touching a stair. No shit."

Somebody, I think it was Dale, bit.

"OK. I'll bite. Show me."

We walked to the top of the stairs and I sailed to the bottom, landed with my feet together, stood up straight and spun around victoriously.

"Hey, come here! Look what Jim can do! Jim – do it again."

Six or seven people wanted in on viewing this little exhibition, but only two or three could crowd around the door at one time. It really didn't take much to get people's attention, I guess. I happily obliged each group, then realized why I'd gone down the stairs to begin with. I hit the head.

Jilly had a son, Willie, who was more or less in charge of the place and was the bartender most of the time. Willie was about my age, maybe a couple of years older, and we became pretty good friends, at least across the bar. I usually didn't get a check but he always made sure I laid a ten- or twenty-dollar bill on the bar in front of me, as if I were running a tab, "in case Dad comes in". He never did.

"Want a burger?"

"Sure."

A few minutes later, a waiter'd bring out a big ol' juicy burger and fries. No charge. I didn't take advantage of this situation. After all, I wasn't Billy Ruben. But once a week or so, sure.

One night I walked in to the empty place and Willie said, "Jim, you're gonna have to sit at that table in the corner tonight", pointing to a table in the farthest corner of the room.

"How come?"

"You shouldn't even be in here tonight, but I asked my Dad – in case you came in – and he said it was okay, but you'd have to sit in the back and stay there. And keep your mouth shut. Don't worry, I'll take care of you, but just mind your own business."

Whoa. Since I was the only customer in there, if a mob hit was in the offing, I'd either be the only witness or else I'd be the victim. Hmmm.

"Don't look so worried. Just a special dinner party tonight. That's all."

Okay. I think.

I sat down, had a drink, looked around at anything and everything, had another drink and looked up to see my burger making its way toward me. Ah, good.

Right then, the front door opened and a half dozen guys walked in. Uh-oh.

I was checking out the group out of the corner of my eye and – Sinatra!

Frank Sinatra was here!

So that was it – Frankie was coming to dinner, the place had chased everybody else out but Willie's friend, who sat invisible in the corner.

The group sat in another section of the room and proceeded to eat, drink and be merry. Just a bunch of normal guys having dinner.

How do you like that?

"Hey, Acuna – guess who I had dinner with last night?" That'd get him.

A random thought hit me. What if I just walked over to their table and said, "Hey, Frank. Wanna see me get from the top of the steps to the bottom without touching a single stair?" They'd either get a helluva kick out of it or I'd get thrown out on my ass by those two goons sitting on either side of him. I decided I'd show him the next time we had dinner together. Tonight, better to just eat my burger in silence.

When I finished, I surreptitiously moseyed on out past the bar and nodded my thanks to Willie. He winked and nodded back.

Me and Frankie- we were "like this".

****

Bill Parker became the super of 264 sometime in the early '70s and lasted until his retirement in the early '80s, after I'd left.

Parker was okay, but was a little on the shy side. He wasn't shy of people – his shyness had to do with work. He was kind of shy of working hard. But he was alright. At least he didn't steal from us. Oh, sure, he nailed everybody, including us, for stuff all the time, just never anything meaningful from us. Supers have a God-given right to steal. Not much, just a little here and there - just enough to make a little extra on the side.

He always wore one of those little "MG" hats, the little cap with the snap on top of the visor. He was forever taking that hat off, rubbing his head, and putting it back on. Must've been some sort of nervous thing.

He walked into the office one day, hat in one hand, the other rubbing his head, and said, "Hey, Cuz (he called everybody Cuz, men and women alike), never guess what happened to me last night."

Your hat blew off and you had a nervous breakdown.

"What?"

"I was drivin' along on the Grand Central, somewhere 'tween Shea and LaGuardia, and I felt a big ol' "thumpa-thumpa-thumpa". I says, 'Oh, no, not a flat tire on the Grand Central!' Yep. Damn right rear tire. Know somethin', Cuz? It was only half flat, though." Here it came. "Only flat on the bottom!" A slap to the thigh.

"Yeah?"

"Well, I pull off to the shoulder – damn, that shoulder ain't nothin' along about there, y'know? I got out, went 'round back, and shit, I got a lotta stuff in that trunk!"

Yep. Most of it probably stolen from the tenants of 264 West 40th Street.

"Anyways, I'm searchin' around in the dark for the damn jack an' all, when I kind of notice another car pull over in front of me. My head's still in the trunk when I see my interior light go on an' hear my hood pop open. 'Hey!', I say, 'What the hell you think you're doin'?"

"Do you believe this? A guy sticks his head around the hood and says, 'Hey, man, all I want's the battery – you can have the whole rest of it.' Can you believe it? Sumbitch thinks I'm tryin' to jack my own car!"

"I says 'Git yer ass outta here! This is my goddamned car!' Only in New York, Cuz. Only in New York."

One year, Parker got it into his head that he would decorate the lobby for the holidays. He went out and bought one of those signs on a string that says "MERRY CHRISTMAS" in alternating green and red shiny letters. He adjusted it just so and it was only maybe an inch off.

Then he got one of those stencil-and-soap kits and put snowflakes and reindeer and Santas all over the walls. By the way, the walls were a blonde marble, so the contrast between white reindeer and blonde wall left something to be desired. But he'd tried and was proud enough of his artwork to come up to the second floor and get me to go down and admire his handiwork.

"Looks great, Bill. Really adds a festive air to the ol' lobby, know what I mean?"

"That's what I was tryin' to do."

"Well, you did it. But, you know something? Most of the tenants in the building are Jewish and don't celebrate Christmas."

"Damn. That's right." A little crestfallen.

"I got an idea. Why don't you just put up a sign that says Happy Hanukah. They celebrate that and it's exactly the same time of year."

"Ah, Cuz. That's why Cuz pays you the big bucks."

When I went down through the lobby on my way home, there was a hand-printed sign, in several different Magic Marker colors that encouraged our Jewish friends to enjoy a "Happy Chanuan".

I don't know what the reaction was from anybody else in the building. Maybe the Jewish people thought Chanuan was an African-American or Puerto Rican or otherwise obscure Christian holiday. Or, maybe they just appreciated the effort and said nothing.

Whatever, everyone passing through the lobby of 264 for the next three weeks was wished a "Happy Chanuan".

Every time Al came in through the lobby and got off the elevator, he wished me and Dale and Jeanne a "Happy Chanuan".

Bubniak asked me, "What means 'Chanuan'"?

"Parker. I think he meant Happy Hanukah."

"Stupid man." John didn't like Parker. Thought he was lazy.

TWENTY-THREE

Dale bought a moped. A Motobecane. Bright orange.

"What do you think of this?"

I had to admit, it was pretty cool. I don't think I'd ever seen a moped before. You could either pedal it like a bicycle or turn on the engine and go tooling along at a snappy twenty. Like a motorcycle, only different.

It was early on a Saturday morning when traffic in the Garment Center is virtually nonexistent.

"Let's go out and take a few spins around the block", he said, hitting the elevator button.

Man, it was fun. Not having to stop at the lights on the corners – hey, it was a bicycle, right? – I made it all the way around the block in about two minutes. I was beginning to see the wisdom in this.

"This is great", I said, exhilarated from my hair blowing back and pretending I had gotten bugs in my teeth, feeling for all the world like Peter Fonda's Captain America in "Easy Rider". I could hear Steppenwolf – "Head out on the highway; lookin' for adventure…"

"Yeah. When you have to go on missions around town, take this. It'll save on cab fares and you can take it just about anywhere."

"Cool."

Early the following week, I had to go all the way across and uptown to deliver some Export Declarations to the Egyptian Embassy, around 59th and First. Daytime traffic always sucked and the moped would be perfect.

On I hopped, Export Decs in my jacket pocket, and hit the elevator button. Out through the lobby and headed east on 40th Street. Because traffic in the Garment Center moved at the rate of about one block every fifteen minutes, I weaved my way in and out of trucks and cars and cabs, slowly but surely, ridin' like a wizard. This was so cool.

The traffic opened up just a little once I got east of Fifth Avenue, the way it always did, and I was moving along nicely. When I got to First Avenue, I turned left.

And was certain I'd be dead inside of four minutes.

First Avenue is about six lanes wide, actually eight lanes but two of them are curbside lanes. For some reason, the traffic going up First was as fast as I'd ever seen it. Trucks were whizzing past me, cabs were missing me by scant inches, cars gave me absolutely no respect at all, busses were changing lanes without even seeing me. I was hating whatever few minutes of my life remained. And my fucking beeper was going off.

Always one to glom on to the newest gadget, Dale had gotten me a beeper the week prior. Because he obviously didn't have enough to do, every time I'd go on a mission, my beeper would go off.

This was in the deep dark time before cell phones, so every time the goddamned beeper would go off, I'd have to hunt down a pay phone, fish for some change, and call the office.

"General Fountains. How may I help you?" Jeanne.

"Hey. It's me. Dale just beeped me."

"Hang on."

Dale would always forget he'd beeped me and was off gallivanting throughout the office or shop or between floors or something. Four or five minutes later.....

"What's happening?"

"Yeah, you beeped me."

"Where are you?"

I'd tell him.

"Great. Just checking."

What the fuck?

I'd just wasted nearly ten minutes just to tell him where I was?

You got it.

Anyway, here I was on First Avenue, hanging on for dear life with my beeper going off in my pocket, next to the Export Decs.

Wanna know where I am, Dale? Do you? Huh? I'm in hell, Dale, that's where I am! I'm about to become a fucking statistic in front of the U.N. Building and you're beeping me asking me where the fuck I am?!?

Of course, I finally made it to the Egyptian Embassy, chained the moped, hands shaking, to the awning post in front and went up to the floor where the Embassy was housed.

I walked in to what looked like a doctor's waiting room. There were several swarthy looking guys with dour looks on their faces sitting in there. They all stared at me as I came through the door. Oh, shit. Spies!

I walked over to the receptionist, who was quite attractive and very pleasant. Not a good time to try and put the moves to her, though. Not with a nest of spies staring a hole in my back. I handed her the documents and asked if it would be alright if I used the phone to call my office. I'd just been beeped, I explained, holding the beeper nonchalantly above the counter so she could see it. That would impress her – not many people had beepers at that early stage.

When I lifted the beeper, all the 'spies' stirred at once. I turned, showed it to them. "Beeper. I have to call my office." They relaxed.

Right. I was in the Egyptian Embassy. They were having a tiff with Israel, weren't they? Those guys probably thought I was gonna blow the place sky high or something. Jesus.

Everything settled down quickly and the receptionist pointed to a phone over by a couch.

"You can use that one. Local call?"

"Yeah – local."

I dialed the office, waited until Jeanne could round up Dale.

"What's happening?"

"I'm at the Egyptian Embassy."

"What's it like?"

"An office." There was no way I was going to start describing the office to him. The 'spies' probably wouldn't cotton to my saying, "the room's about twenty-by-twenty, wall-to-wall windows on the street side…." – that sort of thing. Didn't Dale have anything better to do with his fucking time?

"Oh. See any spies?"

Yes, Dale. And they all have nine-millimeters trained on my back at this very moment.

"Nah."

"How was the ride up there?"

"Piece of cake."

"Good. You know, we're going to start making them. Only we'll just make an adapter you can attach to your bike. Just like a moped, but for your bike."

"Great." Great.

"See you when you get back."

"Right."

On the way back downtown, Second Avenue was a parking lot. Just the way I'd hoped.

I was beginning to question the intelligence of riding around Manhattan on a moped. Within a week or so, we did start to make an engine and driving device that one could attach to one's bike.

Seemed like a very good idea, maybe just not for the streets of New York. Elkhart, maybe, but probably not New York.

We even had a prototype made up and it sort of worked. Not well enough to sell, but we'd try and start selling them anyway.

A few months earlier, Dale had bought darkroom equipment and he decided that we'd pose Jeanne on the bike and take her picture.

Typical "we'll do it ourselves". Why didn't we just go out and get a Brownie Starmite and mail the film to one of those mail-order film developers?

Dale'd develop the pictures and we'd lay out a page for our direct-mail brochure. "Ladies and gentlemen, look in this catalog. What'll it be? A fountain or a gizmo to attach to your bike so you don't have to peddle it?" Dale was taking this diversifying thing just a little too far just a little too soon.

Anyway, Dale couldn't develop the photographs for shit, and that was a good thing. The photos were perfectly lousy. Poorly lit, cruddy product shots – they looked like family photos you'd stick in a box instead of an album.

The page for the brochure got put on hold and the whole idea of a motorized adapter for bicycles faded totally away, never to be pursued again. The prototype sat propped up along a wall in the shop for the next four years.

The idea of motorized wheeled objects would raise its ugly head again in the not-too-distant future.

Right around this time, we were approached by a restaurant in Coney Island that was undergoing a massive renovation. I can't remember the exact name, but it was something like the Lido Manor. The owner, whose name I remember as Armando, had had a restaurant in Coney Island for years and years and was a pretty nice guy. He and his wife owned it and I don't think he was connected to the mob, but I was never quite certain.

As they had come into the showroom, this was one of my five percent babies and the guy was talking an order in the neighborhood of twenty grand – or, a thousand samoleons to me. So I worked hard and diligently to get them the right stuff for the right areas of the restaurant.

There was a potential fly in the ointment. Or should I say pterodactyl in the ointment? He wanted two Eight Foot Extravaganzas to go up on the roof. Great idea, but almost impossible to execute to anyone's satisfaction.

Here were the potential (inevitable) problems as I saw them:

Number one, the wind blows on Coney Island. Hard. The Eight Foot Extravaganza was designed, primarily, for indoor use. The jets of water weren't thick and robust enough to withstand anything but a gentle breeze, and that was stretching it. If the wind blew, the jets of water would blow any which way, meaning out of the bowl. Too much water blows out of the bowl and you lose the necessary water level to keep the pumps cool.

When they overheat, they burn out. Fountain stops.

I took Dale and John aside and said, "This could be a disaster. Those fountains won't work up on that guy's roof. You know that."

"Ah, hell, he'll find a way to make them work", said Dale.

Me: "Why don't we design a custom fountain that will give him what he needs and be a one-of-a-kind item? And, it will work in all kinds of weather."

Bubniak: "Eight-footer no good. Garbage in one month."

Dale: "Just sell him the goddam things."

I went back into the showroom to Armando and his wife.

Armando said, "I really like-a the Eight Foot Extrabaganza. Real nice for my roof, right?"

Me: "Absolutely. They'll be perfect." Somebody shoot me.

To solve this potential problem, we suggested filling the fountains with glycerin instead of water. Glycerin is clear like water, but very viscous and doesn't break up or splash like water. The only drawback is that it feels greasy and kind of puts a greasy coat on everything in touches. Oh, and glycerin ain't necessarily cheap like water, either.

Potential problem number two was that he wanted to run the fountains all year long, winter included. If the fountains are running, the combination of the moving water and the heat from the lights will keep the water in the fountain from freezing. If the water freezes, it can burst the copper tubing and the pumps.

Now that we'd all decided to walk on the wild side, fountain-wise, we simply suggested submersible heaters that could be plugged in and turned on during the winter overnight hours. They'd do the trick. Except I'd never seen them work well enough to heat that much water. Hell, this was only July and they could drop the bomb by midwinter. Let's rock 'n roll!

About the time the fountains were ready to install, which we brilliantly decided would be the Friday of the Labor Day weekend, we had this guy working for us named Wilbert.

Wilbert was worthless as tits on a bull, workwise. Every time I walked into one of the shop rooms, there was ol' Wilbert, taking a break and having a smoke or a soda or a candy bar or an ice cream or a sandwich. Every time. I actually entertained the idea of spying on him to see if he ever did any work and when I caught him just sitting there looking out the window for any extended period of time, I'd fire his lazy ass.

Then I figured Dale or Jeanne would catch me spying on him and I'd get my ass chewed for standing around goofing off. So I let it go.

Wilbert finally earned every nickel he'd ever stolen from our clock that Friday, in my book anyway.

We'd rented one of those goddam big trucks, like the one that choked out on the Jersey Turnpike, and filled it with fountains and all the gear necessary to set them up. Oh, naturally, four or five Polish guys were stuck in the dark in the back, too, along with Wilbert.

John and Al sat in the front with me while I drove.

We couldn't take the truck on the Belt Parkway, which was the only route I was familiar with to get anywhere near Coney Island. We'd have to use the Gowanus or some expressway only people from Brooklyn ever used.

So, onto the Gowanus we cruised. And traffic came to a complete standstill. And why the fuck not? Friday afternoon of Labor Day weekend and we found ourselves on one of the only non-surface streets in all of Brooklyn, along with half the population of Brooklyn trying to get out of town.

"Korek kuravamotch", said Bubniak.

"Korek skoorivissin!", said I.

"What?", said Al. "God, this traffic sucks, doesn't it?"

We'd moved about two exits in forty-five minutes and I was looking at the clock and we weren't going to make it anywhere near our appointed time and it was the Friday of Labor Day weekend and I wanted to get home, too, and life sucked big-time.

I pulled off at the next exit.

"John, doesn't Wilbert live in Brooklyn?"

"Think so. All those guys live in Brooklyn", he said, gesturing toward the back.

"Yeah, but John, your guys only take the subway. Maybe Wilbert knows how to get us there on surface streets."

I pulled over, walked to the back and rolled up the back door. They were all coughing and looking like we'd just crossed the Mexico-Arizona border in the middle of the desert.

"Hey, Wilbert. Can you get us to Coney Island on surface streets? If we stay on the Gowanus, we'll never make it."

"Hell, yes, Jim. This is my neighborhood. I can get you wherever you wanna go in Brooklyn." This was sounding good.

"Okay, you ride up front with me."

Oops. With a cab that only fit three, that meant either John or Al would have to go into the pit with the border-crossers. It meant that Al would have to go into the pit with the border-crossers.

"Oh, no! I can't do that. I won't do that. I get claustrophobia or whatever it's called. No. Not me."

"Al. Get in the back and don't fuck with me. You can't even spell claustrophobia."

"C-l-a-u..."

"Knock it off. Get in there. Take one for the team."

"Fuck the team."

"Come here a minute." I took him aside and quietly told him I pay him double-time for any overtime and the overtime clock had already started.

It worked. Poor Al. Sitting in the dark with a half-dozen Polish guys who were always jabbering and laughing with each other. He was obviously in hell. Double over-time hell, though, so he dealt with it.

Wilbert: "Go left at the next major street and make your way over to Metropolitan Avenue."

Me: "Does the street we're gonna turn onto intersect with Metropolitan?"

"No. But you'll make your way there. We'll find it."

The sonofabitch had no idea where he was or where he was going but he'd wangled his way into the cab.

"Stop over there and I'll get it cleared up. I'm just a little lost. You know, having to sit in the fucking dark sucking diesel fumes and all."

Wilbert went into a corner deli and came back with a big smile on his kisser and a forty-ouncer in his hand. Great. Fucking great. Now he'd be lost and drunk.

"No problem", he said as he climbed up into the truck. "I'll get us there in no time."

"Yeah, well, you'd better or I'll stick that forty up your ass."

Much to my surprise, he meant it. We made a few lefts, made a few rights, went straight a few times and, lo and behold, Coney Island lay dead ahead. Amazing.

That little exhibition of Wilbert's geographic dexterity not only insured his sitting up front on the ride home – because I was totally lost - it also sealed Al's fate to ride home with his new best friends in the back, too. Geez, was he pissed.

It took us a couple of hours to set up all the fountains, but everything looked real good, too, including the two Eight Foot Extravaganzas pumping pure glycerin on the roof. That wouldn't be the end of our trips to the Lido Manor because everything I'd feared might go wrong eventually did.

But, for that day, our work was done and we went smoothly against the outbound traffic all the way home and I dropped the goddam truck off at the rental center at 8:30 at night on the Friday of Labor Day weekend.

But, he'd given me a check for 20K and I had a thousand waiting for me in my next paycheck.

A month later we got a phone call from Armando. Al took the first message. Seems both of his Eight Foot Extravaganzas were on the fritz. The outer spray ring wasn't working on one of them and the inner one wasn't working on the other. Shit. Burned-out pumps. I told Al to call him back and tell him we'd ship another couple pumps out UPS and he could have one of his guys change them. Not quite good enough.

"How my guy change-a the pumps, eh? My guy take outta the trash, sweep-a the floors, unload-a the trucks, OK? He would-a electrify himself if he try an-a change-a the pumps."

Al told Armando he'd have Jim call him. The bastard was probably getting back at me for making him ride in the back with the border-crossers.

Of course I didn't call.

A couple of days later the phone rang and I picked it up.

"General Fountains."

"Is-a Jim there, please?" "Is -a?" Could only be Armando.

"No, I'm sorry, he's out of the office."

"Would-a you tell him I called and-a my fountains not-a working. Big trouble if I-a no hear."

"I'll tell him as soon as he comes in. May I tell him who called?" Like I didn't fucking know.

"Armando. Who's this?"

"Bill Leith."

"Okay a-Bill. An' I better-a hear from him, OK?"

"OK."

"Bye."

"Bye."

Shit.

Again, not quite knowing if Armando had "friends", I finally admitted I had to deal with this head on. See, Dale, being the original fountain tycoon, would have known how to duck this guy until he finally called in an electrician or something. Me, being somewhat of a neophyte, still hadn't perfected the art of completely ignoring a complaining customer.

The next morning, I grabbed a couple of pumps and made my way out to Coney Island, changed the pumps in an hour or two and completely charmed and somewhat conned Armando and his wife.

The pumps had burned out because too much water had blown out of the fountains. The roof was actually slippery from all the glycerin on it. The only hope of keeping the water in the bowls was to turn down the height of the water. Convincing Mr. and Mrs. Armando of this might take some tact.

I had a little "creative design" discussion with them, while we shared some wine and cheese and fruits that they had brought out in my "honor".

"So, Armando. Can you see the fountains on the roof when you drive past the restaurant at night?"

"Oh, yes, Jim. Ever'body inna the neighborhood talks about 'em alla the time. Water ashooting outta the roof. Ever'body say they are-a beautiful."

"Good. Good. Now that they know they're there and they look for them all the time, maybe it's time for us to be just a little more subtle."

"Subtle? Whaddyou mean, a-subtle?"

"Well, Armando, one thing about water and lights at night: sometimes just a little less is just a little more."

Questioning looks. And for good reason.

"Look, if we turn down the sprays, say, no more than twelve inches, the only people who know it's happened will be us. And, if the sprays are just a *little* lower, people will look just a little harder at them and at your restaurant. See what I mean?"

More questioning looks.

"They'll drive just a *little* slower, look a *little* closer at your restaurant and I'll bet just a few *more* of them might stop and decide to eat here, rather than just driving by. More business."

It was like dropping a naked hook in the water, but the hook was in the water, nonetheless.

"More business? You think-a so?" Armando's wife.

"No guarantees, but that's what we're trying to do here, isn't it?"

Slowly, "I like-a the idea, I think." Armando's wife again.

Me: "I know it's a very subtle change, but we have to remember – you put these fountains in to market your restaurant. And, sometimes, marketing uses some crazy psychology. The idea is to draw them in and, by looking closer at the fountains – and at your restaurant – you'll be using some of that marketing psychology."

"Where did-a you learn all about a-marketing?" Armando.

"In college. I was a marketing major." Actually, it was Theater Arts, but that was close enough.

"Well. You know-a fountains and you know-a marketing. Let's try it."

Hell has a special place for people like me.

I turned the sprays down, a little closer to eighteen inches than twelve, but nobody could tell the difference. That was the whole point, anyway – nobody'd ever notice - but my take on Armando was that he'd bought what he'd bought and wanted everything just that way. Hence, the little tango amongst the wine and cheese.

The fountains worked well from then on.

TWENTY-FOUR

"Jim, is blood in stairway. Maybe come quick."

Ah, finally a diversion from totaling up accounts payable and accounts receivable on the infernal adding machine. We never kept the books on a regular basis. But every year, along about mid-February, just before the end of our grace period from the IRS, Jeanne and I would spend weeks entering and adding everything that happened in our business over the past twelve months. We both hated it and if that fucking Leith hadn't skipped, he'd still be doing it.

I followed John to the second floor stairway landing and, sure enough, there was an ample amount of fresh red blood. The blood trail went up toward the third floor and not down toward the street.

Up we went, each of us probably expecting the worst. Probably some guy had gotten mugged in the stairway or shot or stabbed and found his way into the stairwell or something. It wasn't unheard of.

We followed the blood trail up to the fifth floor landing and there, leaning against the wall, was Murphy, the old, perennially-sodden postman.

"Murphy! What the hell happened?"

"Ah, I slipped on the stairs and bumped my head."

"Let's see."

It wasn't a bad cut, thank God, but it was bleeding pretty profusely. His blood was awfully thin, a testament to an overabundance of alcohol in the bloodstream, or so I'd heard.

Murphy used to carry a flask or bottle with him on his rounds, but never talked so nobody ever knew he was half in the bag.

"You'd better get it stitched up. John – get one of your guys to go with him up to St. Vincent's and drop him off at the emergency room."

"No!"

"C'mon, Murph. This ain't gonna stop on its own. You have to get it sewn up."

"I can't." He started to cry. Shit. Another weepy drunk.

"What's the matter?"

"If they catch me drinking one more time, they'll fire me. Ohh. Oh, this is terrible."

I'd never heard of anybody getting fired from the Post Office. Oh – maybe that's why those guys showed up with the sawed-offs and dusted their supervisors and fellow workers – because they got fired for being soused. I didn't think Murph had it in him, though.

I thought for a second.

"Murph – I've got an idea. I'll call your supervisor and tell him that some guy had robbed one of the shops upstairs and was running down the stairs to the street. You just happened to be on your rounds and walked into the stairway just as the guy was coming down. He slammed you against the wall and just kept going. Hell, your boss'll buy that, especially around here. Must actually happen once in a while."

"Ah, I don't know…"

"Sure you do. That bag of your weighs fifty or sixty pounds. You can't maneuver very well with that thing on your back. Shit, he'll buy it for sure. Hell – I know. I'll get Parker up here and we'll tell him the story. I'll get Parker to sit there while I'm talking to your boss and give him a little hell for the building's lack of security."

He thought a little, which was probably a chore, being half-drunk and half-conked from the fall.

"Let's go down to the office. I'll call while you're sitting there so you can hear the conversation, then you and John's guy'll go to the hospital."

We made our way down to the office, John got him some paper towels and some ice and I called Parker to come up. I got Parker off to the side and told him the truth and said I might bitch in his direction a little while I was talking to Murphy's boss. He took off his hat and rubbed his head and said, "Sure, Cuz. No problem."

Al came around the corner and saw the little group. "What happened?"

"Nothing. He fell down."

Al gave a 'so-what-else-is-new' look, snorted, and went back around to his collating. I got Murphy's boss on the phone, I think his name was Carmichael. Told him the story.

"Has he been drinking?"

"Hell, no. Not that I could tell. I haven't seen him drunk in months." A wink to Murphy. "And it wouldn't've happened if we had any goddam security around this place. Parker – how often has this gotta happen before you get a security guard?" A wink to Parker.

"Is he gonna be alright?", asked Carmichael.

"Sure. Couple stitches and he'll be as good as new."

"Ah, that's too bad. The guy's fucking worthless."

"I'll pass along your concern. Anyway, he's on his way up to St. Vincent's with one of our guys. His bag's still here. You gonna send somebody over for it?"

"Ah, fuck. Guess I'll have to. Where are you?"

I told him and off Murphy went to get sewn up with one of John's men.

The next day I saw Murphy on his rounds, head bandaged and sober.

"Hey, Murph. How you doing?"

"Me? I'm fine." Absolutely no indication that he remembered what had happened the day before. Probably didn't. Goofy bastard.

****

Starting in the mid-'70s, after we got the books done, Dale and Jeanne would go to Florida, to Bal Harbour, for a vacation.

The first time they went, they planned – at least they told me – on only going for a week. They were gone five. Left me in charge. Which wasn't all that bad.

They had me stay at their apartment so I could take care of their cats. As they lived at 52nd and Eighth, it was still in my neighborhood so I could stop by on the way home for clean clothes and the like. Besides, it was right across the street from Jilly's and half a block from Gallagher's.

My workload didn't really change any. As a matter of fact, it probably got a little easier – Jeanne wasn't there to give me dirty looks if I was sitting on the couch, my secondary base of operations. About the only additional things I had to do were to get the deposits ready every day and to do the payroll on Fridays.

Jeanne and Dale's friend, Gus Jettner, came to New York from somewhere and stayed with me at their apartment for a couple of weeks. Actually, he was Jeanne's friend from the old days and Dale more or less put up with him. He never would have been able to stay there if they were home. Gus had been in and out of town since I was a kid and I didn't mind hanging out with him. He was very funny and we laughed a lot.

My only worry was that he'd die on me. He had a real bad heart, according to him, and couldn't do too much physical activity. I always pretty much believed that was a crock, because he smoked like a chimney and drank like a fish. Still, I didn't need a dead Gus on my hands.

I don't know what Gus did for a living. A bunch of things, probably. A little of this, a little of that, but nothing that could be construed as a career. I put him on the payroll while he was in New York, working for John, and he sort of worked and sort of didn't, which was probably fine because he sort of got paid – minimum wage plus overtime.

Gus and I would sit around at night and drink scotch and shoot the shit. He usually made dinner, which is to say he warmed up whatever canned glop he'd bought at the store.

The only trouble we ever got into was one night when we both passed out on the matching couches Jeanne and Dale had in the apartment. One was on one side of the room and one was on the other. Gus fell asleep/passed out with a lit cigarette and he awoke in pain.

"Jimmy! Jimmy! Wake up! Wake the fuck up, quick!"

"Huh?"

"Jimmy – we got a fire!"

"What?!?"

He pointed across the room and I tried to focus my eyes, which was no mean feat at that point. His couch was smoldering and smoking.

"Jesus Christ, Gus!"

I jumped up, ran into the kitchen, found a pot, ran some water in it, ran back into the living room and poured it onto the offending cushion. S-s-s-s-s-s. Out quickly and easily.

"What the hell's the matter with you, Gus? Couldn't you have done that? How hard was that? Huh?"

"Jimmy, when I woke up and felt that and saw that, my heart began beating a mile a minute. I thought for sure I was having a heart attack." Bullshit. You were just in a Scotch-soaked stupor and had no idea what to do.

"You okay now?"

"Yeah, I'm fine. Must've passed." Yep, soon as he got the hot potato lateralled into my hands.

"What're we gonna do? That whole side of the cushion is gone. At least it hardly touched the foam rubber."

Ah, fortunately that was true. The cushion itself was fine. It was the covering that was burned. But only on one side.

The coverings had been expensive in their day and were black and white checked, like a chessboard. Over time, the white had become greyed. If we were to get one cushion re-covered, it'd stand out like a sore thumb. If we went and got both couches recovered, meaning about six seat cushions, four back cushions and four bolsters, it'd cost a fortune.

What to do?

"Gus – how much money do you have?"

"Shit, Jimmy. You know how much I've got – you wrote the paycheck, remember? And more than half of that's gone."

"Yeah. That's what I was afraid of. Me, too."

"Jimmy. Why don't you tell them you did it. Like it was an accident with a candle or something."

"What? I had nothing to do with it. You almost burned the fucking place down, not me."

"I know. But you and I both know Dale hates my guts and he'd have my ass if he finds out I did it. C'mon, you're their nephew and they really love you. You know you can't do anything wrong in their eyes. Tell 'em it was an accident and nothing'll happen. Come on, be a pal."

"Oh no you don't, Gus. Don't even begin to think that way. Don't even *begin* to think." "Fine. What the hell are we gonna do then?"

"I don't know." Wait a minute.

"Gus, go turn it over."

"What?"

"Turn it over. Go turn the cushion over."

"Oh, no."

He walked over and turned the cushion over. Good as new.

"Good as new."

"Jimmy, are you nuts? First time they turn that over, they'll flip."

"Gus, my bet is that that cushion hasn't been turned over in five years. And if we're lucky, it won't get turned over for another five years.

Hell, even if they turn it over in a few months, whichever one of them turns it over will probably blame the other one."

"That's probably true. It's a wonder more of 'em don't have holes in 'em already." "So, we just keep our mouths shut and don't burn another one. If they notice it in the next couple of months, I'll just say you did it and you'll be a thousand miles away."

"Jimmy, don't tell them I did it!"

"Just relax, Gus. Trust me, they won't notice."

And I don't think they ever did. At least they never mentioned it.

But, the next morning in the office, Gus said to Al, "Al, did Jimmy tell you how he almost burned down Jeanne and Dale's apartment last night?"

"Gus. Just shut the fuck up about it or I'll have Little Joe fiberglass your fucking head!"

Gus laughed and walked around the corner into the hallway.

Al, to me: "What? You almost burned down Jeanne and Dale's house?"

"No, Al. Gus did. But just don't ever say anything about it again. Everything's fine. Just fine. OK?"

"Sure, Jim. Everything's fine." And around the corner he went. Sometimes Al could get this infuriating look on his face that was half confusion, half accusatory. The word "skeptical" comes to mind. Bastard.

The week Dale and Jeanne were to be gone stretched into three, then four, then five, then six. Hell, they were gone from the middle of January and here it was almost the first of March. I didn't really mind at all, though. The place had settled into a nice, smooth rhythm and things were going along nicely and quietly.

Dale and Jeanne were staying at an empty apartment in Harriett's building in Bal Harbour. Harriett was the "rental manager" or something and it was a beautiful apartment building right across Collins Avenue from the Sea View and Ivanhoe Hotels.

The Sea View was chock full of rich, elderly people, mostly from the Midwest, like Chicago and Minneapolis. There were a whole lot of rich widows whose husbands had made their fortunes in the ball-bearing or metal turning or brake lining business or something equally as exciting.

The Ivanhoe had maybe a little younger demographic – sixty-five instead of eighty – and it seemed like most of its guests were from New York. The Ivanhoe had a deal with Harriett's apartment building that allowed her seasonal renters the use of cabanas by the Ivanhoe's pool. That's where Dale and Jeanne hung out all day.

There was one cabana that was off limits to everyone, even if it wasn't in use. It belonged to Arthur Godfrey, who was almost never there, but he was thought of as some sort of god around the Ivanhoe.

There was another guy who had everything pretty much his way, too, and he was a state senator from Illinois. I think his name was Bob-something. Seems he always had an oversized jug of scotch in his cabana that dispensed the nectar with a spout, like a beer keg.

Dale would call me every morning around eleven.

"What's happening?"

I'd tell him any good news that had come our way in the last few hours, namely whatever checks may have been in the early mail. There wasn't any really bad news, other than the occasional very last ditch attempt by some company to get paid before they sued us.

If that happened, Dale would tell me to send them two hundred on account and that would keep them quiet for another couple of weeks.

He'd tell me to call him at the Ivanhoe if anything came up. Like the noon mail with a tally of whatever checks that had brought.

I'd call the Ivanhoe's front desk, ask for Dale and tell the operator he was probably out in the cabanas. He'd come on in a few minutes and we'd shoot whatever shit needed shooting. I didn't realize until later that every time I called, the operator would page him and the page would be heard all over the hotel. He'd have several people, including

Jim Lucey, Iz and some drinking buddies from Gallagher's call a couple of times a day, too.

"Mr. Dale Hodge. Call for Mr. Dale Hodge, please."

See, the more pages people got in a day, the more important they became in the eyes of their friends around the pool. Dale'd probably get twelve to fifteen calls during a five or six hour period. That's something like three an hour. Man, this guy must be one of the pillars of capitalism! Of course – General Motors, General Dynamics, General Fountains – the names were interchangeable.

Hey – it was fun for him, so what the hell, right?

Around the middle of their sixth week down there, they did something that blew me away. They told me to take a couple of weeks, come on down and hang out with them. I'd been working hard, the weather in New York sucked, and we'd have a good time. I flew down, Harriett gave me my own place behind her building, in one of the vacant maid's apartments, and there I was in Miami. First time I'd ever seen a palm tree.

I had a great time. Up early. Nice breakfast. At the pool by eleven. Cocktails at noon. Back to the room around four. Shower and dress. Smoke a joint. Cocktails around seven. Nice dinner. Meet some old rich widows at the Sea View around nine-thirty.

I thought I was really going to get lucky one night. Over at the Sea View, they had a big dance floor with a live band that played songs from the forties. It was ghastly to me, but I was sailing along not caring about anything in the world, so what the hell.

Dale introduced me to the women from the Johnson family. Johnson, as in Johnson Outboards. There was the matriarch, who was probably in her fifties and two daughters, maybe just a little older than I, who were both pretty decent looking. Oh boy, I thought, I'd take either one of them.

Alas, they were both snobs, probably as a result of having been told their entire lives that their respective shit didn't stink. The mother, however, kept sweeping me off to the dance floor. Dale said, conspiratorially, "Jim, you might have yourself a hot one, there. She's got more money than God!"

"Dale, she's fucking ancient!"

"Ancient and rich!"

The whole deal worked itself out soon enough, though, as the daughters whined long and loud enough that Mom gathered them up and they all left.

I finally met the senator. Or, as everyone around him referred to him, the Senator. This guy was a piece of work. He drank continuously from that scotch spigot, from the time he got there 'til the time he left. Big, strong drinks, too. But he never once looked like he'd had an ounce. I don't know how he did it.

He never got paged over the phone. He never seemed to do any work. Never had a briefcase or sheaf of papers that you'd expect a senator to have. Never made a call that I know of. Sure as hell made me want to enter politics, if this was how it worked.

We all went to Joe's Stone Crab for dinner one night. It was jammed, but the Senator had a reservation for about twelve and we walked straight in, straight through the place to our table, with the whole place bowing and scraping in his wake.

He sat at the head of the table and I sat to his left. Not once during the dinner did a political issue spew forth from his lips. The one thing I remember is that when he ordered a drink, he ordered two. "Always order a back-up, m'boy. You don't want to run out while you're looking around for your waiter."

I wonder whatever happened to that guy. Never made a big name for himself, as far as I know, but he probably milked being the Senator for decades.

By the time we got back to New York, two weeks later, Dale was talking about buying 264.

Right, I'm ducking Joe Jaboni from We Just Got Chumped and his seven hundred dollar invoice and Dale and Jeanne are going to buy a twenty-story building. This was, very obviously, another of Dale's pipe dreams.

It was all he talked about at Gallagher's. Dale was always one to tell people what he was going to do before he ever did it. Like the bikes with the motors and the Henry Ford book. Most of the time, those things just disappeared into thin air. Made for good bar conversation, though.

I was standing there talking to Bernard Brill one night and excitedly asked him what he thought of Dale buying the building. He gave me his best Ben Franklin look and said, "Jimmy, I don't think Dale will ever buy that building."

"How do you know?"

"Because he hasn't asked me for any money yet." Everybody asked Bernard for money – he's the one that really had it.

"What's this about Dale buying a building?", asked Manny, obviously on the ear.

Manny was Manny Manishor, a dapper, elderly gentleman from Brooklyn who had made his living the past sixty years as a bookmaker. Everybody at Gallagher's bet with Manny. But you could only pay up or collect on Tuesday or Friday evenings. Those were the nights Manny used Gallagher's as his 'office'. Where he spent the other five nights he never said, but he probably had three or four joints that also served as his office.

Manny was pretty curmudgeonly, had impeccable manners and hated it when people didn't follow suit.

He sure didn't like Billy Ruben. He knew Billy was King of the Mooches and that rubbed him the wrong way. But what he really hated about Billy was whenever he had to take a bet from him. True to form, Billy had recently bet in the neighborhood of two hundred bucks to show on an overwhelming favorite someplace. The horse won and paid like a dime to show. Billy was due a whopping twenty bucks.

He waddled into Gallagher's, went straight to the bar to get a handful of nuts or whatever was being offered. Then, he surveyed the room with his big old bug eyes and announced in a too-loud voice, "I'm looking for Manny. He owes me my winnings."

Everybody in his immediate vicinity winced and, somewhere along the bar, Manny muttered some Yiddish obscenity under his breath.

When Ruben spotted him and broadly approached him, grinning from ear to ear, Manny said to him, "Listen, you. How many times I gotta tell you to keep your voice down about this stuff? You think I been in this business over sixty years with guys like you letting everybody in the room know I make book? What the hell's the matter with you?"
"Oh, Manny, you're just upset that I took your money."

"Took my money? Listen, you cheap putz, you think I need action like that from chalk bettors who bet show? I don't want that kind of action. I don't need that kind of action. Next time you get the urge, just tell me – I'll *give* you twenty bucks. Here." He handed him a twenty. "Now – Mr. Hotshot Gambler, you gonna buy me a drink with your winnings like a gentleman?"

With that, grin still in place, Billy turned and walked down the bar to see if he could get somebody to buy *him* a drink. The man had absolutely no shame.

"That sonofabitch. Jimmy, how can you put up with that guy?"

"For one thing, Manny, the little exchanges you two guys have are always fun to watch." "Ah! I gotta go. I always like to catch the subway by nine."

"I know. Have a safe trip home. See you Friday."

"Good night, Jimmy. Zie Gezundt." He always said Zie Gezundt.

Some guys, unlike Billy Ruben, bet pretty big with Manny. He and Bernard would often exchange a couple thousand dollars on occasion. It's funny, Bernard would pull an unruly pile of money from his left pants pocket and another from his right and lay it on the bar. "Manny – you count out what I owe you."

One night, there were a bunch of us in there and we were discussing the new disco that had gone in next door – had taken over the space that Fornos Restaurant used to be in. Fornos was run by two Greek brothers, Vincent and Julio. Vincent, aka Don Vincenzo, was a slight man who really ran the place. His brother, Julio, had had brain damage or something as a young man and did a lot of wandering around, trying to look like he had something important to do, but he also looked like he couldn't remember exactly what it was.

They decided to sell because they weren't getting any younger and Don Vincenzo wanted to move to Florida or somewhere with his wife. That was kind of sad because Julio would now wander around without looking like he had something important to do. He just wandered around.

Our group that night also included a friend of ours who only made it around once a month or so, Billy Canterino. Canterino was a detective. As a matter of fact, he was one of the guys who hit that apartment with Frank Serpico when all hell broke loose and Serpico claimed they'd all deserted him or something. Canterino didn't talk much about it, but it was pretty obvious he thought Serpico was pulling everybody's chain. Canterino was in on some of the toughest things in NYPD history.

We all decided to wander next door to check out the place.

Imagine – a dozen or so middle-aged inebriants accompanied by an equally inebriated kid in his twenties hit the door to one of the West Side's hottest new discos. It wasn't Studio 54, but it wasn't far behind.

The guy at the door said, "No way. We're full." No sign of trying to be civil, but that was also part of discos' charm, I guess. "Ooh, be rude to me. But, please, just let me in." Somebody, probably Bernard, pulled out a wad of unruly bills and the guy still said no.

Canterino made his way to the head of our line and whispered no more than one line to the guy at the door.

"Right this way, please. Enjoy yourselves."

"Billy, what the hell did you say to that guy to get us this kind of treatment?"

"I just showed him my badge and told him if he didn't let us in right now, I'd have a dozen squad cars and a posse of fire inspectors here in the next five minutes."

Worked like a charm.

Sometime in the next year or so, Canterino got sick. Some kind of terrible kidney problems. He had to go on dialysis two or three times a week. He'd stop in every once in a while. He looked terrible. His face had blown all out of proportion due to the steroids that were keeping him alive. Nobody, including him, thought he was long for this world. He finally stopped coming in.

Wouldn't you know, a few years later I was reading the Sunday Times and picked up the magazine section. There on the front cover was Billy Canterino. He had survived and had gone on to become an angel for hundreds of people who had terrible kidney problems. He had started a nationwide donor-recipient program, had developed a counselling program and was a fixture in the New York City hospital system. He had become a real hero. God, that made me feel good.

TWENTY-FIVE

I went to the New England Restaurant Show three or four times, total. Now that I had the van and the lay of the land, I could get my stuff unloaded, carried in and set up in no time. I'd even gotten smart and had confiscated a dolly from the shop so I didn't have to carry all that stuff.

The problem with Boston in April is that it rains a lot. Seems it always rained while I was there. Sometimes it hurt attendance and sometimes it didn't.

One year, it did.

It was dead as shit for pretty much the whole show. And there's nothing more boring than hanging around a booth with nothing to do for eight hours. You can't even make deals. At least if it's a deadbeat crowd, you can make deals. No crowd, no deals. I met this guy named Dennis. Dennis was a salesman for one of those companies that made big meat-cooking ranges – the kind that makes steaks smell extra good while they're cooking, if you know what I mean. Dennis and his pals had a big booth, were throwing a lot of flame, but were not too generous with the meat samples, what with no crowd and all.

My booth was about fifty feet from the bar and about ten-thirty on day number two, I decided that I might as well have a Bloody Mary. Another guy came up and ordered one, too.

"How's the show?"

"Whaddyathink, man? It sucks."

"Sure does. My name's Jim."

"Dennis."

We got to shooting the shit, had two or three more apiece and decided we'd better get back to our respective booths. Actually, Dennis decided he'd better get back to his booth. I was fine – I could see if anybody was wandering up to mine and could make a break for it in time to intercept them before they moved on.

"Let's reconnoiter back here at noon."

"Done."

Well, by five o'clock, both of us were three sheets to the wind.

I decided to pack it in half an hour early because if I drank any more I wouldn't be able to drive back to my hotel. For some ungodly reason, I was staying at the Hilton at Logan Airport. I think I chose that place because it was an easy drive from the Convention Center.

I had to drive through a tunnel and had the presence of mind to realize that if I were any drunker, I'd stand a good chance of piling up the van in the middle of the tunnel at the middle of rush hour. That would not have been good.

Off I went and, miraculously, found my way back to the hotel in one piece.

I passed out on the bed – somewhere around seven, I think.

I woke up around ten, wondered where the hell I was, remembered and decided ten was too early to go back to sleep. I was probably still a little under the weather.

I went down to the bar and ordered a drink. This was right around the time of Saturday Night Fever and the Bee Gees' hits were booming from the juke box. I danced a number of dances with some chick that was also at the bar, me thinking I was John Travolta or something. I hate to admit it, but I actually had an off-white suit and was wearing it.

What a jamoke.

Natch, I tried to pick her up but she gave me some song and dance about having to get up early to go on sales calls or some such bullshit and left.

So, there I was, sitting at the bar two or three stools down from some guy with longish hair.

Two strangers – two guys – sitting at a bar a few stools from each other do not talk to each other. If one of them tries to strike up a conversation, it's incumbent upon the other guy to assume the conversation striker is either a nutcase or gay.

Therefore, both guys strike up conversations with the bartender. That's safe. And, if a customer-bartender conversation turns interesting, it's perfectly acceptable for the guy not involved in the conversation to get involved. That way, you can have a three-sided conversation and if the bartender walks away, it is still legitimate for the two customers to carry on the conversation. No harm, no foul.

That's how it happened in this particular instance. Just that way. The other customer and I carried on a two-way version of the three-way conversation that included the bartender who had walked away and it was about music, probably because the disco was blaring in our skulls.

"By the way, my name's Jim."

"I'm Gene. What do you do, Jim?"

"I'm a fountain tycoon, Gene, how about you?"

"I'm a singer."

Ho-ly shit! Is it who I think it is? Hell, yes it is!

I couldn't believe it!

It was, though.

"You're Gene Clark."

"Yep."

Gene Clark was one of the vocalists of the Byrds, probably one of the greatest bands of all time. "Mr. Tambourine Man", "Turn, Turn, Turn", "Eight Miles High", "All I Really Want to Do", "He Was a Friend of Mine". The fucking Byrds, man! Jim (aka Roger) McGuinn. David Crosby. Chris Hillman.

What in the living hell was Gene Clark doing in the Airport Hilton at Logan International Airport in Boston-by-God, Massachusetts?!?

"What in the world are you doing here? In this place?" He should be at the Copley Plaza or the Four Seasons or something. Or somewhere other than Boston.

"I'm helping to produce an album, doing a little singing on it."

"Whose album?"

"Ah, you wouldn't know them. If it's any good, then you'll know."

"What happened to you and the Byrds?"

"Well, you know, I left and rejoined and around and around. We finally broke up several years ago."

"I couldn't believe it. Man, you guys were the best! You, like, defined my youth."

"Yeah, sort of defined ours, too. I guess a lot of people, huh?"

"Hey, know what one of my all-time favorite songs is? 'He Was a Friend of Mine'."

"Ah, yeah, the song about Kennedy. I really liked that song, too. Good harmonies."

I thought to myself, wow, how the mighty have fallen.

I said, "You know, when McGuinn changed his name from Jim to Roger because of some numerology shit, I figured something was happening."

He just snorted.

I'd about had it. Not drunk, just kind of all in. And depressed, too, seeing Gene Clark in the bar of the Airport Hilton and knowing he was just bumping along.

"Hey, listen, Gene – can I bother you for your autograph?"

"Sure, man, glad to oblige."

And he signed his autograph on a cocktail napkin replete with the Hilton Rainbow. I was rummaging through some stuff the other day and there it was. I still have it.

Although I'm happy to say I no longer have the off-white John Travolta-knock-off suit.

****

There was this woman who came around the office every few weeks. Her name was Ming and she was a sort-of friend of Jeanne's and an Avon lady. Ming was married to JoJo Moore, a bartender that had worked back at The Garden in Jamaica a number of years earlier.

JoJo had died by this time, but I remember him saying to me, several years earlier, while he was still alive, "Jimmy, if you're ever gonna punch your wife, hit her in the belly. See, the belly don't bruise." At the time I didn't know if he was shitting me or not but, knowing Ming, there wasn't a court in the country that would've convicted him for doing so with impunity.

Ming could drive you nuts. Whenever she came in, Dale would split for the shop or somewhere, I'd head for the presses and Jeanne would have to sit there making small talk with Ming. Hey – it was her friend.

Ming personified small talk. "Ooh, Jimmy, it's cold today, isn't it?"

"Yep. Cold."

"Nice to be warm."

"Real nice."

"That's a nice shirt."

"I stole it off a dead guy."

"What?"

"Nothing." Around the corner.

To get rid of her, Jeanne would give her a couple of drinks. After about her third, she always split.

She had this weird red-face thing going on, though. After her first drink, her face would start to get a little flushed. By the middle of her second, it'd be approaching red. By her third, it looked like she'd fallen asleep on the beach for about three hours. I used to wonder if her head'd pop if she ever had a fourth.

During the course of the half-hour it took her to polish off two or three drinks, the small talk got even worse.

Tiger, the cat, would waltz on through the office.

"Ooh, Tiger! Hi, Tiger. Come here, Tiger."

Tige: "No fucking way."

"What a pretty cat, huh Jeanne?" This was maybe the twentieth time she'd seen Tiger and she said it every goddam time.

"Yes, she is, Ming. Just beautiful."

"And that's a pretty blouse you're wearing."

"You think so?", Jeanne'd say automatically, hands flying on the adding machine.

"Oh, yes. It brings out your eyes. Oh, and what pretty pants."

"Thanks."

"It's cold out today, isn't it, Jeanne?"

"Yes it is."

"Nice to be warm."

No answer.

"Glad I have a nice warm coat."

No answer.

"And gloves. I got them last year. Do you like gloves?"

"Jim – will you get over here and fix Ming another drink?"

Shit. I'll bomb the hell out of her. Maybe she'll get real goofy and do a striptease or something. I wouldn't even go around the corner to get her glass. Simply pour the drink in another one. That'd mean I only had to come in contact with her once.

"Oh, thank you, Jimmy. Are those new pants?"

"No."

"They're nice. Pants are nice, aren't they Jeanne?"

"Mmm."

"How come Tiger never comes to see me?"

Because she knows you're stone crazy, you old bat!

Dale would walk back in, frowning.

"Oh, Dale, that's a nice shirt. Is it new?"

No answer, whatsoever. Just a frown.

About this time, Ming would try to pawn off some of her Avon crap on Jeanne. Here's why Ming kept coming back: to get rid of her, Jeanne would write her a check for fifty bucks and tell her to order whatever she thought Jeanne would want.

So, Ming gets a fifty-dollar sale for talking about the weather and shirts, getting half a snootful, and annoying everybody in the place. Didn't have to sell a thing. Maybe she wasn't crazy.

Off she'd go, coat on, gloves on, buzz on, face like a turnip.

Then there was Rose. Rose Martini. Rose was a close friend of Auntie Barb's up on 51st and Eighth. Lived in the same building. In her seventies, or so it seemed. Rose was a bookkeeper and Jeanne hired her to do what she and I used to do. She was around far too often.

Rose meant well but she was half-dingy, too. Always walked in with a cane in one hand and a full shopping bag in the other. That bag would hold her purse, shoes, whatever books she had taken home, lunch and various and sundry crap.

Rose had trouble keeping her trap shut, too. And she always had issues with something or other. The buses. The grocery store. The newsstand on the corner. The rent control board. The failure of General Fountain Corp. to do its business to suit her bookkeeping.

And when she wanted to talk about one of her issues, she'd catch you off guard and kind of pin you into a corner. It wasn't easy waltzing around Rose to get out of one of those corners because she had a bad hip – hence the cane – and I always felt if I really juked her, she'd go down in a heap.

She'd get all conspiratorial on you, voice down real low, like whatever she was saying was a secret. "Jimmy, do you know what happened to me last night on my way home?"

A gang bang?

"No. What?"

"Well. I stopped at D'Agostino's to get some nice fish. Do you like fish, Jimmy?"

"Fish is good."

"Well, there was a store coupon for a dollar off fluke. And, guess what? By the time I got there, they were out of fluke."

"Maybe they never had any. Maybe the fluke was a fluke."

"What?"

"Never mind."

"Anyway, I asked for a rain check on the fluke. When I asked if the coupon would be good on the rain check, they told me, 'No, the store coupon's only for today', so I got hold of the manager and asked him. I got the same response, can you believe it? I told him, 'Why, you're the manager, you can make the decision.' Know what he told me? 'It's a corporate decision. I can't do anything about it.' Jimmy, why do they have a manager if he can't make decisions?"

Right then, if Jaboni from We Just Got Chumped called, Harry Hyatt, Bill Leith and Jim. all would have been there fighting to take his call. Please, phone – ring. "I was so mad. Jimmy, what's this world coming to? And I've always liked D'Agostino's.

Do you like D'Agostino's?"

"Never been there. I do my marketing at Deli – Good Food."

During the conversation, I'd head-faked to the left once and to the right, twice. I thought maybe she'd take the bait. No way. She was good. I was actually contemplating a hip and shoulder fake to the right and a quick spin move to the left when Jeanne saved me.

"Those books done yet, Rose?"

"Oh. Almost Jeanne. Jimmy, I'd better get back to work. But watch out for D'Agostino's. They're crooks."

Sometimes just existing can be exhausting.

TWENTY-SIX

Dale began to get serious about buying the building.

The management company who ran the building, Newmark & Co., also owned the building. Generally, the management company collects the rents, pays the building staff, makes the repairs, attracts new tenants, and so on, but does so for the owner or owners.

Newmark not only managed a slew, but also owned a number of buildings itself – it's still one of the largest real estate companies in New York.

Newmark assigns the oversight of its buildings to young men and women agents. In the Garment Center there is a tremendous turnover of these people. It's not an easy job. There are hundreds, if not thousands, of small companies that are just scraping by, living from hand to mouth, year after year.

There are also companies that emerge and disappear with any particular year's fashions. In the mid-seventies, stretch polyester was big. No, not leisure suits, but shirts and blouses. There were a lot of loud, weird designs. The cuts of the clothes were tight and form-fitting. Given all that, specialty houses popped up all over the place to fill the demand.

And, because of that fashion trend (if one were to call it fashion), a lot of the more traditional places either adapted, laid low for a few years if they had money, or went out of business. This type of transitional clientele was and is the norm for the Garment Center.

That made it hard on the young agents. Everybody wants to hondle the price. Nobody pays on time. Everybody demands more than a place has to offer. And Newmark & Co. didn't get paid until the money came in, except for a monthly retainer. Its management beat the hell out of these young kids to get the most per square foot, then to deliver the money each month. Most of them washed out or moved on.

We had a kid around this time, though, who was pretty good. His name was Rob Kozlow. Kozlow never got into heated discussions with tenants and had the gift of gab. And he was persistent. And had no visible shame.

If a guy didn't have money for the rent, Kozlow'd ask him what he had on hand. The guy might say a hundred bucks. Good, give it to me. He'd get it and two days later, the same scenario would play itself out again. It was a tough way to make a living and, even though Kozlow wore a suit and tie, he was a warrior at heart.

Dale and Jeanne took a liking to him and pumped him for all the information they could get on the building. Natch, Kozlow jumped at the chance, because if the building changed hands under his watch, he'd make a ton of dough. He even turned copies of the rent rolls and monthly expenses to us. He said he'd had to sneak copies of the originals to us without telling his bosses, but I always thought that was a line of shit. Newmark & Co. didn't become one of the largest real estate firms by allowing junior birdmen to sneak copies of anything out of the building to give to existing tenants.

Looking at the numbers, Dale thought he might be able to turn a yearly profit on the building, particularly now because General Fountains was renting the better part of three whole floors. That in itself would be quite a savings.

Jeanne was skeptical. She realized Newmark bought everything in bulk, from floor cleaner to paint to toilet paper to major and minor outside repair work. If we took the whole thing private, we'd probably have to pay close to retail. Robbie countered that if we kept Newmark as the rental agent, they'd pass their pricing on to us.

Jeanne still didn't trust that Newmark would do anything out of kindness and we'd pay for it somewhere, in hidden charges that would be almost impossible for us to find. Either way, Dale had a bunch of meetings with Jim Lucey, ol' "Hole-in-the-Head", the VP of the bank. Oh, these meeting were over lunch so I expect most of the business was conducted in the first twenty minutes, just as the second round was being delivered.

Lucey liked Dale and Jeanne, though, and it seemed he was ready to help if and when anything got serious.

One day, Dale popped the question to Kozlow: "What kind of money are we talking about?"

"I'll find out."

Well, once his boss smelled a little blood in the water, he insisted he get involved. His name was Stan Roth and he was the president or something. Roth looked and acted like a Hollywood mogul. Smooth. Smiling. Accommodating. Confident. Friendly. Like a fucking shark.

Another round of lunches ensued, but this time at better restaurants.

Dale finally got the number – six hundred thousand dollars.

Six hundred thousand? I didn't know if that seemed like a lot or a little. It was a helluva more than I knew we were good for, but had always thought in terms of millions when it came to Manhattan real estate.

Over the next few weeks, Dale had Jeanne prepared P & L statements 'til the cows came home. Each time, he'd show Lucey and Lucey would give his advice. That advice always was, "Dale, you can't make it work with these numbers."

Jeanne'd do the numbers again. Same drill. Why Lucey never just put a stop to Jeanne's creative number writing was beyond me, but I gathered that the banking and investment industry didn't really care if the numbers were correct, they just had to look good. Over the years, this has been proven out time and again.

Enron.

The saga of the potential building purchase was cause for daily discussion among the regulars at Gallagher's. Everybody was pulling for us, I'll say that. Especially Sal, one of the bartenders.

Sal Spinelli was a real good, solid guy from Western Pennsylvania. He felt as if he'd adopted Dale and Jeanne and me and would always engage us in that confidential tone only bartenders and gangsters can.

Sal had a real, good dry sense of humor. He'd lean over the bar, motion for me to put my ear close to his mouth and say something like, "Remember, Jimmy, you get no bread with one meatball."

"So, Dale. What's the news on the building?"

"Looks like it might just happen, Sal."

"Good, Kid. Now, tell me – you kids aren't stretching yourselves too thin by doing this, are you? You got a good thing going and I don't wanna see you fuck it up." "Don't worry, Sal. The numbers look good." Sure, the numbers that Lucey told Jeanne to put down so the bank wouldn't flinch, I thought.

Sal would generally have his own glass of scotch and water hidden behind some bottles on the back bar and every once in a while it would get the best of him. The manager, Dick Conlin, really liked Sal, though, and would simply tell him to take the rest of the night off. He'd been working hard and he deserved it. And he'd pay him for the entire shift. Conlin was a good guy.

And Dick Conlin was known far and wide as being a good guy and one of midtown's movers and shakers, if only because he seemed to know everybody.

Joe DiMaggio came in on occasion and he and Dick would stand there and shoot the shit for hours. Politicians, sports stars, actors, actresses, politicians – everybody knew and liked Dick Conlin.

He was a member of The Friar's Club and they decided to roast him.

We were all invited, but Jeanne and Dale couldn't make it that late afternoon. Maybe they had a meeting with Newmark or something, I can't remember. However, I was chosen to carry our flag and that suited me just fine.

Once I got there, I realized I probably should've stayed back at the office. For one thing, I was probably the youngest guy – and there were only men there - in the place by at least forty years. Second, I knew maybe two people. Seems most of the regular guys from

Gallagher's had been to one of these before and had chosen, rightly, to stay away, Dick Conlin or not.

The "roasters" were old-time song 'n dance-type guys or Borscht Belt comedians. Guys like Freddie Roman and Jack Carter. "Dick Conlin's pretty old. How old, you ask? Let's see…Lincoln was killed in 1865……Haha!" Those guys were about as funny as a sore dick.

Or the weatherman from one of the non-network local television stations. Or the sports anchor from one of the other non-network local television stations. No DiMaggio. Well, maybe DiMaggio was there, but I didn't see him. Really, the place was packed with a bunch of good-ol'-boy elderly businessmen and I didn't have a clue who any of them were. Conlin obviously did, though. They were probably guys from the Gallagher's lunch crowd.

I did recognize one star, if 'star' is the word. He was a fellow who, at the time, was recognizable as the principle actor in a series of Preparation H television commercials. We found ourselves standing facing each other. Quick, Jim – small talk!

"Hey, I really like your Preparation H commercials." Smooth.

"Uh, yeah", looking over my shoulder as if he saw someone to talk to rather than me. Hey, those Prep H spots had made him a rich man. The least he could do was to make some little half-witted small talk joke about them. "Ah, they're a pain in the ass." Or some such thing.

I finally saw Brill across the room and lurched through the old men toward him. I think I'd taken to lurching because that's what they all seemed to be doing. Lurching around the room, slopping their drinks down their wrists.

"Hey, Bernard."

"Hello, James."

"Just get here?"

"Thankfully, yes."

"Gonna stay long?"

"Hopefully, no."

"Good. Been here long enough?"

"Too long."

"Wanna go to Gallagher's?"

"I thought you'd never ask."

We hopped in a cab and were waltzing in the door past the hanging meat in ten minutes.

As we elbowed our way through the pre-theater crowd, there was a commotion at the front door.

All of a sudden, the place exploded in the scream of a full-blown bagpipe. Christ, it was loud. As we looked, here came a guy fully decked-out it Scottish regalia, kilt, jacket, bearskin hat, spats, the whole nine yards. And he was blowing that pipe for all it was worth. He marched all the way around the bar with that thing just a-screaming.

He stopped abruptly and snapped to attention. The place went nuts, cheering and applauding. He bowed slightly, made a smart military about-face, brought the pipes to his lips and started in again. Only this time, he headed straight for the front door and out into the street, never missing a note.

"What the hell was that all about?" was the general question on everybody's lips.

Sal motioned me over and said, conspiratorially, "Dewar's promotion." Ah.

Sure beat the hell out of old, tired Freddie Roman Borscht-Belt jokes, though.

Dale made his way over. "How was the roast?"

"It sucked."

"I knew it would. That's why you went instead of me."

"Thanks."

I got to thinking, I'll bet the Preparation H guy could've had the place in stitches if he'd stood up and compared Conlin to a hemorrhoid or something. "I was showing Dick the new package design of a tube of Preparation H, but the top came off, somebody jostled me and it squirted all over Conlin. Guess what? Next thing I knew he was a midget! Hahahaha!"

Sal interrupted my reverie. "Here, Jimmy, have a drink."

TWENTY-SEVEN

That December, we decided to exhibit at a show that was out of the ordinary for us, but it was held in New York, down on 22nd Street, so our costs would be minimal. I always went to restaurant or hotel trade shows and the occasional home and garden show, which always sucked. Selling to Mr. & Mrs. Homeowner was a pain in the ass and they didn't have any money anyway.

If I recall, this particular show was called N.A.D.I., which I think stood for National Association of Display Interiors. The clientele was primarily composed of retail store designers, architects, and retail store display executives. We figured, what the hell, maybe we could score something fairly big out of this and in that industry, they didn't nickel and dime you.

I had the basic show display, five or six fountains, including a modified "Satellite" job, albeit a lot smaller than the one we'd had at the Coliseum a few years earlier. I guess I was used to selling merchandise right at the show, that's the way it always happened at the shows I'd been to. Not this one. I was majorly disappointed because if I'd written a thousand dollar's worth of orders, it was a lot.

One of the most interesting things about the show, though, was the booth next to mine. Two guys from Jacksonville had developed this pair of pseudo-robotic manikins. Actually, one was a dummy and one was a manikin. I learned that at that show: the female of the species is called a manikin and the male is called a dummy. Cute.

They had a joystick hooked up to the dummy that would enable the operator, standing a number of feet away, to manipulate the dummy's head and arms. The dummy was nicely dressed in a suit and tie. As somebody walked past, the dummy's head would turn to follow the person's progress and the dummy'd lift his arm as if to wave. Not bad in and of itself.

But they also had a microphone attached to the operator and a speaker in the dummy's head, so it would appear as if the dummy were speaking.

Example: A woman would walk past with a bright red blouse. The dummy's head would follow her as she passed and the dummy would say, "That's a lovely red blouse, m'dear." The woman would turn around to see who may have been complimenting her and the dummy'd wave at her. "I hear that style's coming back in again." It was fun.

The guys from Jacksonville were okay guys. Seems they'd grown up with the guys from Lynnyrd Skynnyrd and had always stayed close. They used to go on tour with them, sometimes. Naturally, they had been devastated when most of the group was killed in that plane crash.

Anyway, these guys had good senses of humor. Their little shtick with the dummy was just a little irreverent, enough to delight people. And I think they did pretty well at the show. It was a very small show, as far as the number of exhibitors and attendees went. After all, it was a pretty targeted group. All the exhibitors got to know each other and the whole atmosphere was quite communal. When things got slow, people would mosey on over and converge at the Jacksonville guys' booth, if for no other reason than to screw around.

Everybody wanted to become the dummy's operator and most people got the chance. Naturally, it turned into a junior high school humor fest.

Some guy – some exhibitor – would walk by and the dummy would say, "Hey you! Bite me." Or, "You're full of shit." Or, "Fuck you." Real inspired stuff. Or, one of the female exhibitors would be subject to "Hey baby! What're you wearing under that dress?"

One of my personal favorites was, "Ooh, hey you! Come here and scratch my ass. I can't scratch my own ass and it itches like hell. C'mon over here and scratch my ass, willya? I'll give you a dollar if you'll scratch my ass!" The other was, "Aw, jeez. I just farted and shit my pants." Real quality stuff.

By the time the show was over I was convinced it had been a dud. A lousy thousand bucks, too few brochures given away, and a ton of expensive business cards had been snapped up.

A month or two later, though, my opinion of the show changed dramatically.

I received a call from the design director at Macy's. The *real* Macy's – the one on 34th Street, not some big box mall Macy's.

They were going to institute an annual flower show the first week in April. The entire store would be festooned with Spring flowers and plants, particularly the main floor and the basement, which contained more contemporary merchandise. He thought it might be a nice touch if they had fountains interspersed in among the flowers everywhere, too. He wanted to meet with me and suggested he come to our showroom.

NO! I didn't want the design director from Macy's, replete with an open-ended purchase order setting foot in our place. All we'd need is for him to walk in and get accosted by Acuna or Rose Martini or for John to tell me Smolinski had fallen down drunk in a stairway again or for Tiger to present him with a dead mouse at this feet or something. I suggested to him that I meet him at the store so he could show me what his thinking was and that way I'd be able to more efficiently present him with a couple of concepts quickly. He bit. Not only that, it made sense.

His name was Palmer Atkins and he was a Palmer Atkins.

I met him at his office on the executive floor at Macy's. Nothing modern and fancy about those offices – Macy's was an old building and the offices reflected that age. Nice, but old.

I had walked down Seventh Avenue in a cold rain. It certainly didn't feel much like Springtime and flowers on that day in February. I could've walked down Eighth Avenue, it probably would've been a little quicker, but hey, I was going to the executive offices at Macy's and deserved Seventh Avenue instead of Eighth.

Palmer and I took and elevator to the main floor. You know, when Macy's used to bill itself as The World's Largest Store, they weren't kidding. The part of the main floor that was to be a big part of the Flower Show's focus was in the area of the cosmetics and perfumes and handbags and watches and jewelry, that kind of stuff.

Palmer wanted the fountains to be up high on the islands around which the retail countertops ran. The tops of the islands were already pretty high – about eight feet above the floor level. The islands were usually used to display merchandise and could be seen from around the store floor.

His idea was to have the fountains surrounded by flowers with the water jetting up into the air as the centerpiece. I suggested plain white lights in the fountains and got easy agreement from him.

This looked like it might be pretty simple, at least this part of it.

We could use our standard 36" white fiberglass bowls with a single 16" diameter spray ring and a single 150-watt light. The water would rise to about 36-40 inches above the bowl and that'd put the top of the water spray in the neighborhood of twelve feet high.

I explained my thinking and he agreed.

"Good. So, Palmer, how many do you think you'll need? Looks to me like fifteen or twenty."

"Let's go with twenty-four." Yes!

"Now, the windows."

The windows? You mean I might actually get my fountains featured in the windows of Macy's, Herald Square, New York City?

If this all worked out, I might just get a promotion from fountain tycoon to fountain mogul.

There were six windows on the Seventh Avenue side, three on either side of the main entrance, the part in front of which all the performers lip-synch and dance and all during the Macy's Thanksgiving Day Parade.

Those were the windows that would be decorated in the Flower Show motif.

Palmer said, "We'd like to make it a preview of what customers will experience once they enter the store." Good. That meant fountains.

I stood back and cased the windows. "Palmer, why don't we use somewhat smaller fountains in the outside windows and increase the size of them as we move in toward the doors?"

"Help me, here, Jim." I'll help you alright, Palmer.

"Look. In the two outside windows, we'll put two 24-inch fountains in each, on differing levels or something. We usually make those bowls in black, but we'll make these in white to go along with the white bowls inside the store.

"Then, in the middle two windows we'll put a thirty-six inch fountain in each. Same fountains as we have inside.

"Then, in the two windows closest to the entrance, we'll put fifty-inch fountains with white bowls. The whole effect will be a graduated one, with bigger fountains leading people to the door." Man, I was on fire.

He thought about that for a minute.

"Nah." What?!?

"Remember, the theme is the Flower Show, not the Fountain Show. The fountains are there to complement the flowers, not dominate them."

"Right."

"Let's put one of the thirty-six inch fountains in each of the six windows. Our merchandising display people will make each window look entirely different – you know, move the fountains around in each window, have different flowers and flower arrangements in each. It'll look great."

I did a little quick calculation in my head and realized the price of the two ideas was about the same. Great. No argument here.

"That's why they pay you the big bucks, Palmer."

"I wish. Now, let's go in and down to the basement. That's where we'll have a real challenge."

Needless to say, I was loving this. Just as we went through the door, my beeper went off. Naturally.

"Palmer, I'm afraid I have to call my office. Where are the pay phones?" Actually, getting beeped probably impressed him and helped to seal my position, at least in his mind, as a true fountain tycoon.

"Right over there, along that wall. I'll meet you right here." And he went off to admire the purses and such.

I dropped the coin in and dialed.

"General Fountains."

"Al, Dale just beeped me."

"He's on the other line." Dale was always on the other line, about half the time doing business and the other half bullshitting with somebody.

"Motion to him that it's me."

He came right on.

"What's happenin'?" Must've been one of those bullshit calls.

"Dale, this is going great. So far, we're talking about thirty, thirty-six inchers with a single spray ring and white lights."

"Hot damn! What else?"

"We're doing down to the basement now and I have no idea what that's gonna bring."

"Hey, we just might be able to swing this building yet. Call me as soon as you're done."

"Yep."

I rounded up Palmer and we took the escalator downstairs.

The area of this part of the store that was targeted for the Flower Show treatment was at the bottom of the main escalators and featured contemporary housewares and home decorating gizmos and the atmosphere and the offerings seemed geared toward a much younger demographic than the more traditional feeling one felt in the rest of the store.

"As you can probably tell, we're trying to attract a little younger crowd down here. Ultimately, we'd like to make Macy's Basement the place young people think of when they're moving into a new apartment or remodeling what they already have. That's why the Flower Show motif has to be different down here than it is upstairs."

"Got it."

"What we'd like to do is to create a contemporary focal point, right here, so when people come down the escalator, it draws them right to these departments."

We were standing in a wide aisle.

"Right where we're standing?"

"Right here."

Okay, this wasn't gonna be some stock stuff, that was for sure. And whatever we came up with had to be some sort of long rectangle, certainly not round. People still had to walk down the aisle, wide as it was, and it was about twenty feet wide.

I contemplated the situation for a minute. "I'm thinking of a large rectangular pool – a big one – maybe twenty feet long and eight or ten feet wide. We'll design a contemporary water display inside of it and maybe put some large rocks throughout the pool – you know, two or three different elements in the same unit. There'll be a lot of real estate in that pool and you want to keep it as interesting as possible. And your guys can do all kinds of things with flowers in there, maybe even water lilies, y'know?"

"And we could mask the outside of the pool with flowers."

"Exactly."

"Oh, and Jim. We can't have any water splash onto the floor. All we'd need is for somebody to slip and fall."

"Right. I'll tell you what. Give me a day or two and I'll get back to you with an idea that'll work. We'll start working on it as soon as I get back."

"Good. And I'll need a cost estimate on that. What'll happen is that you'll give me a proforma invoice for everything we've talked about and we can issue a purchase order from that."

"Okay. First I'll get you the idea and cost for this. Once you agree, I'll put together the pro-forma. Oh – hey, when will you want the fountains delivered?"

"The Flower Show opens on Sunday morning, April first. We can't close down to set it all up so everything, flowers, fountains – everything – will have to be set up between eight o'clock Saturday night, when we close, and nine o'clock Sunday morning."

Fu-uck. That sounded like a total pain in the ass, but hey – this was a big deal and we'd make it work.

Walking back to the office – this time up Eighth Avenue because I was in a hurry, I thought maybe two or three of our Satellite units would look good in that big pool in the basement. They were contemporary and pretty original-looking and didn't look anything like our standard-type fountains that were going in on the first floor and in the windows.

I gave Jeanne and Dale the complete rundown when I got back. Sat on the couch and everything and didn't even get a dirty look from Jeanne. Even Al stood in the doorway so he could listen in.

Dale liked the idea of the Satellites, but was afraid of the splash factor. "Wait. We can build those with only half of the 'satellie' so they lie right above the water level."

"Will you be able to see them alright?"

"Hell, yes. We'll make the diameter of the 'arms' a little bigger and they'll look great."

"How many units can fit into the pool?"

He thought for a minute. "Three. If each unit measures four feet from end of arm to end of arm, you'll have two feet on the narrow side of the pool. That's plenty of room to catch any splash. We'll place them so, end to end, there's three feet between the outside of each unit. That's eighteen feet altogether. In a twenty-foot pool, that's pretty dominating. Go get John in here."

I went next door to summons Bubniak. Dale and I could talk in a kind of shorthand, but when it came to John, it took infinitely longer. That made sense, though, he was the one who'd have to make it work, so it was almost necessary for him to get bogged down in details.

The thirty, thirty-six inch units were no problem. "I have Joe make bowls and we put together up on seven. Use Tadeusz and Piotrowski. We have ready in four days. Must pack?"

"Well, we have to deliver them ourselves and we don't want them to get all dinged up, so we'd better put them in cartons."

"Good. We finish and break cartons down and bring back." Good for John – he was always thinking of ways to save money.

Then Dale started to explain the basement fountain to him.

It was just like John to piss on the idea.

"Can't do. Can't make twenty-foot pool. How you move?"

The sonofabitch had a point. There was no way a twenty-foot anything could be moved out of our building, not with all the corners and ceiling heights and all. Besides, we'd need a tractor-trailer or something to move it and that was beyond me to drive and expensive as all hell to hire.

Me: "How we do?"

John thought for a minute. "We make two ten-foot sections and put together in store."

"But, John, we only have from nine o'clock Saturday night to six o'clock Sunday morning to get it all done." I lied about the six o'clock deadline. I didn't want to have to explain a bunch of Polish guys working on a fountain at 8:45 in the morning, with a passel of Macy's executives standing there looking at their watches.

"We move in sections first. Bring wood and nails and glass and resin and put together. She set up while we put other fountains in place. I stay with big fountain and run electric and set up Satellites. Where we get water?"

Good question. I'd have to check that out with Palmer. "I'll get that taken care of." Christ, I could see myself now, carrying buckets of water from some slop sink at six in the morning.

I'd need Al the night of the set-up. I had to have somebody else around who spoke English.

"Al, can you work with us to set up on that Saturday night?"

"Tooling around Macy's in the middle of the night? Sure, be glad to." Al saw ten hours of time-and-a-half, too.

"Al, we won't be 'tooling around', we'll be working our asses off."

"Just kidding." I knew he was, too. Al was as conscientious as they came.

The next day I went down to Macy's again and met Palmer in the basement. I outlined our idea and showed him some photos of the Satellite in action. He bounced up and down on his toes and clapped excitedly. My guess was that he liked it.

"Ooh. That's good. That's real good. Can you give me a line drawing of what the thing will look like so I can give it to our designers? That way, they can have everything ready to go when it's finished."

"Sure." Gulp. How the hell was I going to get a drawing done? We never had any drawings done. "I'll have it for you tomorrow."

"Oh. And when you bring the drawing, bring the pro-forma. I'll have the P.O. cut the next day and you're good to go."

He had yet to ask me how much this entire project was gonna cost. I had the number in my head, but was thinking of adding to it by half when he asked, "Oh, just by the way, what are we looking at in terms of total cost?"

Ah, he was a nice guy, it was a huge order anyway and it *was* Macy's. I told him, "Right around twenty-three thousand."

"Fine." Not an instant of hesitation. Shit, I should've said thirty-three. Shit.

On the walk back to 264, I decided I could probably do the drawing myself. I wasn't terrible at that stuff and he'd only asked for a line drawing, not some fancy thing with water colors and people milling about and all that. I'd get Dale to scrawl the basic look of it and take it from there.

I spent the rest of the afternoon working on the drawing and I'll be damned if it didn't look pretty good. It wouldn't win any contests, but the proportions were right and I'd put in the dimensions with drop lines, like an architect.

The next morning I typed up the pro-forma, called Palmer, set up a meeting and the whole deal was taken care of. He looked at the drawing and kind of smirked. "At least our designers will have an idea of what it'll look like. And you have the dimensions, so that's good."

We were good to go.

It didn't overtax us to prepare the Macy's order. Everything was pretty stock. Even the Satellites were easy.

Palmer called a couple of days later and said he'd been talking to his designers and they had asked if we could add three or four small rock waterfall affairs into the big Satellite pool.

"Sure. It'll be pretty easy and we do have extra room in the corners of the pool."

"Good. How much extra are we talking about?"

I thought for a minute. "Probably another twenty-five hundred."

"Fine. Just send a pro-forma and call it 'additional elements to Basement fountain."

Damn. Did it again. Should've said five grand.

"Got it."

I told Dale and John about the new additions. Dale looked a little concerned.

"Y'know, we don't want to have to use real rocks and cement them together. The damned things'll weigh a ton and we'll never be able to move them. And we can't be putting them together in the middle of the night while you're setting it up. Let me think about this for a few minutes." And off he went to another floor, whistling away. He was always whistling.

A little while later he strode into the office. "Got it."

Whew.

"What?"

"We'll use volcanic rock. We can get it down in the Flower District. It's really lightweight – a two-by-two-by-two piece of volcanic rock won't weight twenty pounds. We'll drill a hole down through the middle of four big ones, slip in a piece of copper pipe down each hole, and hook each to their own pumps. We'll get a few more rocks to put around each one and it'll work just fine."

Dale was a genius at fountains, there was never any doubt about that.

I got on the phone and located a place that sold those things down on 29th Street, off of Sixth. I had no idea volcanic rock was ever used for anything. Seems a lot of flower shops and decorators and so on use them all the time, because of the weight.

I hopped on the moped – I was getting pretty good on it by now – and headed downtown. Even though I was getting used to driving it in traffic, I couldn't get comfortable around speeding trucks no matter what.

Just as the elevator doors were closing as I was leaving our floor at 264, Dale yelled something that sounded like, "Better take some gloves!"

I didn't have the faintest idea what he meant by that. I hadn't worn gloves while I was riding the moped all winter long and on this day the temperature was up around fifty. I'd manage.

When I got to the place, I asked the fellow at the front desk about looking at his volcanic rocks and he sent me around to a big room that was strewn with them, all different sizes and shapes.

I walked around knowing pretty much what I was looking for that would serve as the four main rocks for the waterfalls. As far as the other rocks to go around them, I'd just pick out a miscellaneous bunch of sizes and shapes.

I saw one that caught my eye over in a corner behind some smaller ones. I stepped over and between a few dozen as I made my way through what appeared to be a misplaced lava field. When I got to it I reached down to move it around so I could get a better look at it.

Ouch! Christ, what the hell was that? The tips of my fingers had little droplets of blood on them. What was that all about? I reached down again and OUCH! – same damned thing.

It's then that I realized that volcanic rock is sharp as hell. Every square inch of it. It's like coral. Basically, all you have to do it touch it and you'll get cut. And it stings for hours. Nasty, nasty stuff.

Now I knew why Dale mentioned the gloves.

I went back to the front desk. "Hey, dude. Do you have any gloves I can borrow for a few minutes?"

"First time with volcanic rock, eh?", he said without looking up from whatever he was doing. No, asshole. I'm gonna rob the place and didn't want to leave my fingerprints anywhere.

"Yeah."

I learned to hate volcanic rock over those few weeks. From moving that shit around, even with gloves, I had scrapes on my hands and arms that didn't heal 'til May.

The set-up night finally came and I'd rented a truck from Avis, down on Eleventh Avenue. Big thing, and like always, had several guys riding in the back.

I said to Al, "Why don't you hop up in there with John's guys. It's only a few blocks." Just screwing with his head.

"Oh, no. I'll walk down and meet you there. I ain't getting in the back of one of those things again."

"Well, you can stand on the running board on the passenger's side if you want. Hang on tight, though."

"Fine. Anything but back there. Wait a minute. Who's riding in front with you and John?"

"Smolinski."

"Smolinski?!? Why, you're letting that drunken piece of shit ride up front and you want me to ride in the back?"

"Well, he's got a good buzz going and I don't want him to puke on the fountains or anything."

Al began sputtering in Spanish and I let him go for a minute. It was fun to watch Al get pissed. He was such a good guy it was simply fun to tease him.

"Nah. C'mon, Al. Jump in. I was just shitting you. You think I'd take a drunken Smolinski into Macy's in the middle of the night? He'd disappear somewhere, pass out, and nobody'd find him for a week. Least not 'til they smelled his corpse."

Al was torn between still being pissed and being relieved he was riding shotgun. "What, I hear 'drunk'. Al drunk?" John, just adding to it.

"No, I'm not drunk!"

"Al peeyock?"

"Al peeyonnie."

"What are you guys talking about?"

"Shouldn't come to work drunk, Al."

"I am not drunk!"

"For twenty bucks, I no tell Dale", said John.

"Fuck you guys."

We placed each of the main floor fountains up on their perches and asked one of the Macy's guys where the nearest water sources were. Thankfully, they had closets with running water all over the place. It's funny, when you go into a store as a shopper, you never notice those little doors.

We'd brought our own buckets and each fountain held about two buckets, so with each guy armed with a pair of buckets, we had the whole thing set up in no time. As each was filled with water, we turned it on. Damned if it didn't look good in that three-quarter darkened gigunda room with those fountains all over the place!

The window merchandising guys were there and we just showed them how to add water and told them to plug the fountains in and turn them on. They didn't really want our help. My guess is that they didn't really want a bunch of scruffy-looking Polish guys traipsing around their window décor. Anyway, they didn't seem the type of guys that would want a bunch of scruffy-looking Polish guys traipsing around their window décor. Let's just say the two lifestyles weren't particularly compatible.

John and a couple of his guys put the pieces of the pool together and the fiberglass took less than an hour to set up. We put the Satellites in place, ran the cables through compression fittings on the sides of the pool, and put plugs on the end of the cables. There were also more than enough electrical outlets flush with the floor right where we needed them.

We put the goddam lava rock waterfalls in place – with gloves - and ran the electric the same way. Just about ready to go.

The thought hit me that Christ!, if we have to fill this thing with buckets, we'll be here forever. I found one of the Macy's engineers and told him the situation. I'd forgotten to check with Palmer. I thought, "I should write stuff down once in a while."

"No problem. We'll run hoses from two of the water closets. Should be able to fill it in an hour or so."

Yes!

We were done with everything and had an hour to kill. John sent most of his guys home and just he and two of his guys and Al and I were the only ones left.

We decided to investigate the store. After all, it was buzzing with dozens of people working anyway and we just began wandering.

John said, "Where are couches?"

"Huh?"

"Where are couches? Need new couch for house. Maybe get here."

We looked at one of those store directories and saw that the couches were on the fifth floor. We walked over to the freight elevator and asked the guy to take us up to five. The fifth floor was almost totally dark except for the few lights they leave on at night for security. We wandered around until we found the couches. As John was looking, the rest of us decided to rest our weary bones and spread out on several of them. A couple of minutes later, we heard voices and I looked around to see the beams of two or three flashlights coming in our direction.

"Hey! Who's over there?"

"It's just us guys setting up the fountains for the Flower Show", I said.

"What in the hell are you doing up here?"

"We've got about an hour to kill and one of our guys is looking for a couch. We thought we'd come up to check them out."

"Well check your asses back downstairs. You ain't s'posed to be up here at all."

"Oh. Okay. Nobody told us."

"Well, I'm telling you. Let's go. Now."

He led us back to the freight elevator and down we went. Maybe we shouldn't have been up there, but with his nasty attitude, Macy's cost themselves a possible couch sale that night.

Before too long, the pool was full and we were ready to turn everything on. I had just realized how nervous I was. Would the goddam thing work? Please, God, just this once. Make it work right.

We went around and plugged all the elements in. One by one, they started up. The thing was working and it looked sensational! Fucking sensational!

Within two minutes, there must've been twenty-five or thirty people, Palmer included, standing around admiring the fountain. This floor was also operating with minimal overnight lighting and the fountain looked stupendous. We had maybe twenty-four lights in the thing and the way the lights and water played off the ceiling was incredible.

The little crowd of workers – and Palmer – started applauding!

Palmer came over to me and gave me a big hug. "Oh, Jim, this is super! Just super!

It's perfect!"

It was, too.

Everybody in the place was beaming. I was so proud, especially of John.

"Tell John. He's the artist who built it."

Palmer gave John a big hug. "Oh, thankyouthankyouthankyou!" You shoulda seen the look on John's face.

You could see how proud John was, even if he was a little taken aback by Palmer's effusiveness.

We began packing up our stuff and the merchandising guys began placing flowers and plants around and in the pool. Wow. I couldn't believe it myself that the thing looked so good.

Al, who'd had absolutely nothing to do with designing or building the thing, drew himself up like a peacock and said to me, "Nothing to it."

"Fuck you, Al. You ride in the back on the way home."

He just laughed.

TWENTY-EIGHT

The next day, Sunday, April 1st, was a beautiful day. The sun was shining and it was nearly seventy degrees.

Jeanne and Dale and I had brunch somewhere and wandered down to Macy's.

The place was jammed with people and the fountains were working and there were literally thousands of flowers. All those flowers weren't there when we'd left about three in the morning so there was an awful lot of work done between then and when the store opened.

We went down to the Basement. The fountain was the center of attention. I looked into the pool and there were hundreds of coins. People were tossing coins in like there was no tomorrow.

"Jim!"

I wheeled around to see a beaming Palmer walking toward us with a couple of guys in suits.

"Jim, I want to introduce you to my boss, Anton Fiske, and the head of display merchandising, Cody Dworkin." We made introductions all around and it was obvious the Macy's folks were more than pleased. The two guys fawned over Dale and Jeanne which made me happy, too.

I took Palmer aside.

"Palmer, look at all the coins in that thing. There must be close to a hundred bucks in there."

"Wow. Yeah."

I had an idea.

"Hey, do you guys have a favorite charity or something? If you do, we could put a sign up telling people that all the coins in the fountain will go to that charity. You might be able to raise a few thousand bucks during the show. And, it'll make you look good."

He thought a moment.

"Perfect. Yes, we have several charities we're involved with. Just a minute."

He walked over to confer with his bosses and came back with a big smile on his face. "They love it. First thing tomorrow morning, I'll get with the right people and we'll decide which charity we'll use. Maybe we'll change it every day so they all benefit. What a perfect idea. Oh, by the way, I told my boss it was my idea, if you don't mind."

"Great idea, Palmer", I said loudly enough for his boss to hear. I shook his hand. "Great idea."

Over the two-week period, they took in over $3500 for their charities.

The next day, Monday, I decided to check on the Macy's fountains in the morning. They had assured us they would have people to replenish the water in the fountains on a daily basis, but I didn't trust that it would happen. With that cavernous room full of dry air, coupled with the heat from the underwater lights, evaporation was going to be a problem.

If too much water evaporated, two things could happen. First, if there wasn't enough water in the fountain to keep the spray going high enough to hit the light and keep it cool, it would get hot as hell. Then, somebody'd pour cold water on top of the hot light and the bulb would break. That would mean a minor on-site repair job, but nobody wanted one of our Polish guys in their finest 14th Street work wear standing high atop one of their counters in the women's handbag section.

If too much water evaporated and the pump overheated, the pump could burn out. It would also mean an on-site repair, but would take longer.

When I walked into the store late Monday morning, I could see all the fountains were low on water. Not a real good sign. That meant they'd need to be refilled at least once a day.

This was a job for glycerin!

My beeper went off and I went to hunt down the pay phone.

"Good morning. General Fountains, how may I help you?"

"Jeanne. Me."

"How're the fountains?"

"OK, but I think we're gonna need to put glycerin in each of the ones on the main floor. Probably about a gallon in each. We'll need about twenty gallons. Can you order it? I'll get one of the guys and we can pick it up in the van and then bring it over here to Macy's."

"I'll see if we can't get it delivered. They're way out in Long Island City somewhere and you don't want to be driving around all day."

"I'd like to get that stuff in these fountains today, though. Think they can do it?"

"I'll see. Let you know when you get back."

"OK."

I went to the water closet, retrieved my buckets and spent the next hour and a half filling the fountains. Man, the dirty looks those salespeople gave me. Lady, you're selling fucking wallets. You got no right to look down your nose at anybody!

The big fountain in the basement was cool. It still looked great. And, there was a guy who worked at night whose responsibility it was to fill it each night with a hose. That one I didn't worry about.

When I got back to 264, Jeanne said they could deliver the glycerin, but not 'til the next morning. Great. When people told you "the next morning", they really meant sometime during the daylight hours. Nothing ever got where it was supposed to "in the morning". Dale was sitting in his base-of-operations chair. "Those fountains'll be alright 'til we get the glycerin into them. Don't worry."

Dale always said not to worry when there was something to be worried about. Of course, he didn't have to worry. He wasn't the one that had to deal with whatever problems came up. That was my job. And I was worried.

"I think it'd be a good idea if I go back down there late this afternoon and top them off. That way, they'll be good until whatever time we get there with the glycerin tomorrow."

"Nah, you don't have to go. Send Acuna."

The phone rang and Dale picked it up. "General. Who? Just a minute." He put it on

hold, handed me the phone and started for the door, whistling.

"Who is it?"

"I don't know. Some guy for Bill Leith." Thanks, Dale.

After I'd lied to whoever it was that had called, I told Jeanne that Acuna wouldn't work for this mission. He would hit me up for cab fare ("Jeemy, that's a long way. I might wear out the soles of my choes. Hahaha."). Then, if I knew Acuna, and I did, he'd wander around the store for an hour, surreptitiously glance at the fountains until he saw one that obviously had enough water in it and report back that they were all fine. The next day, if we had burn-outs, he say, "But Jeemy, they were all working efine when I monitored them." And, he'd use the word 'monitored', too, the asshole.

"I'd better go myself."

I did. And I didn't really mind it. It gave me a "mission" to a nice place and it gave me a chance to kind of mog around the store. It sure beat the hell out of driving to Fort Lee for acetone.

The glycerin arrived early the next afternoon and I took Al and Little Joe with me to take care of the job. Actually, because there was no where to park, I drove and dropped them off with the glycerin. Al knew where all the fountains were and Joe knew how to fix anything that needed fixing.

I simply drove the van, looking for all the world like a fountain tycoon. Joe loved it because he never got to go on a mission. Al loved it because he could importantly show Little Joe where all the fountains were. So, that little mission worked out well for everybody.

The glycerin worked, too. We only had to have water added every other day and Palmer had arranged for a couple of guys to follow us around to learn how to do it and they took over the responsibility.

The First Annual Macy's Flower Show was one of the largest, smoothest jobs we'd ever had and I was proud to have been the driving force, at least on our side, of the whole thing. If I wasn't careful, I'd progress from fountain tycoon to fountain magnate before too long.

One night along in there, Jeanne and Dale and I stopped at Dempsey's on the way from the office to Gallagher's. Jack Dempsey's was on Broadway between 49th and 50th, if I remember correctly. Dempsey was still alive and he'd be in the restaurant a night or two a week.

Jeanne and Dale knew him pretty well because he was friends with Roy and Harriet, particularly Harriet. When we were kids, he'd order us frappes. He still remembered me and had seen me grow up. "Hey, kid – you trade those frappes for scotch yet?"

Dempsey didn't really own the place, at least he wasn't the majority owner. The guy that owned it was a fellow named Jack Amiel. Amiel had a ton of dough, was a big investor in Broadway shows and had owned Count Turf, the horse that won the Kentucky Derby at odds of over a hundred to one.

Amiel was fat. Real fat. And he used to wear his suit pants up real high, almost under his armpits. I used to wonder how long the fly on his trousers was. It must've been almost three feet long.

Amiel was a tough old bird, too. This particular night, we were standing at the bar and he was buying us drinks and so on, when one of his maître d's came over and whispered something to him.

"I'll be right back. Gotta step outside for a minute."

"Everything all right?", asked Dale.

"Yeah, I just gotta take a gun away from a guy."

What?!?

And off he went.

"Dale, did he just say he had to go take a gun away from some guy?"

"Yep. That's what he said."

"Jesus."

A couple of minutes later, up strolled Amiel, looking none the worse for wear.

"Jack, what was that all about?"

"Ah. I fired some asshole today for stealing tips. He came back and told one of the guys at the front he was here to get me."

"What the hell happened?"

"I just walked up to him before he could do anything, slapped him across the face and told him to get his ass out of here before I got mad."

"What about the gun?"

"He didn't have no gun. Just said he did. Little prick."

Speaking of guns, I was threatened with a gun one night in Gallagher's.

There was this guy named Billy Baxter. He had something to do with the Marlboro Cup, the big thoroughbred horse race that used to take place every October. Maybe he worked for Philip Morris or something.

Anyway, he was at the bar and skunk drunk. I was standing next to him, about five or six feet away, and talking to Bernard and Sal the bartender. I could hear Baxter behind me, trying to insult me or swear at me or something he probably wouldn't have done if he were sober. I just ignored him.

This went on for several minutes and still I wouldn't turn around and acknowledge him. All of a sudden, he's standing right at my shoulder and said, "Listen, you. I got a gun in this holster and I been talking to you and you been ignoring me. How'd you like it if I shoot you right here?"

Bernard and I both looked at him and Sal took off. Sal had gone around to tell Dale what he'd just heard.

As Bernard and I were standing there like a couple of frozen goofballs, I saw Dale come around the bar and head straight for Baxter.

He grabbed him by the tie, right under the throat, and lifted him up onto his toes. "Listen, you sonofabitch. If you don't apologize – right now! – and get your lousy ass out of here in the next ten seconds, I'll smash your fat face into this bar until even your wife won't recognize it. Then I'll rip off your fucking head and shit down your throat! You got that, asshole?"

Baxter's feet were barely touching the floor and his face was turning bright red. Still, Dale wouldn't let him go. Lifted him up a little higher, maybe.

"Now!"

"I-I'm s-sorry", he whispered hoarsely.

Dale threw him down by the tie and Baxter reeled across the floor and fell in a heap.

Dale was over him in an instant. "Move, goddam it! Move! Out! Out! Oh, and give me the fucking gun!"

"I-I don't have it on me."

"Get out of here, goddamit, before I get really mad!"

And he lurched on out the door.

I thought, What's with guys spouting off about having guns when they don't?

"Very nice, Dale. Really very nice", said Bernard. "Is that something you learned in Indiana?" Brill always rode Dale for being from Indiana. Bernard thought of New Jersey as "Out West".

I saw Baxter a number of times after that, sober or relatively close, and he was always quite civil. Some guys, though. Demon rum just lets out the monster lurking inside.

TWENTY-NINE

Jim Lucey's assistant vice-president at the bank was a woman named Joanie. Joanie was a petite woman with hair so blonde it was almost white. You could tell it didn't come from a bottle because her eyebrows were almost white, even the hair on her arms was almost white. That's as far as I was ever able to check.

Joanie was our champion, not only because her boss really liked us, but because she did, too. We all became good friends. That came in particularly handy for me when I was late in getting the payroll ready on a Friday afternoon.

Between two-thirty and three on a Friday afternoon, the teller lines went on forever. If I gave all the guys their checks and they all went to the bank to cash them, they could all be gone for an hour.

I worked it out with Joanie so I'd call her with the amounts for each guy. She'd have the money put in individual envelopes and the guys would all go down and march right up to her desk. She looked like a quartermaster, especially with a small army of Polish guys and Al and Acuna crowding around her. I had her put my money in a sealed envelope that Al would bring back. I had her seal it because I didn't want Al and Acuna to find out I wasn't making much more than they were.

As Dale and Jeanne were getting down to the short strokes on their quest to buy the building, Joanie became invaluable to Jeanne. Helped her fill out forms, prepare good-looking P&Ls, and generally served as her coach.

In June of that year, push had finally come to shove.

The price was cemented at $600,000 and Dale and Jeanne needed to put down only ten percent, or sixty thousand.

That was a problem.

See, the bank actually wanted sixty grand in cash. Dale suggested they borrow it. Lucey said, "Dale, are you nuts? You're borrowing five hundred and forty thousand! You can't borrow any more money. We need the cash."

The most they could come up with was about forty-eight thousand. Twelve short. And that was stretching it.

Dale thought and stewed about it for a day or so, then had an idea.

His brother, Paul – PL – had plenty of money. Not only did he have the farm down in

West Memphis, Dale knew he'd opened small savings accounts in cities and towns across the country. The magazine business could reap quite a lot of cash on occasion and PL would just as soon hide the money from the world when he had the chance. PL was notoriously tight with a buck.

"Hell, twelve thousand to Paul is pocket change. I've seen that suitcase he carries with him with all those bank books. Jeanne! Find out where Paul is and get him on the phone."

Jeanne tracked him down to a motel in Louisville. Dale spent a half hour or so on the phone with him and nonchalantly spelled out the deal. He knew his brother would smell a good deal and try to buy into the building with his twelve grand if Dale wasn't careful. Dale's fear was that PL would figure that if he was putting up twenty percent of the down payment, he was in for twenty percent of the building - even though Dale and Jeanne would carry the mortgage. That's the way PL thought.

Dale finally made it somewhat clear that he actually wanted to borrow the twelve grand.

"Borrow? Dale, I don't lend money, you know that."

They went around for a few more minutes and Dale suggested to PL that he'd send me down to meet with him and give him a little more 'insight'.

Me? Why me?

Dale said, "Because Paul likes you and he doesn't trust me. Maybe you'll get lucky."

"Why doesn't he trust you?"

"Because I don't trust him."

Nice tight family.

I was on a late afternoon flight to Louisville and got in around eight. PL was there to meet me. I'd expected one of his goons. PL knew that would get fucked up because the guy wouldn't know me and wouldn't make a sign or anything and he'd have to come and get me eventually, anyway.

We got back to the motel and I was expecting to check into a room of my own.

"How long you expect to be here, anyway?"

"Well, probably at least overnight."

"Ah, we'll be busy all night and if you need to sleep, lay down on one of the beds in my room."

Cheap shit.

"Hungry?"

"Yeah, sure."

"There's a fast food burger joint at the end of the parking lot. What do you want?"

Man, this was first class all the way.

"A cheeseburger, fries and a Coke."

He had a couple of his guys hanging around the room, doing nothing but smoking cigarettes.

"Mel, go get his dinner. And get me a black coffee. Here." He handed him ten bucks. "What about me?", asked Mel.

"You got paid yesterday. You want something, buy it yourself. Ah – you can have whatever the change'll buy you."

Off he went. "Oh, and get me two packs of cigarettes." There went Mel's dinner.

"Cheap bastards always want me to buy 'em dinner."

Magazine kids kept rotating in and out almost all night. Every once in a while PL and I would wander around the motel, looking in on people. They slept two to a room.

"Shirley. You've gotta be up by six to get gas in your car. Call it a night, huh?"

"Goddam it Preston! Clean up this dump. And get those clothes off the floor."

"Not stoned tonight, are you Diana? I'd hate to see the cops come and toss this room."

"No, Paul. I'm clean. Really."

"Doesn't smell like it, Diana. I'm gonna look in here every hour and it better not smell like this again tonight or I'll have the cops here and won't even take your call if you get busted."

"Don't worry, Paul."

To me: "Nice kid, but can't keep off the stuff."

Maybe I'd go visit Diana a little later. Nah, that'd be stupid.

Around three in the morning, PL pulled a suitcase out from under the bed. When he opened it, I noticed piles of bank books held together with rubber bands. He spent the next hour looking through almost all of them, squinting through his cigarette smoke and not showing a single sign of emotion.

We kept up a conversation about everything under the sun but the building and whether he was going to help Dale. We talked about cows, racehorses, baseball, my Mom, life on the road, the drain on the federal fucking gold reserve – everything imaginable except the reason I was there. Every so often, I'd try to adroitly steer the conversation to the building. He'd reply with "Unh", squint through the smoke, and continue looking through the bank books.

I thought maybe he was trying to find one of the bank books that had a deposit in the neighborhood of twelve grand. Say, like an account at a bank in Nashville with $12,500 or something. I don't know why I thought that, other than it was real late and I was now relying on hope.

Sometime in the wee hours before dawn, PL would begin nonchalantly throwing out a question or two about the building.

"When was it built?"

I could be nonchalant, too.

"When was what built?"

"The building. 264."

"Sometime around 1920, I think."

And that would be that for then.

Fucking PL never slept.

And I stayed right with him. For all I knew, at any minute he could say, "OK. Tell Dale I'll do it." At least that was what I was hoping for.

We'd been drinking black coffee and smoking cigarettes all night long. PL had this strange habit of not using an ashtray to put out his cigarettes. He'd stand them up on end, on the filters, on a windowsill or something. Once he got ten or twelve lined up, he'd sweep them into the wastebasket.

Just before dawn, he stood up and stretched.

"Well, College Boy (he always called me College Boy), I think I'm ready."

Oh boy. Here it came. He was going to part with the dough.

"OK", I said, somewhat enthusiastically.

"You ready?"

"I sure am." Maybe I could catch an early flight and be the hero that saved the day.

"The diner opens at five. 'Bout that now. Let's go get us some breakfast."

What?!?

Was he fucking with my head or was it too much coffee and not enough sleep on my part?

"OK."

As we walked across the parking lot, it hit me that he was probably torn between being cheap, not hearing any sort of deal in it for him and wanting to help Dale, as distasteful as that probably was for him. He was either still trying to make up his mind or he was just wasting time until I gave up and left.

We were the first ones into the diner and sat in a booth. The waitress came over, handed us each a menu and poured us coffee.

"I'll just have coffee", said PL.

This was breakfast? I decided I wasn't going to show him any sign of weakness. I didn't want him to be telling Dale, "College Boy came all the way down here on your behalf and all he wanted to do was eat."

"Coffee's fine, thanks."

So, our little coffee klatch had moved from room 211 to the diner. At least it was a change of scene.

Around six, the magazine crew kids starting wandering in. At least there was some action, now, and I started to wake up out of my daze.

"Morning, PL."

"Unh."

"Hey, PL. Looks like a good day to write some business, huh?"

"Better be."

Some guy wandered over. "PL, I got a favor to ask."

"Yeah?"

"See, Louis, he's my roommate, right? Well, that sumbitch snores the whole goddam night. I ain't had a good night's sleep in a week. 'Spose I could switch roommates with somebody?"

"Everybody knows Louis snores and nobody's gonna switch with you."

"Suppose I could get my own room?"

"You do that and I gotta pay for two singles – his and yours."

"I'll chip in."

PL thought for a minute.

"Tell you what. If both of you – not just one of you, both of you – write two thousand each today, I'll buy you individual rooms for a month. How's that?"

"Two thousand?"

"Seems to me, you want your own room bad enough, you'll get your ass in gear and bring in the two, right?"

"But Louis doesn't give a shit about getting his own room. He's the one who's snoring. He don't know he's keeping me awake half the fucking night."

"Didn't you tell him?"

"Sure, but he says he can't do nothing about it."

"Here's an idea – tell him you're gay. That oughta work."

The guy stood there for a minute, contemplating what PL had just said. You could tell he was torn.

"I'll figure out something. Ain't gonna tell him that, though."

"Then tell him you're a fucking axe murderer. Just bring in the two thousand each."

With that, the guy turned and walked away, looking both perplexed and determined at the same time.

"Fucking guy. He won't do eight hundred today", PL said through his cigarette smoke. "Hell, Louis is good for fifteen hundred a day, every day. He can snore all he wants, for all I care."

The next two or three hours were taken up getting the crew ready to hit the road for the day. PL had several minor calamities to take care of.

A car wouldn't start.

"You didn't know this fucking car was on the fritz before you brought it back here last night?"

"No, PL. Honest. It worked just fine all day."

"Get two guys and push it over to the gas station on the corner."

Some girl couldn't find her sweater, was accusing everyone of stealing it and refused to leave before it was returned.

Her enterprising car handler found it in the back seat of the car. Away they went.

"Christ, it's like herding cats", said PL.

I asked him if it had always been like this, you know, with so much of this juvenile shit.

"Always. Long as I can remember. Don't forget, most of these guys ain't college boys", he said with a sidelong glance and a smirk.

"Bite me, Mister Arkansas Fucking Cattle Baron."

He laughed hard.

Somewhere between eight-thirty and nine o'clock, I told PL I was going to have to call Dale.

"What'll I tell him?"

"Tell him I haven't figured it out yet."

I called.

"General."

"It's me."

"What's happening?"

"I don't know."

"You don't know?"

"No. We sat up all night, he went through maybe fifty bank books, and hasn't said anything, other than to ask me a few random questions about the building, like when was it built – things like that. I just told him I was going to call you and asked him what I should tell you. He said he hasn't figured it out yet."

"Goddam it."

"He hasn't said no, though, or even made any negative comments. I just don't have any idea."

"Tight-assed sonofabitch. Let me talk to him."

"Just a second, he's out in the parking lot."

PL came in and, from what I heard of the conversation, it was nice and friendly. At least Dale hadn't blown it with a temper tantrum or anything. PL was still nonchalant as hell and equally noncommittal.

He handed the phone back to me and walked out the door back into the parking lot.

"What do I do?"

"Just hang loose, I guess. We'll see if something happens in the next few hours." We hung up.

We screwed around the motel for the next hour or two when PL said, "Let's go to the track for a couple of races."

Wow! That's right – we were in Louisville, home of Churchill Downs. I was certainly up for that.

Off we went to the track. Being midweek, it was hardly crowded and certainly wasn't all jazzed up like you see it on the first Saturday in May. But it was Churchill Downs. PL was of the Billy Ruben school of betting. He put fifty on each of the favorites in the first two races – albeit to win, not show, like Billy. Both horses ran third.

I, on the other hand, bet ten on a 7-1 shot in the first and that horse ran out of the money.

In the second race, there was a horse that had run in New York, but had been beaten rather soundly up there in the big leagues. I figured he was good enough to win in Kentucky, though. Worth ten bucks, anyway. Especially at 11-1. He won by three and I went looking for the cashier's window to collect my one-twenty.

When I got back, PL said he'd had enough. Shit, I thought, this is just getting good.

Back to the motel.

Over to the diner. I finally broke down and had a bowl of soup and a Coke. PL had black coffee and four cigarettes, which he lined up on the windowsill.

Around three in the afternoon, I finally asked him.

"Paul. I've been here almost twenty-four hours. Dale's closing on the building is tomorrow. What's it gonna be?" At this point, I felt I already knew the answer.

"Well, Jimmy, it's like this. I don't trust New York City. Don't trust bankers. Truth be told, I don't trust Dale all that much. What the hell's he know about running a building in New York City? Huh? It's all he can do to keep that fountain business running. What's he need with another distraction? I can't see him keeping all those balls in the air. See what I mean?"

Deep down, I did see what he meant. But.....

"Paul, that building pretty much runs itself. And there's a management company that handles all the rents and renters and such."

"When did you ever know Dale to leave well enough alone? He'll have that management company gone in six months. Nah. I don't trust it."

"He's got me."

"That's the only thing he's got going for him. You and Jeanne." Wow. A compliment.

"I can't do it. Just can't do it." Dead serious. Looking me straight in the eye.

"Okay. I'll call him. Can you get me to the airport? I've got a six o'clock flight booked." I'd done that when buying the round-trip ticket.

"Course."

I called Dale. He didn't sound surprised. Nobody was.

"What're you going to do for the money for the closing tomorrow?"

"I've got one last shot. I have a call into Don Winters. He owes us four thousand and I'll ask him to give us eight toward his next orders. He's got plenty of money."

"Think he'll do it?"

"He should, goddamit – he's made a fortune off of us."

Don Winters owned Fountains of Wayne, a huge lawn and garden decorating center on Route 46 in Wayne, New Jersey. He did do an awful lot of business with us and was one of our largest distributors.

Winters could be a pain in the ass, especially when he wanted something. If he wanted it now, he wanted it now. And he could be real pushy. But he was a decent guy and an honest guy. And we'd done business with him for over ten years. If Dale leveled with him, it just might work.

"My flight doesn't get in until almost ten (I knew both he and Jeanne would be stewed by then.) so I'll call you first thing in the morning."

"Call me around seven. We'll figure out our game plan then." With a closing on a twenty-story building in New York City scheduled for eleven o'clock, a good four hours should give us plenty of time to figure out how to come up with twelve thousand dollars.

Jee-sus.

I called Dale at seven. The office phone also rang in their apartment. They were there. "General." He sounded awake.

"Hey."

"How was the flight?"

"Not bad. At least it was on time."

"Paul drive you to the airport?"

"Yeah."

"That sonofabitch. The more I think about it, the madder I get. He let you waste two days sitting around in a goddam motel room waiting for him to make up his mind. I'll bet he had no intention of lending us the money anyway."

"Hard to say. He's a hard guy to read." I couldn't bring myself to relate PL's reasoning for not lending Dale the money. He'd made some pretty good points but it sure as hell wasn't up to me to outline them to Dale. "He sure has a lot of bank books, though." "Who knows? Maybe he's broke and those bank books showed zero balances. Ah, I sincerely doubt that, though. He's got money salted everywhere – his is a cash business and if he wasn't making any money, he'd get out. Nah – he's just cheap. Always has been."

"Well, whatever. What're we going to do?"

"I talked to Don Winters and it sounds like he'll help us out. He said we could pick a check up this morning. I called Lucey to tell him and he told me we couldn't use a check. Has to be cash, certified check or money order. When I called Don back to tell him that, he'd gone for the day."

"Oh. Nice."

"Yeah. Listen, why don't you get the van and drive out there? By the time you get there, I'll have talked to him and, hopefully, he'll have the cash. We really don't have any time to waste. You'll probably have to meet us at the closing and give me the cash."

"Kind of down to the ol' wire, isn't it?"

He laughed. "Isn't it always?"

"Where's the closing? I'll drive directly there from Don's place, cash in hand, I hope."

"I don't know. Jeanne has the address and she's in the shower. Call me from Don's and I'll let you know."

"Okay. I'd better get going. Oh – and hey, is there gas in the van?"

"Damned if I know."

"I'll call you in a little while."

"Right."

We kept the van in a garage on 44th Street, just west of Eighth, so it only took me a couple of minutes to walk over there. I knew the guys there pretty well and told them I was in a hurry, so they brought the van down right away, even though the place was filling up with early morning commuters.

I checked the gas gauge. Three-quarters. Whew. That was a good fifteen minutes saved.

I swung into the Lincoln Tunnel a couple of minutes before eight. Even going against the inbound traffic, the trip would probably take me forty-five minutes to an hour each way. Figure fifteen minutes at Don's and I should be back in midtown around ten or a little after. That'd give me almost an hour to drive to wherever the closing was and get the money to Dale. And that was with no delays anywhere along the line.

Christ, it was going to be close. If I had to follow Don to a bank or something to get a check certified or something, we were screwed. Oh, well – onward.

I took Route 3 west and it would hit 46 a few miles ahead. Actually, I think 3 became 46 at some point. Don's was a few miles further ahead, right where 46 and 23 merge.

It was a bright, sunny day. A beautiful day, really. But I couldn't pay too much attention to the weather. I was a man on a mission.

I pulled into the parking lot of Fountains of Wayne about ten to nine. It wasn't open yet, didn't open until ten on weekdays. I saw a car parked by the back door and hoped it was Don's.

I tried the back door and it was locked. I pulled the old New York City bread delivery guy trick of rapping on the window with a coin. A couple of minutes later, Don Winters opened the door.

"Dale didn't tell me it had to be in cash." Enough for the niceties.

"I think he tried to call you back but you'd gone."

"Yeah, whatever. You guys think I've got thousands of dollars in cash just laying around?"

Yes, Don, we do. Yours is pretty much a cash business, you're open until seven and you haven't had a chance to get to the bank yet this morning to make a deposit. Stop fucking with me and hand it over.

"Dale says you keep all your money in a mattress. Says you've got the first dollar you ever made, too."

"Aw, fuck me. Fuck him, too." There was just a hint of a smile.

"Listen – I looked over my orders with you guys last night. You still owe me four pumps and three 'Olympias'. Don't have 'em with you, do you?"

"No. I just flew in from Louisville last night. Didn't get in 'til after ten." Whoa, was that a fountain tycoon story or what? "I didn't stop by the office this morning. We'll get 'em to you in a couple of days."

"Well, tell Dale this little transaction will cost him four additional pumps and one more 'Olympia' – free of charge. And I need everything by the end of the week."

"Done. I'll see if John can deliver everything tomorrow or the next day."

"Yeah, sure. I know you guys. The fucking season'll be over before I see anything."

"No, really."

"Don't 'no, really' me, Jim. You guys can be a pain in the ass, you know that?"

"Ah, but Don. You're making a fortune off our stuff, aren't you?"

"Not when I can't deliver them to my customers, I'm not."

It always went this way with Don Winters.

"Now. Take your goddam money and get outta here. You don't want to be late for your closing. You fucking guys are late for everything else."

He handed me an envelope full of hundred-dollar bills. I counted them.

"It's all there."

"Just checking." Yep. A hundred-and-twenty of 'em. "I'd better get going. And, really, Don, thanks a lot. Oh – can I use the phone to call Dale?"

"It's on the wall."

I dialed and Dale answered on the first ring.

"General."

"Yeah, it's me. I got it."

"Good. He gave me some song and dance on the phone and bitched and moaned a little bit, but he said he'd come through."

"Where's the closing? I'll have to meet you there."

"Right. Let's see….here it is."

He gave me an address on 50th Street, between Fifth and Sixth. Right across from Rockefeller Center. Shit. Parking in that neck of the woods was a real pain in the ass. There weren't many garages in that neighborhood. Oh well, maybe I'd get lucky. "It's on the 28th floor. When you get off the elevator, the law firm's right in front of you." "I'd better get moving. I'll be there just as soon as I can get there."

"Okay." We hung up.

"Don, I'd love to stand around and listen to you bitch, but I gotta move."

"Go on – get outta here."

I walked to the door, opened it, walked through and just as it was closing, Don said, "And hey – congratulations on the building. Really." He was smiling.

"Thanks." I was smiling, too.

I hopped by into the van and retraced my route back to the city. I was right on time.

All was going really well until I hit the spot where 3 merges with the Jersey Turnpike traffic. That spot's always a pain in the ass, but today it was really sluggish, even though rush hour should have been about over by now.

This sucked.

We just crawled. It was ten after ten. Fifty minutes to get the last three miles of this mess, through the tunnel, probably up Tenth Avenue (it wouldn't be as crowded as one of the more midtown northbound avenues), and over 50th Street to find a parking garage.

It was nearly ten-thirty when I reached the toll booths. This was rough on the nerves.

I got to thinking while driving through the tunnel. By the time I get up near Rockefeller Center, it's going to be eleven, anyway. If I have to find a garage, park the van and walk to the building, that'll chew up another ten, fifteen minutes. I had an idea.

As soon as I got on the Manhattan side of the tunnel, I looked for a phone booth. Found one at 40th and Ninth. I jumped out and called the office.

"General Fountains." Al.

"Al, you gotta do me a favor."

"What?"

"Leave right now and meet me on the northeast corner of 40th and Eighth. I'll be driving the van up 40th and'll make a left on Eighth and pull over and pick you up."

"Sure, but why?"

"I gotta meet Jeanne and Dale at the closing and I'm running late and you'll have to sit in the van down in front of the building where the closing is so I can run up with something they need."

"Yeah, but who's gonna answer the phones?"

"Fuck the phones. Just move. Now."

"Right."

I jumped back into the van and made my way up 40th between Eighth and Ninth. This block always sucked because a lot of the tunnel traffic used it to head east. That, and the fact that the Port Authority Building was the whole block long. Between Jersey drivers and cabbies, I thought I'd lose my mind. I was almost screaming at cars by now. It was ten minutes to eleven.

I finally made the corner and there was Al.

"Quick! Get in."

"What time are you supposed to be there?"

"Eleven."

"Never make it."

"Fuck you, Al."

Eighth Avenue wasn't too bad. We whizzed right up to 50th Street and turned right. As we were about to cross Broadway, the downtown traffic slowed and a bus ran the yellow, thoroughly blocking our way across. We were three cars from the corner.

"Shit!"

By the time the bus had moved, only one car made it through before our light turned red.

Two minutes to eleven. This was terrible.

The light changed and I laid on the van's horn. We made it through and moved pretty well down 50th until we were almost at Sixth. Sixth Avenue was fast becoming a parking lot. If we made it through this light, though, the place I was going was in the next block.

It was two lights before we made it through and then 50th Street was full ahead of us. There was a truck blocking the right lane a little ways into the block and two lanes of traffic had to merge into one.

"Traffic's pretty bad, huh?", Al said conversationally.

"Thanks, Al. I hadn't fucking noticed."

Ten after eleven.

We made it past the truck and I started looking for the building. It was going to be up on the left and, dammit, nearer Fifth than Sixth. I was now hoping there was a "No Parking" zone or something in front of it so I could pull into it. I didn't want Al to be blocking a lane of traffic and it wasn't like he could drive around the block. He was a city kid who didn't know how to drive and didn't have a license.

There was a "No Parking" zone in front. At least it wasn't a "No Standing" zone. Cops would make you move it if they saw somebody in the vehicle in a "No Standing" zone. It was the squad car guys who would do that. If a car was parked in a "No Parking" zone, that was the purview of the "brownies", or parking enforcement assholes. And if there was somebody in the vehicle, he could generally buy three or four minutes.

"Al. Wait here with the van. I gotta run some money upstairs to Jeanne and Dale at the closing. I'll put the flashers on and if anybody asks, I'm just dropping off a pump for the lobby fountain." I didn't know if they had a lobby fountain or not, but it was exotic enough to sound good if necessary.

We had "General Fountain Corp.", along with our address, in big letters on the side of the van. We might be okay.

"I'll be back just as quick as I can. Shouldn't be more than five minutes. And if somebody gives you shit, take the ticket. You don't wanna get popped for driving without a license. Besides, I'd say you stole it."

"Gee, thanks."

I literally ran into the building and an elevator was in the lobby. I got in, hit '28' and exhaled. Just as the doors were closing, somebody stopped the door with his hand to get in. It was a coffee shop delivery guy and he gave me a dirty look for not holding the door for him.

"What floor?" The least I could do.

"Seventeen." Shit, why couldn't it have been thirty or something?

The doors closed again and I looked at my watch. Ten-twenty. Ouch.

The elevator finally made it to twenty-eight and I stepped off. In front of me was a big set of glass doors with the name "Meter Dicker and Lever" or something on them. This was the place.

I walked up to the receptionist, who smiled coolly at me. I could feel the sweat running down my temples and my shirt was sticking to me.

"Good morning. How may I help you?"

How 'bout a shower and a change of clothes?

"I'm looking for the closing on 264 West 40th Street."

"Ah, yes. One moment, please."

She picked up the phone and said something I couldn't hear. A few seconds later, a guy I'd never seen before came down the hall toward me.

"Hi. I'm Martin Levinson. Are you Jim?"

"Yes. Nice to meet you." We shook hands.

"We've been waiting for you."

I'll bet you have.

He led me into a big conference room with a large table in the middle. There must've been twelve people sitting around it, though the only ones I knew were Jeanne and Dale and Jim Lucey and Stan Roth.

Jeanne smiled sweetly. Lucey raised his eyebrows. Stan got up, smiling and smooth as shit, and came around the table. "Jim. Nice to see you. Glad you made it."

"Me too."

Dale and I walked over into the corner for a minute, two fountain tycoons looking for the world like this stuff happened to us every day of the week.

"Got it?"

"Yeah, here it is", I said, surreptitiously slipping him the envelope that he tucked into his inside jacket pocket. "Look at you. Got a tie on and everything."

"Gonna buy a building. Good thing you showed up when you did. Nothing happens until all the money is accounted for, so we've been sitting here making small talk for about twenty minutes. These guys were starting to look at their watches. A couple of minutes ago, Stan whispered in my ear that we had about another five or ten minutes and the jig was gonna be up."

"Hell, I had a good two or three minutes to spare, then. If I'd known that, I'da stopped for coffee."

"Excuse me, Dale?" One of the suits.

"Yep. Coming. Jim, you want to stay for this?"

"Love to, but Al's downstairs in the van and he's probably shitting a brick by now."

"Okay. This shouldn't take much more than an hour. I'll see you back at the office."

"Okay. And, Dale – congratulations."

"Thanks. A big part of this is thanks to you, too."

"Thanks. See you later." To the assembled room: "I'd love to stay, but some of us fountain tycoons have to keep the ship of state afloat."

I made my most graceful exit, waved cavalierly to the receptionist and headed back downstairs to the van.

Thank God it was still there.

"No ticket?", I asked Al as he climbed out of the driver's seat to go around to the other side.

"Nah. Piece of cake. Some nice looking girls up in this neighborhood, though."

"D'you do one in the back of the van while I was gone?"

"Nah."

"Ah, Al, I'm disappointed in you. I thought you were a stud."

"I am. But I couldn't watch for cops and pick up girls at the same time."

"You coulda scored the daily double if you'd a done a female 'brownie', though."

"You know, I never thought of that."

We drove back to the garage and headed back to the office.

John met us as we stepped off the elevator.

"Where you go? Phones ringing and nobody answer."

"Nobody?"

"Maybe Acuna."

Great. Even though John's English was spotty, at least he could take a message.

Check that – he could write down a phone number. Acuna could have sold the place for lunch money.

I walked into the office and Tige was asleep on Jeanne's desk, under the heat of the desk lamp.

"Acuna?"

From the back: "Jeemy?"

Acuna swept around the corner.

"Jeemy. Thee phone rang a lot. Al, why deedn't you tell me you were a-livving?"

"Jim told me to run right downstairs."

Acuna looked at Al like he smelled.

"Acuna, who called?"

"Eet's on thee desk. I wrote down some messages. Does that gato always sleep there?"

"Every day."

I looked at the messages. Names and phone numbers. Couldn't ask any more of that from ol' Acuna, could I? Nothing that looked urgent. All was well.

"Who ees Beel Leet?"

"Who?"

"Beel Leet. He had two or three calls. Beel Leet." What the fuck?

"Oh – Bill Leith!"

"Yes, Jeemy."

"He's a private investigator retained by the FBI and immigration. He's been around a couple of times asking for you."

"That's not funny, Jeemy. That's not funny at all." His face twitched.

"Ah, take it easy, Acuna. It's just a name I use when I'm ducking people. You better watch out or I'll start using William Perez Acuna."

"Only eef eet's a lady." He pulled a Groucho Marx with his eyebrows. "Hahaha!"

THIRTY

I got the call from Dale and Jeanne around one-thirty.

They had bought themselves a building.

I thought about that for a few minutes. They had really come a long way since he had that idea for a fountain in a hotel in Memphis. They had gone from renting a tiny space on the eleventh floor of 264 West 40th Street to owning the damned thing. Not bad for a couple of kids from the sticks.

Anyway, they were having lunch with Lucey and Joanie and would be back later. I told Dale I'd pass the word around the shop.

I went around the corner. I said to Al and Acuna, "Well, it's now the General Fountain Building."

"Really. They really pulled it off, huh?", said Al with real admiration in his voice.

"Very good, Jeemy", Acuna chimed in. "Maybe I can leev here rent free, eh?" The eyebrows were going up and down.

"Sure, Acuna. We'll get you a pup tent to put on the roof."

"What's a poop tent?"

"A tent with its own bathroom."

"Sounds syuperb, Jeemy!"

I went next door to the shop to tell John.

John was becoming disenchanted with America. Back in the Ukraine and in Poland, they were led to believe that the United States was perfect. Everybody had a job, a house, a car, lifetime security, the best health care. The streets were paved with gold. Since he'd been here ten or fifteen years, he realized that just wasn't the case. He worked like a dog six days a week and saved money like a miser, just to be able to finally afford a fixer-upper in a shitty section of Queens.

He was becoming acutely aware of the difference between the haves and have nots. And he knew which of those he was, too.

From where John stood, Dale's buying the building didn't mean any more money for him, but he was certain it would mean a whole lot more work. Oh, he was happy that the business was succeeding, but he was becoming a little disappointed that very few of the spoils were coming his way.

His reaction was mixed.

"Good. Maybe he get rid of Parker. Parker naygoose. Strashny naygoose. Biggest naygoose." John was pissed because Parker was in the building employees' union, Local 32B and 32J. That gave him a slew of benefits John didn't have. And Parker was a lazy bastard, there was no getting around that.

"Maybe he will, John. He can do about what he wants, now."

To Dale's credit, one of the first things he did was to put John into the union. That took place within the first week of their taking over the building. John was now thrilled he'd bought it.

Dale and Jeanne and Lucey and Joanie stormed in around three-thirty. It was pretty obvious that most of the lunch had been of the liquid variety. Lucey and Joanie were three sheets to the wind, but Jeanne and Dale were surprisingly sober. I thought it must have been the excitement that kept those two from being affected too strongly.

"Jim! Drinks all around!"

"Hey, Dale", I said somewhat quietly, "what about Al and Acuna?"

"Hell, yes. Them, too!"

"We need ice."

"Send Acuna."

"Hey, Acuna!"

Around the corner he came. "Yes, Jeemy?"

"If you'll go get some ice, I'll buy you a drink."

"I'll be back before thee cubes melt a seengle drop!"

I gave him a five and he headed for the stairs. Acuna always waited for the elevator. I think he hit the stairs before one of us changed our mind.

Al ambled around the corner.

"Hey, Jeanne and Dale – congratulations on the building." Al was really a nice kid.

"Why thank you, Albert", said Jeanne. "We couldn't have done it without you." I think she meant it, too.

Al beamed from ear to ear.

"Al", said Dale. "How's it feel to be a landlord?"

"Who, me?"

"Well, we're all in this together."

I piped up. "What he means, Al, is that you have to go around and collect the rents. You're our 'muscle'. You gotta intimidate some of these guys. You know, put 'em up against the wall once in a while, just to keep 'em current."

"Now, wait a minute."

"Jimmy, leave Al alone", laughed Jeanne.

Dale got on the phone and called just about everyone he knew. He was really on a roll. He even called Gallagher's. By now, it was around four-thirty. He asked Mario, the maître d', if anyone was around.

"Just Bill Ruben."

"Put him on the phone."

When Ruben got on the phone, Dale invited him down to the office. I guess that made sense they had been neighbors on 48th Street, up over Jack Monte Rosa's. They went back as far as anyone.

Bill said it would take him about half an hour to walk down.

"Just hop a cab. I'll pay you back when you get here." Billy Ruben never gave an inch. By the time he got there, we were on our second drink and Lucey and Joanie had gone back to the bank. Or home, I'd hoped. Al had had one drink and he'd left, too. He always did.

Acuna, on the other hand…..well, he wouldn't shut up. He had poured his own second drink and completely bombed himself. There was virtually no room for water. He was prattling on about how Dale should turn the building into condominiums or something and I could see Dale had just about had enough.

"Hey, Acuna", he said. "Here's a hundred. Go get yourself a nice meal."

"Thank you, Dale. With thees, I might have a leetle wine and eef I'm lucky, a leetle love, eh? Hahaha." With that, he downed his drink, swept out of the office and hit the down button on the elevator and was gone.

Billy got there a minute or two later.

"Well, Jeanne. Dale. You really did it this time, didn't you?", said Ruben, toasting them. "It's a long way from 48th Street, isn't it, Bill?"

"I'll say."

Jeanne said, "Billy – remember Miss Viola?"

"You know, she was the spookiest person I've ever known. I used to tip-toe past her door praying she wouldn't jump out at me." The image of Billy Ruben tip-toeing was one I was having a hard time conjuring.

"I got an idea", said Dale. "Let's go celebrate."

"Where?"

"How about the Rainbow Room?"

The Rainbow Room? Where did he come up with that?

"The Rainbow Room? Where did you come up with that?", I asked.

"We walked past it on our way to the closing today. I hadn't thought about it in years. Come on, let's go. We can afford it now, we're landed gentry!"

"Dale", Jeanne said, "with what we now owe, we've never been poorer."

"Oh, stop thinking like a bookkeeper. Get yourself together and let's get out of here."

We took a cab right to the door. Took the elevator up to the top floor and walked to the bar. The view from the Rainbow Room is unique in all the world. It looks out over midtown Manhattan and you could see all the way to the World Trade Center. The Chrysler and Empire State Buildings soared majestically to the south.

The sun was beginning to set over New Jersey and New York never looked better. "Can you see our building?", asked Dale.

We couldn't, but it was pretty heady knowing one of those buildings out there in the Greatest City in the World belonged to us – them – us.

When we turned around, Ruben wasn't there. I looked around and saw him waddling back in our direction, with a plate piled massively high with food.

"Hey – this is some spread", he said, obviously in Nirvana. "This happy hour puts every other one to shame." I hadn't thought the word 'shame' was in Billy's vocabulary. "We should come here more often."

Billy said 'we', because at twelve-fifty a drink, there was no way he was coming here on his own. He'd need a sponsor.

He set the plate down in front of him on the bar and was adopting a stance that meant 'everybody keep your hands off'.

"That's okay, Billy. We don't really want any."

"Hey, help yourself", he said around a mouthful of deviled egg. "There's plenty enough for all of us."

We finished our drinks and decided to head for Gallagher's.

Billy had just brought over his second plateful. He was truly torn. More free food here or more free drinks at Gallagher's? I could see the wheels turning. He knew we'd be at Gallagher's for an hour or two. He'd finagle it both ways.

"You guys go ahead. I'll be along in a few minutes."

And he was.

****

My cousin Diane – Iz – had cleaned herself up nicely after her bout in rehab. She was living on the twentieth floor at 888 Eighth Avenue, the same building as Jeanne and Dale. Dale supported her, financially, while she worked as a counselor at Veritas, the rehab placed she'd been in.

She'd gotten herself a little dog, a Lhasa Apso named Whitey. I'd met the dog a couple of times and, for a little barker, he seemed okay. He was a happy little guy.

A few weeks after the closing on the building, Iz had gotten an invitation to spend from Sunday 'til Wednesday at a friend's place on Fire Island. She asked her Mom and Dad to keep Whitey for her while she was away.

Jeanne and Dale took Whitey into their apartment on Sunday afternoon and all hell broke loose. Their two cats absolutely freaked over Whitey and attacked him from the minute he got in the front door.

Two hours later, the battle still raged and Dale figured the only thing to do was to take Whitey down to the office and leave him there for the duration. We'd be there all day during the week and Tiger wouldn't bother with him. She put up with so much shit around there anyway, a little dog wouldn't phase her in the least.

Dale called me on Sunday evening to tell me and that I should walk him first thing in the morning and "for Christ's sakes, don't let anything happen to that dog – Izzy'd kill us!".

I awoke Monday morning and turned on the news. New York City was just beginning the worst heat wave it'd seen in seventeen years. It was going to be between a hundred and a hundred-and-five all week long.

I got to the office a little before eight and as I unlocked the door, probably the worst three-day period I'd had in years opened with it.

As I opened the door, Whitey ran out between my legs. "Whitey!"

As I turned to catch him, he ran into the elevator just as the door closed.

"Jee-sus Christ!"

I hit the stairwell door at a dead run and took them two at a time to the lobby.

Nobody I knew was in the lobby! No one to ask if Whitey had run out!

Maybe the elevator Whitey ran onto was going up. I'd wait in the lobby 'til all three came down and opened and prayed that he'd be in one of them.

First one....nope. Second one....no dog. Third elevator....NO!

I ran back up the stairs and into the shop.

"John! You see white dog?"

"Dog? What dog?"

"Did you see a little white dog anywhere in the last couple of minutes?"

"I no see dog."

"Shit! Diane's dog is staying next door in the office. When I opened the door, the dog ran out and into the elevator. Can you get one of your guys to stand in the lobby to watch for it while you and I go up to twenty and check all the floors?"

"Sure. Hootch-pan!"

Frantic Polish and one of the guys made for the door.

John and I hit the 'up' button.

"Christ, John, that little shit was gone before I could do anything. I sure hope it's running around peeing on the walls somewhere in this building."

John and I went to every office and every rest room and slop sink in the building. Even down to Parker's in the basement.

Nothing. The dog was gone. And there were thousands of commuters walking up 40th Street on their way from the Port Authority.

I decided maybe Whitey was somewhere on the street.

I alerted another John, the super of the building across the street. I ran into the two parking garages right next door and across the street. It's amazing how blank a human's face can be when you ask him or her if they've seen a little white dog running around.

I ran-walked all the way up 40th Street to Broadway. Nothing.

I finally had to face the music. I dropped a dime in a pay phone and called Jeanne and Dale and told them.

"Jesus Christ! You sure you looked everywhere in the building?"

"Everywhere. The dog is on the street somewhere. I'm going to walk around all these blocks and see if somebody's seen him."

"That's the best you can do. We'll be there in a little while. Jesus Christ."

"Yeah."

It was now about a quarter to nine and I had walked 39th Street from Broadway to Eighth. I figured the little guy hadn't tried to cross Eighth Avenue with all that traffic. I did look up and down it though, praying I wouldn't see a little white and red puddle in the middle of the avenue. I didn't.

Now 38th from Eighth to Broadway. A time and temperature sign on a bank said it was a hundred-and-one degrees and I was dripping sweat like I'd just run five miles. Now 37th from Broadway to Eighth. Now 36th.

There was a precinct station on 36th Street – Midtown South – and I went in and up to the desk officer.

"Officer, I'd like to report a missing dog."

He was writing something. When he finished writing, he said, "Can I help you?"

"Yeah, I'd like to report a missing dog."

"A missing dog?" Great. This guy was no Kojak.

"Yes. A missing dog."

"Can you be more specific?" Touché.

"I work in a building at 40th and Eighth. My cousin's dog was in the office. When I opened the door, the dog ran out and into the elevator. I looked everywhere in the building and no dog. I have a feeling the dog ran out of the building. It's small and white – a Lhasa Apso, I think. Maybe somebody found it and reported it."

"Doesn't the dog have any identification?"

"I don't know."

"Too bad. The little guy's probably scared as shit if he's out running around the Garment Center somewhere."

"Yeah."

"Okay, here's what we'll do. You fill out this form and I'll get on the walkie-talkie to the patrolmen in the area. Give me your name and phone number in case we get lucky." I gave it to him and filled out the form, which was mercifully short.

"What's the dog's name."

"Whitey."

"Like in Whitey Ford?"

"Like in Whitey Ford. Can you give me the number here so I can check with you guys later? Your shift will change and the next guy might not call me right away."

"Yeah, here's a card."

"Okay, thanks. I guess I'll go out and walk around some more."

"Good luck."

"You too."

I walked out of the precinct house and retraced a lot of my earlier steps. Still no Whitey.

I had an idea.

I'd go back to the office and make up a paper 'plate' and print up a bunch of "Lost Dog" flyers and blanket the neighborhood with them. A 'paper plate' can be used on a printing press for very short runs and we had a bunch of them in the office.

When I got to the office, Jeanne and Dale were there. So were Al and Acuna. I was dripping sweat and nearly in tears.

Everybody understood that it might have happened to any one of us who opened the door first – just happened to have been me. At that moment, I wished I weren't so goddam reliable. If I'd strolled in around nine, I might not be feeling so responsible for this little crisis.

Dale sent Al and Acuna to go out and walk around the neighborhood some more and go into coffee shops and lobbies and freight entrances to ask if anyone had seen Whitey.

I outlined my flyer idea and it was agreed it was worth a try. We decided to offer a reward – two hundred dollars for Whitey's return. We figured somebody might rather want the cash than the dog and by putting the amount on the flyer, it would maybe create some interest. The largest words on the flyer were "$200 REWARD". I put our phone number and the phone number of the Midtown South precinct house on it, too.

Al and Acuna were instructed to be back in forty-five minutes to pick up their supply and some tape.

Within half an hour, I had a few hundred printed and, armed with my supply and a roll of Scotch tape, hit the streets.

I put up flyers on light poles, mail boxes, blank walls and blanketed street corners. I put them under delivery trucks' windshield wipers and taped them to the outside of street level windows.

When I got to the corner of 40th and Seventh, I realized I hadn't even walked any of the uptown streets. I had gone block after block downtown, but not uptown. I guess I didn't think Whitey would make for Times Square and also knew that most of the people walking from the Port Authority worked in the Garment Center and not in Times Square.

At this point in the '70's, Times Square was at its absolute raunchiest. It was X-rated movies houses separated by peep shows, with the occasional bullet-proofed glass closet-sized cigarette-soda-beer-lottery ticket shop thrown in. And there were a fair amount of nasty-assed topless joints peppered throughout. And the crowd it attracted was not church ladies from Des Moines.

I hadn't really ever considered finding myself in a Times Square topless bar at eleven in the morning, but these were not ordinary circumstances.

I went into one on Seventh Avenue between 41st and 42nd. I was blind when I walked into the darkened bar, coming in from bright sunlight. The music was blaring and there were more people at the bar than I'd thought. Actually, I'd thought there wouldn't be anybody at the bar and was quite surprised by the hustle and bustle.

Speaking of hustling and bustling, there was a babe, bathed in red light, doing her stoned-out version of the hootchie-kootchie on a postage stamp-sized stage. Upon closer inspection, 'babe' was a stretch. It was hard to estimate her age, but she looked like ten miles of old bad road. She was naked except for a G-string and ratty old shoes, but I couldn't bring myself to look any closer. Let's just say the word "sagging" would've been in any reliable description of her.

The thing that was kind of sad was that no one was watching her. Seems the patrons' lust was stronger for demon rum than what was attempted to being passed off as erotica.

I gave a flyer to the bartender, who looked at me rather askance.

"You think a dog would come in here?" Sure, asshole, if he was thirsty and wanted watered-down drinks for eighty-nine cents a shot.

"No, but one of your patrons might've seen it or found it and brought it in. There's a two hundred dollar reward."

"Hey!", he shouted. "Anybody seen a little white dog? Two hundred bucks to whoever finds it."

There was a semi-collective, "unh" from along the bar.

I thanked the guy and left.

I walked into every sleaze ball operation in Times Square. The two hundred dollar reward drove me onward in this neighborhood.

Nothing. I put up a lot of flyers, though.

I got back to the office mid-afternoon and Al and Acuna were back, too.

Nobody had had any luck. We were all pretty dejected and coming to grips that little Whitey was probably gone for good.

The phone rang.

"General." Pause. "Hang on a minute." He put the phone on hold.

"Jesus Christ, it's Izzy! What'll we do? What'll we tell her? Here, Jim, you talk to her." With that, he handed me the phone, got up and disappeared around the corner. He wasn't whistling this time.

Well, I was the one who'd lost Whitey, so I guess I had to be the one to talk. I was about to take the phone off hold when Dale came back around the corner.

"Listen. Don't tell her the dog's missing. She won't be back for a couple of days and he might show up by then. Just tell her he's fine." Gone again.

I hit the button.

"Iz!"

"Well, hello, Jim."

"Dale had to take another call. How's Fire Island?"

"Great! I never realized there were so many gay guys out here, though."

"It's kind of famous for that. You having fun, though?"

"Oh, yeah. It's like a constant party out here. I have to watch myself, but I'm having fun. A single girl out here draws straight guys like bees to honey. How's Whitey?"

Gulp..

"He's just fine. He and Tige are getting along and he seems pretty happy."

"Can I say hello to him."

Fucking great.

"Sure. Whitey? C'mere, Whitey. Good boy. Mommy says hello."

"Put the phone up to his ear so he can hear my voice."

I wanted to die.

"Okay, here he is."

"Hi, little baby boy. How's Mommy's little baby boy? Hmm? Are you being a good boy?

Well, Mommy misses you and I'll see you day after tomorrow."

I put the phone back to my ear.

"Iz, it's me. I'm back."

"Do you think he recognized my voice? Did he hear me?"

"Oh, yeah. His little ears perked right up when he heard your voice and he licked the receiver." There was no doubt in my mind that I would go to Hell for this.

"Good. Okay – gotta go. I'll call you guys tomorrow. And give Whitey a big kiss for me." "There's nothing I would rather do, believe me."

"Okay, 'bye."

"Bye."

Shit. This was reminding me of the old joke – 'Grandma's up on the roof'.

We did our best to get through the rest of the day and I went straight home. I wasn't in the mood to hang out at Gallagher's or anywhere else.

The next day, the Al, Acuna and I went back and re-traced our steps, replacing flyers that had disappeared. It was about all we could do.

Thank God Iz didn't call on Tuesday. I couldn't have gone through all that again. The office was a lot more normal than it had been the day before, but the atmosphere was decidedly subdued.

About four in the afternoon, Jeanne said there was a call for me.

I picked up the phone.

"Hi. This is Desk Sergeant Wilkins at the Midtown South Precinct."

"Yes?" My heart skipped a beat.

"We might have found your dog."

"What?!?"

"Yeah. A lady called and said she found a dog that matched the description. Seems she took it home with her to Jersey. She saw a flyer and called us."

"Great. When can I get him back?"

"Well, there's a little issue there. Seems she thinks you don't deserve the dog 'cause you lost him."

"What?"

"I know. He's your property and you reported him lost and she reported finding him, so we'll work things out. But you have to go meet with her. Tomorrow morning."

"Meet with her? Where? Why? Can't you guys just get the dog back from her and I'll get him from you? We're good for the reward money – I'll drop it off in a few minutes." "It's not that. She wants to meet with you to make sure you're 'worthy' of the dog."

"Worthy of the dog?!? What is this?"

"Ah, she's a lady who loves dogs and wants to make sure they have the best homes or something. You can't blame her."

"No, you can't. But Whitey has a real good home."

"I know that and you know that. But she doesn't know that and she has the dog."

"Christ."

"Listen to me. You want this dog back in the easiest, fastest manner?"

"Well, yeah."

"Okay. Then meet with this lady at her office tomorrow morning at ten." He gave me an address on Sixth Avenue between 36th and 37th. How'd Whitey get all the way over there? "I'll have a patrolman meet you at the entrance to the building and the two of you go up and talk with her. Be nice to her. And bring the money. And I'll see to it the officer gets you your dog back, okay?"

"Yeah. Sure. Okay. Tomorrow at ten."

I told everybody in the office about my conversation and that Whitey was in good shape and we'd get him back in the morning. Nobody could believe it. It was as if Whitey had come back from the dead.

The next morning I met the cop at the entrance to the building and the building's super was there, too. The cop said we were going up to the super's office on the roof and the woman would meet with us there.

"Why his office? Why not hers?", I asked the cop.

"I guess she works in a fancy office and she doesn't want to be seen meeting with a police officer there."

"Whatever. Does she have the dog, though?"

"The super, here, says she does." The super nodded in confirmation.

Up we went. When we got there, the super went down to the lady's office and brought her up. It was reminding me of a spy novel.

She came in all stone-faced. "How do you 'lose' a dog?", she demanded.

Nice to meet you, too, babe.

I gave her the whole story. About keeping him for Iz. About him not getting along with her parents' cats. About him running out. About us running through every floor, scouring the Garment Center, going to Midtown South, printing up and distributing flyers all over the place. The whole shootin' match.

"Seems like this fella had a little bad luck and they went through a whole lot to get that little dog back", said the cop helpfully.

"Well, the Garment Center is no place for a Lhasa Apso", she said.

"I totally agree, ma'am", I said. "I can't wait for him to get back to his nice little apartment uptown."

"Is the owner good to him? Why didn't she take him with her if she loves him so much?"

"She dotes on him hand and foot. And she didn't think Fire Island would be a good place to take him."

"Mmph. I suppose not."

"So, lady. Can he have his dog back? Not to try to rush this, but we have a little crime in this part of town and I'd better get back to trying to keep it down." The cop.

"Okay. He's down in my office. I'll go get him and bring him back up here." I told her I had the two hundred dollars.

"It wasn't about the money. It was never about the money."

"I realize that, but it's yours. I'll give it to you when you guys get back up here."

Five minutes later, Whitey was in my lap, panting happily. Not any happier than I was panting, I'll give you that.

I carried him in my arms all the way back to the office. No way I was letting that dog get away again.

When I got back to 264, I tied his leash to the couch leg. Everybody gathered around and welcomed him back. He didn't seem any the worse for wear. Just a little thirsty, so we got him a big bowl of water and we all went back to work.

A little while later, I was walking through the office and he was sleeping peacefully on the couch. I wondered if his last two days had been anything like ours.

Iz came back in from Fire Island that afternoon and stopped by the office around four to pick up Whitey. There was a big reunion.

"How was he? Did he behave himself? Did you guys have fun with him?", she asked in rapid-fire succession.

She didn't need to know.

"He was a perfect gentleman. Not a bit of trouble."

THIRTY-ONE

Now that we owned the building, we started exploring every part of it.

Up on the roof, there were two large wooden Rosenwach water tanks, just like most buildings have. They weren't very interesting other than seeing one up close and touching it. They always seemed like these things that had landed on rooftops all over New York and nobody really knew anything about them.

The 'elevator' room was, naturally, right above the elevators and housed the big elevator motors and gears and fuse boxes and the gigantic cable winches.

Over the next few years, I'd become all-to-familiar with elevator fuses. They were huge – over a foot long and a couple of inches in diameter. Whenever one would blow, the attendant elevator would come to a screaming halt and the lights would go out. We could always tell when this happened because the on-board alarm bell would sound. You could always tell how nervous the passenger or passengers were by the insistence of the alarm bell.

We always had two or three spare fuses lying around – nobody wanted to explain to terrified passengers that somebody'd had to go across town to get one while they were stuck in the dark.

I could go from hearing the alarm bell to replacing the fuse within five minutes. It was something I was especially proud of.

Once the fuse was replaced and the elevator working again, it didn't always stop directly at the floor level the first time. I had to help hoist any number of people up two or three feet or help them jump down two or three feet. They were always so goddam glad to get out of there they seldom got pissed.

There were between fifty and a hundred army-green-colored barrels in the elevator room. They had the word "For Emergency Use Only" stenciled in yellow on the outside. We wondered what the hell was in them. One day, Dale and John and I pried one open, not knowing what we'd find inside.

We found saltine crackers.

We had nearly a hundred barrels of thirty-year old saltine crackers. There must've been half a million of the things. We opened one of the packages. They were stale, to say the least. Certainly inedible.

"What the hell are these things doing here?", I asked.

Dale said, "They must've distributed these things to all the buildings in town either during World War II or at the beginning of the Cold War. In case we got bombed or something."

"If this building were bombed, don't you think the roof was probably not the best place to store these things?"

"They were probably in the basement for years and were moved up here. Why they weren't just thrown away, though, is beyond me."

"Maybe it was Parker. He might've been waiting for the building's allotment of cheese and he'd fence the whole load as cheese 'n crackers."

There was a huge expanse of the roof that was flat and had a wall that was maybe three feet high. From that part of the roof we had a real good view of the Hudson River and New Jersey to the west. The other views weren't much as the view on north side of the roof was blocked by the elevator room and the water tanks. To the east, just more Garment Center buildings, most of which were a few stories taller than ours. Same to the south.

Several times that Summer, we'd take a few chairs up and have drinks at the end of the day. It was nice being alone up so high with the street noise pretty much blocked out. Watching the sun start down over Jersey was very pretty and relaxing.

One day, Dale said, "Why don't we put a roof garden up here? We could get a couple of those tables with the umbrellas, a few chairs, maybe even build a bar."

So we did.

Or rather, John did.

Now, John was a terrific worker and had a great practical sense, but like with the table down in the back room, most of what he built was always just a little off. It had a lot to do with the raw materials he had to work with and the fact that Dale always wanted everything done yesterday.

Over the next few weeks, John built a bar – with running water - that backed up to the elevator room, put a wooden slanted roof over it, and put in an okay back bar. Naturally, he had to use inexpensive wood and stained it a nondescript color.

John put up stockade-type fencing around the whole area. Good thing, too. We'd have probably lost two or three friends without it. You know, liquor and all. He painted the floor a dark, forest green and we put in some artificial trees and a few fountains.

Dale got a few bar stools, three tables with umbrellas, some extra chairs and side tables, and bought a refrigerator and gas grill. He had phones put up there, too, so we could go up whenever we wanted and not feel like we were playing hooky.

By early September, the place looked great. It really was a roof garden with all the fixin's.

We had a barbecue party one Sunday and probably fifty people were there. Dale was the grill meister and I was the bartender. All the gang from Gallagher's was there, along with a lot of other friends and acquaintances. Believe it or not, the whole thing went swimmingly and we had no problems.

To enter the building on a Sunday, people had to reach between the bars on the grill that covered the freight entrance on the weekends and push a hidden button which rang in the freight elevator. One of us would hear the bell and go down and let people in.

Worked like a charm.

Over the next few months, Dale and John added clear Plexiglas walls around the bar to keep the cold out, men's and women's rest rooms, and extended the structure further down one wall to make a living room. Dale even put in a pot-bellied, wood-burning stove in that room.

Somewhere, he'd found an old one-armed bandit that took quarters and put it in the corner of the bar. I think maybe he got it from Fritz.

I was always afraid that somebody'd stumble out the front door onto 40th Street after dark and get nailed by some hopped-up asshole but, miraculously, it never happened.

Eventually, Dale added the piece de resistance – a hot tub.

I gotta tell you – sitting in that hot tub, drink in hand, watching the snow swirl around only a few feet away, was pretty sweet.

The roof was cool.

When we took over the building, General Fountains had several spaces on several floors: most of the second floor, half of the fifth, seventh and twelfth, and a pretty large space up on nineteen.

In looking at the monthly printouts that Newmark provided, Jeanne realized they added a surcharge to every tenant's electric bill. The more electricity you used, the higher the surcharge. She didn't like that, didn't like it at all. At least where we were concerned. She called Robbie Kazlow, who was still our Newmark guy, and asked him about it.

"This surcharge reverts back to the owner of the building, right? In other words, it's another profit center for us, isn't it?"

"Well, ah, no, not really", said Kazlow.

"Then who gets it?"

"Ah, Newmark gets it."

"What do you mean, Newmark gets it? Why shouldn't we get it? It's our building."

"Oh, it's one of the methods we use to cover our administrative costs."

"Your administrative costs? Then what's our monthly retainer cover?"

Kazlow was caught and he knew it.

"Furthermore, you're charging a percentage of the electricity for all the common areas – the hallways, lobby – that sort of thing, to each of the tenants, too, right?"

"Right. After all, Jeanne, somebody has to pay for it."

"Fine. Just take our surcharges off."

"What?"

"Take our surcharges off – anything General Fountains uses – take those surcharges off."

"I, uh, I don't think I can do that."

"What." It was a statement, not a question.

"You see, Jeanne, every building and every building owner we have does it this way. We can't make exceptions for just one building. And I know Stan doesn't want to start a precedent. It's where Newmark makes a large part of its revenue."

Jeanne was furious. Furious. From that moment on, she hated Newmark. From that moment on, she would pore over the monthly printouts and she and Robbie would sit and go over every question she had. Sometimes, it would take hours.

Dale was equally as furious. Thank God neither one of them was furious enough to fire Newmark, though. The administrative labor was horrible – and that was with computers. I was always afraid Dale would say we were going to do it ourselves and Jeanne and I would be forever bogged down in accounts payable and accounts receivable. Hell, we couldn't keep up with General Fountains already. How would we do that, too?

But Dale had an idea.

"Goddamit, we won't use their fucking electric."

"Huh?"

"We'll get a gas-powered generator and put it up on seven. We can run everything we have off that. Our only costs will be fuel."

So we did.

We got a generator the size you see running ferris wheels at a carnival. A huge diesel job. When we took it up in the freight elevator, I was certain the cable'd break and we'd all end up crushed in some dark pit on the south side of 40th Street. Made it, though. We had to put huge springs under it so it didn't shake itself through the floor. Then, a flooring of about twelve inches of sound-proof insulation. Then four-by-four beams held together with six-inch bolts.

Because the goddam engine was so loud – stand next to one at a carnival sometime - because the engine was so loud, we had to build a sound-proof room around it. Walls, ceiling, door, everything. Everything was over twelve inches thick.

But it worked.

We ran all of General Fountains' electricity off that generator, as well as the hallway and stairwell lights, the lobby lights, bathroom lights, everything but the elevators. And it only cost us for diesel fuel. Saved us a fortune.

There was a slight downside, however.

Somebody had to take regular trips over to Fort Lee in the van to pick up four fifty-five gallon drums of diesel fuel. I took on that mission many more times than I'd liked. Riding around – and through the Lincoln Tunnel - with 220 gallons of highly flammable liquid sitting two feet behind my head was always unnerving. All I needed was for some goofball babe putting on her makeup or some delivery driver who'd washed down his lunch with forty ounces of Olde English 800 to rear-end me and we'd have made the national news.

The generator came in real handy in the Summer of '77, though.

I was sitting at home on a Tuesday evening, sipping on a can of beer. For the first time in history, I had bought pork chops and was going to cook myself a meal at home. I was looking forward to Shake 'n Bake pork chops, a tomato-and-onion salad and Ore-Ida french fries. Had the television on, almost ready to rattle those pot and pans. All of a sudden, everything went black. Black. Black-black.

I looked out the window. No lights on in the buildings behind me. Looked down at Joe Allen's. Nothing.

Blackout?

I went down to the street to see if "Restaurant Row" was dark. It was. Eighth Avenue, too. No traffic lights, nothing.

Definite blackout.

Uh-oh. I had an electric stove. Don't tell me – no pork chops?!?

I didn't have a transistor radio, so I called Gallagher's. Dark, too. I asked if Dale was there.

A minute or two later, he came on the phone.

"Guess we got a blackout, huh?"

"Guess so. How big is it? Have you heard?", I asked him.

"Sal has a transistor radio. Seems all of New York, Jersey and Long Island are dark, too. They didn't mention Connecticut."

"Wow. Whaddya suppose it is?"

"I don't know. Probably some ancient Con Ed switching station or something gave up the ghost."

"So, you don't think it's the end of the world?"

"Nah, Jim. I doubt it. World can't end tonight."

"Why not?"

"'cause it can't, that's why."

"Right. What're you guys gonna do?"

"Don't know. They brought out some candles here, can't go eat anywhere, might just as well have another drink."

"What about the generator?"

"I thought of that. No sense going down there tonight. Who knows, the power might come right back on any minute now. I'll meet you there first thing in the morning and fire it up. At least we'll have power – and air conditioning."

"Okay, I'll be there around seven."

"Right."

"Jeanne okay?"

"She's fine. Once she realizes it, she won't like the idea of trudging up six flights of stairs to get home, but she'll make it."

"See you in the morning."

"Yep."

Next, I called my mother. She and my stepdad still lived outside of Syracuse and I wondered if they had power. I remembered 1965, when the whole northeast went dark.

They had power. If the world was going to end tonight, I figured Syracuse had been spared.

Nothing else to do but continue drinking beer and go to bed. Shit, I was looking forward to those pork chops, too.

I woke up around six. It was hotter than hell. New York had been having another heat wave and this blackout happened right in the middle of it. Man, was I uncomfortable in that little studio apartment. How the hell did people live like this before air conditioning?

Checked on the pork chops. The refrigerator was warm. Pork chops do not do well in warm. I threw them away. Didn't need trichinosis on top of a blackout.

I got dressed and walked down to 264. It was weird. Almost every store on Eighth Avenue had some sort of neon light or something. None of them were on. Either were the stoplights.

Cops were standing in the middle of every other intersection, directing whatever traffic there was. Traffic was very light, though, like on a Sunday morning. It was funny – horns weren't blaring. Maybe people actually thought of each other during times like this.

I ran into Jeanne and Dale on the street. We had Jeanne wait by the front door until we could walk up to seven and start the generator. No sense in her standing in the dark. Within ten minutes, 264 West 40th Street and General Fountain Corp. were open for business. None of the guys came in though, the subways weren't running. Best of all, we had the air conditioning blasting and a radio. The radio stations had their own generators and were on the air.

Dale had been right. Some Con Ed thing had gone flooey and exploded. They were expecting everything to be back on line by early afternoon.

Thank God for that generator.

But, dammit, I'd lost some perfectly good pork chops. Stupid Con Ed.

****

There were a few various and sundry people that were always coming around, maybe once or twice a week, generally to get a free snootful and to shoot the shit.

Jack Horn, the Gray Line Bus Tour guy; Irwin Rubin, the lawyer; Jack Mohr, one-time honcho at Revlon; Jim Lehner, one-time voice of Mr. Magoo, probably in a knock-off not sanctioned by Jim Backus. There were many others, but these guys were always underfoot, though not usually at the same time.

I don't know how Jeanne and Dale hooked up with Jack Horn. He always said he was an executive with Gray Line, the bus tours that took tourists, primarily foreign ones, on trips around Manhattan. I think Horn was actually one of the guides, the guys who stood in the front of the bus with a microphone and spouted canned drivel about the sights of the City.

He always looked over-stuffed. He looked like he was about to burst out of his vest, his suit, his skin. He looked like a balloon that had been blown up nearly to the bursting point. I don't know why, other than he probably thought he was a thin guy so he bought smaller-sized clothes. He wasn't anything of the sort. Hence, the sausage visage.

He smoked those nasty Phillies Tiparillos and had a dry, loud, raspy laugh that seemed just a little too forced. Instead of a chuckle, like most people would give, he just simply laughed too hard and long to be completely sane.

He had never married and there was general consensus that none of the guys who worked at the Gray Line ever did, either.

After about a year of his twice-weekly visits, they suddenly stopped. Two or three weeks later Jeanne, who had a soft spot in her heart for everyone, called the Gray Line to see what was up. Seems Horn was in the hospital with some dread disease. He died a week or two later of some obscure fungus of the lungs.

Irwin Rubin was in his mid-seventies and was a lawyer at a pretty top-notch firm. He and his wife lived in the same building as Jeanne and Dale and they had gotten friendly. I think Irwin did some work for us regarding the building, but he was happily, though unknowingly, on the downslope of his career.

Once you're "made" in a big law firm, I guess you can hang out there forever. Seems that was what he was doing. I don't think he could've handled anything too strenuous, he kept falling asleep.

He'd come by the office around four in the afternoon (that was a clue that he wasn't urgently needed on a big case), unread Wall Street Journal tucked under his arm, and he'd plant himself on the couch with a big, benevolent smile.

"Jim, fix Irwin a hot dog", Dale'd tell me. "But first, bring him a scotch."

"Oh, really, I shouldn't", he'd say every single time. "Maybe just one of each."

Wrap the dog in a paper towel, give it thirty seconds. Put some ice in a glass and pour in a more-than-generous helping of scotch. Put the dog in the bun, another thirty seconds. Splash of water in the scotch. Take out the dog, throw mustard on it and… "Here you go, Irwin. A dog and a tail of the one that bit you."

"Oh, why thanks, Jimmy. I really shouldn't." He'd glom onto both.

I'd go back about my business, Dale would head for parts unknown, and Jeanne and Irwin would engage in some trite conversation.

A few minutes later, I'd go to check on Irwin's refreshmental progress and he'd be fast asleep, sitting there on the couch, dog gone and glass of scotch tipping precariously in his hand.

"Hey, Irwin, another hot dog?"

"Hmmph? Oh. Oh, why yes, Jimmy, I think I'll splurge today."

"And I'll top off the drink, too."

"Oh. Oh, why, sure."

The scene repeated itself. Eat the dog, sip the scotch, saw the wood.

Pretty soon, he'd rouse himself and announce he'd better get headed home.

"Why, gee, Irwin, it sure was nice of you to stop by", Jeanne would say. "Better take a cab – you don't want to be walking up Eighth Avenue. And give our love to Doris."

"Okay, Jeanne – and thanks for the advice. See you all in a few days."

And he'd waddle off.

Jack Mohr was kind of an enigma.

He was second or third behind ol' Charlie Revson at Revlon during its glory days in the '60s. Big job. Huge job. You could tell Jack had been at the top. He was smooth, sophisticated, knew virtually everybody in the fragrance business.

But he was in his seventies and his time had passed, too.

He was always trying to make the next big Houbigant score for us. We'd fashion some prototype fountain as per his design idea and he'd have a slew of meetings with "the top people" at this company and that. He had a few decent sales – nothing on the scale of the Houbigant order, but a dozen fountains here, a dozen there.

I always thought his problem was that he looked down at anything resembling mass market. That was the old Revlon in him coming out.

He'd spend his time trying to hustle fountains to Princess Marcella Borghese or Chanel or something of that ilk.

They'd end up buying five or six fountains to use at press conferences to announce a new line or something. But they didn't want anything to do with putting three thousand of 'em on fragrance counters in mid-America. Building five or six specialty fountains always ended up costing us money, not the other way around. Add to that Jack's commission, and it was an upside-down deal.

But ol' Jack was always out there swinging away.

We wouldn't see or hear from him for a couple of months, then he'd be hot on the scent of something, then we couldn't get rid of him.

I had fun watching him trying to explain "elegance" to Bubniak when it came to creating a fountain.

He'd hang in the shop with John, half-glasses perched on his nose, hands gesturing lyrically, waxing eloquently about how "the water must 'caress' the fragrance decanter" when John would say, "You crazy? You want water to hit bottle? She splash!"

"No, John. I want the water to gently cascade down the face of the decanter, as if it were the fragrance running down the aristocratic neck of a lovely cosmopolitan woman." "She splash. Make mess."

It was obvious John wanted no part of this and was busting Mohr's ass to the max. Time to spin on the heel and head for parts unknown to find Dale before I got hauled in to officiate.

Jack would come back into the office a little later, little parts of his face twitching, trying to hold his composure in place the way Charlie Revson did. He bitched to me, not Dale or Jeanne. For one thing, neither would listen.

"Boy, John can be frustrating. He just doesn't understand what I'm trying to convey with this fountain."

Yes he does and he thinks you're full of shit.

"Did you guys come up with anything?"

"Well, uh, yes, but it was certainly a challenging experience."

"Nothing good ever comes easy, Jack."

"We built the greatest fragrance empire the world has ever known with less wrangling."

"Ah, but you may have built the greatest fountain ever known just now, too. How 'bout a drink?"

"I think I need one."

One day he came in with what I thought was a brilliant idea.

Some company he was working with had been able to infuse fragrance into polymers. In other words, the basic structure of an object could be made to smell like whatever one wanted it to.

Jack had a small cloisonné apple lapel pin. The backing and the pin and the apple's stem and the little leaf were gold-plated metal. The apple itself was a bright red, a polymer-based paint that had been infused with the scent of an apple.

He had the apple only as an example of how the new process worked, but I saw a huge opportunity for him and for us.

Up on the nineteenth floor was a woman named Elizabeth Kennedy and that was also the name of her company. She made small, pretty high quality cloisonné picture frames, that were gold-plated metal filled with various polymer-based colors.

"Jack. Here's an idea. You know how Ed Koch is pushing the 'Big Apple' theme everywhere? Hell, the red apple logo is everywhere you looks nowadays."

"Right."

"What if we were to sell this scented apple pin idea to the City of New York? I don't know if the city'd buy them or if you could work out a licensing deal or what. But I think millions of these little babies could be sold. Big Apple lapel pins that actually smell like apple? If a fucking natural!"

"And – if you could get a big enough order, we could probably work with Elizabeth Kennedy up on the nineteenth floor to make the things. We'd just sit in the middle and rake in the money."

"You think so?"

"Hell, yes, I think so. Who wouldn't buy one of these? It's got 'collector's item' written all over it."

"But how do we go about selling it to the City?"

"I don't know, Jack – I guess that's where you come in."

He thought for a moment.

"You know – I used to know John Lindsay. We were on several panels together. Why, I remember one time – " uh,oh, here he went, just stepped onto an express train to the past.

"Jack. Start there. Start with guys you used to know. Somehow, you'll find your way to the right guy."

"I'll get on it first thing in the morning."

Whether he got on it first thing the next morning or not, I don't know. I do know nothing ever came of a great idea. No thanks to me, either, I suppose. But Jack was the one working on commission, not me.

No sir. I was a first-class fountain tycoon working for an hourly wage.

THIRTY-TWO

One day Dale came around the corner wheeling that bicycle with the motor he'd put together a couple of years earlier. The one that had been leaning up against the wall, collecting dust and, most recently, serving as a pseudo-clothesline for the Polish guys who'd wash out their dirty socks in the slop sink.

"I have an idea."

Jeanne didn't dare look up from her work.

I bit.

"What?"

"There are a lot of people in wheelchairs, right?"

"I guess."

"And there are a lot of people who either can't or don't have the strength to move themselves around in them. Especially if they want to go somewhere, like down the street or something."

"True. A lot of elderly, paraplegics, like that, right?"

"Exactly. What if we built motorized wheelchairs so those people could go wherever they wanted? Within reason, of course."

"How would you do that?"

"By putting reversible motors on each wheel – sort of like on this bike - that would be controlled with a joy stick attached to the armrest."

"Would it work?"

"Hell, yes, it would work. Jake," he always called Jeanne 'Jake', "see where we can find a good wheelchair. What's the name of the best kind? Everest…..Everest and Jennings, I think. See where we can get a couple of Everest and Jennings wheelchairs."

"Oh, Dale."

"And see if Jim can go pick them up somewhere. I want to get started on this today." Jeanne and I looked at each other. Wheelchairs?!? Electric wheelchairs?!? "Jimmy, you see if you can find them. I don't want anything to do with this." Great. The whole idea of wheelchairs freaked me out and now I was going to have to hunt them down and go buy two of the goddam things. I'd have rather been dealing with the spies in the Egyptian Embassy.

I looked in the Yellow Pages, made a couple of calls and found a place that had a couple of Everest and Jennings wheelchairs that I could go pick up. When I got them back to 264, I gave them to Dale and tried to forget about the whole idea. Often enough, this type of idea just dissipated on its own. I was hoping this was one of them.

A few days later, the elevator door opened and there came Dale, riding in his motorized wheelchair, turning into the office and doing a pretty graceful pirouette in the thing right there in front of us.

Cool.

"Can I try?"

"Sure. You'll figure the joystick out right away. Nothing to it."

Dammit, it worked! It worked well. Backwards, forwards, left, right. It'd turn almost directly all the way around.

"This is great!"

Al came around the corner. "What's this?"

"Try it, Al."

He did. And, other than running into the coffee table and slopping some day-old half drunken coffee all over that day's checks in advance, did pretty well.

Even Acuna got into the act.

"Maybe you should keep that and use it all the time, Acuna. The FBI'd never look for you in an electric wheelchair."

"Stop eet, Jeemy. That's not funny."

The only thing that seemed ungainly was the platform in the back that held two automobile batteries.

"Dale, what's up with the batteries?"

"Those motors use a lot of juice. Only way we can figure to keep the power up."

"They look like shit."

"I know, but I don't think anybody who's in a wheelchair and hasn't been able to move around by themselves for years will care if there are a couple of batteries in the back."

"Good point."

We all tested the thing around the building for the next few days. All except Jeanne. I even took it down to the street and went around the block. It worked really well. I was still freaked about being in a wheelchair, but thought of it as a new form of transportation, not as a wheelchair, and I was okay.

A couple of days later, Dale said, "C'mon, Jim. We're going on a field trip."

"Cool. Where to?"

"Goldwater Hospital over on Roosevelt Island."

I'd never heard of Goldwater Hospital but he explained that was where a lot of the worst paralysis cases were and they did a lot of work that wasn't being done elsewhere.

"Are we going to take the chair?"

"No. I just want to walk around and get the lay of the land. See how wheelchairs are being used, what kind of people are using them, if there are any electric chairs already on the market – that sort of thing."

"Do we have an appointment with anybody?"

"No. We'll just walk around. Act like we're visiting somebody or something. If we get stopped, we'll tell the truth, but I don't want to tip my hand if I don't have to."

"Okay."

Off we went.

Roosevelt Island is in the middle of the East River, between Manhattan and Queens. It's two or three miles long and maybe a mile wide at its widest.

I'd been there a couple of years earlier to pick up some guy Izzy was seeing. A good portion of the island had been revitalized and had a bunch of high rise apartment buildings and a nice little commercial center. A lot of young people who couldn't afford the Manhattan rents were living there. To get there, you either had to drive over the 59th Street Bridge or take the tram. So, I pictured Goldwater Hospital somewhere along in that new area.

Wrong.

Goldwater Hospital is hidden off in the far corner of the island, and approaching it down the long driveway, reminded me of one of those movies where detectives go to visit some demented serial killer hoping for clues to a string of murders they're working on. Even the weather seemed to change for the worse.

We parked the van and walked in the front door.

It was dark and institutional. There were people lying on gurneys lining the hallways. Many were groaning or making incoherent sounds. Some were lying on their stomachs, trying to stretch their necks up. Under the sheets, there was no evidence of arms or legs.

We walked down a hallway toward windows that had sunlight streaming in.

Sitting in the sun were about a dozen guys, all young, probably in their twenties. They looked robust enough, but there they were – in wheelchairs being moved about by orderlies. I sidled up to one of the orderlies.

"Excuse me, and without sounding more stupid than I look, what's the matter with most of these guys? They're real young."

The orderly looked a hole right through me.

"Gunshot victims. Knifing victims. Violence is what brought 'em here."

"Oh. Thanks."

Christ. You read about shootings in the paper and saw the stories on TV, but you didn't think about what happens next. Now I knew. Whoa.

I asked him, "Are many of these guys here?"

"A few hundred."

Oof.

"What happens to them next?"

"This is it. They're here for life. Families can't take care of 'em. Can't take care of themselves. Somebody gotta take care of 'em. The state pays for 'em."

"You mean they might be here for forty or fifty years?"

"They never last that long, but yeah, that's it."

"There are probably people in a lot worse shape than this, too, right?"

He snorted. "These guys are in the best shape in the place."

Good God.

We left.

"Dale, that is the single most depressing place I've ever been in in my life."

"I'll say."

Then he brightened. "Well, there's gotta be a lot of people that aren't in that bad a shape who'd be happy to have an electric wheelchair."

He seemed to be able to leave Goldwater Hospital when we drove out the driveway. It has stayed with me to this day.

Sometime within the next week or se Dale had set up an appointment for me to meet with some administrators at some Catholic hospital in Queens. I can't remember the name of it, but it wasn't too far from the 59th Street Bridge.

I was at a little of a loss as to how to proceed with these folks. Was I selling them? Was I just gathering information? How hard should I push? I was a little uncomfortable, not setting up the appointment myself and kind of going in as a hired gun.

Dale said, "Hell, yes, Sell 'em. These chairs are the wave of the future and if they're really all about providing their patients with the new and best care, these chairs should be at the top of their list."

Armed with my pep talk and a chair in the back of the van, I was good to go.

I kicked myself for not personally getting the directions and relying on Dale's directions.

Of course I got lost. Not bad lost, you can't get too lost in that part of Queens, but I was becoming dangerously close to being late for my meeting.

When I finally saw the hospital looming up among the three-story buildings that comprise that part of the world, I knew I was okay. What wasn't okay was getting in to the hospital. They had construction zones everywhere. All the directional signs put me into places I couldn't go. After about ten minutes, I parked in a loading zone – hey, I was unloading a wheelchair bound for the hospital, wasn't I?

Out came the chair. Then the platform the batteries sat on. Then the batteries. Then I had to hook up the batteries. Properly. Failed on my first attempt at that. The damned thing wouldn't go. Switched some wires around and was in business.

But I was fifteen minutes late.

By the time I found my way to the administrator's offices, I was almost twenty-five minutes late. Shit. And shit again.

Jim Gath

I checked in with the receptionist and she informed me, ominously coolly, that the three people I was meeting with were waiting in the conference room.

Into the conference room. I introduced myself to the two women and one guy and handed each person a business card. That, I shouldn't have done. The cards, of course, said "General Fountain Corp." and I was "National Sales Manager".

It was obvious the most imposing woman was the boss and the other two had something to do with people who needed wheelchairs.

The guy looked down his nose at my card and said, "'General Fountain Corp.'? What do fountains have to do with wheelchairs?"

"Well, the fountain business is our main business, but we have several others. We haven't given a name to the wheelchair company yet, but we wanted to show this chair to you at your earliest possible convenience. Sort of an 'advance preview'."

He just snorted.

"What do you know about wheelchairs?" It was the other woman, not the administrator.

"Well, I have to admit, we may have a lot to learn about the nuances and variables of the industry, but we believe we've developed a viable new method for people who use them to get around."

"Why are you using an Everest and Jennings chair?"

How the fuck do I know? Better yet, what the fuck does it matter? Lookit the goddam way it moves, you bimbo!

"Because we heard they're the best."

"Well, you heard wrong."

"Oh."

"And look at this seat!"

What?

"The seat?"

"Yes! Do you know what will happen to someone who's incontinent and uses this seat?"

"No."

"This seat's made of naugahyde – plastic! The acids in urine will not only give the person terrible blisters and ulcerated sores, they'll eat through this seat in no time!"

"Oh. Well, it's just a prototype. We figured each individual would use the seat that's right for him or her." Man, I was pulling this directly out of my ass, now. We'd never thought of the fucking seat.

"You've never thought of the seat, have you?" It was the guy.

"Well, uh –"

"And this backrest. A person who's quadriplegic can't use a soft back like this. They'd slouch. And if some patients slouch, they'll die of asphyxiation! Don't you know something as elemental as that?!?"

They hit me with three or four other problems in a staccato back-and-forth manner. I'd had about enough of this. These two were ganging up on me and I didn't like it. Whether it was because I was late or because they knew it would make extra work for them or because their lives revolved around the very real, very minute details of the disabled, I didn't know. But I didn't like taking it in the teeth, either, especially from a couple of mid-level geeks.

"Look. You're right. We don't know much about the needs of people with chronic disabilities. But we do know mechanics. And what we're showing you here is an idea that might work for some, if not all, of your patients. We also know that a machine such as this will afford some people a modicum of freedom they may have thought unattainable."

I turned to the administrator.

"Ms. So-and-so, I'm not here to try and sell you folks this chair, such as it is. That would be more than presumptive. I also realize we have a lot to learn. But what I'd like is your honest opinion as to whether you feel a vehicle like this has viability for your institution and your patients. That's all.

"As a matter of fact, you folks could be invaluable to us in helping to develop it so it has the tactical elements necessary to be something useful to a lot of people."

"Well, Mr. – uh – (she looked down at my card) Gath, the answer is 'perhaps'. Perhaps you may be on the path to something useful. Certainly not in its present state, however. My colleagues have just touched on a few of the issues. And there are many.

"Our suggestion to you and the people at General Fountain Corp. (ouch!) is that you spend considerable time and energy researching the needs of our patients and those like them. Incorporate what you learn. Make adjustments and course corrections. "Then, once you're satisfied you've developed a product that fully meets our needs, bring it back to us and we'll gladly revisit it."

"Can we work with you people in helping us with our research?" I figured if they helped develop it, not only would they buy into it, I could use the Saint Whatever It Was name in marketing it.

"I think not. Our people are extremely busy keeping up with the considerable needs of our existing patients. I'm sure you understand."

Shit.

"Sure. I understand. Well, thank you all for your time and input this afternoon. And don't worry, I heard everything you said. And, be assured, I'll be back with something that you'll be really happy with."

"Certainly. And thank you for coming." The other two just scowled. Assholes.

I left.

Well, I thought, that went real well, didn't it? I got my ass handed to me. In no uncertain terms.

At least the van was still there.

When I got back, Dale said, "So, how many'd you sell?"

"Dale", I said, "this is gonna be harder than it looks." I went on to explain the whole conversation, such as it was.

"Fuck 'em. They're one of those City hospitals anyway. They can't say 'boo!' without checking with a hundred people. Maybe we'll go straight to retail with these things."

"Straight to retail?"

"Sure. We'll run some ads in those nursing home magazines. Worked for fountains, right? Ought to work for electric wheelchairs."

He had a point.

But there were two things troubling me about his thinking on this one. First, I had heard loudly and clearly that we didn't know jack shit about the needs of the wheelchair-bound and that was kind of key.

Second, an image flashed through my mind of a bunch of elderly people engaging in games of 'bumper-chairs' in the hallways of nursing homes across the country. That'd go over big in the administrative offices.

Man, I wished to hell I could just get back to selling fountains, but Dale was like a dog with a bone on this one.

Next thing I knew, I had an appointment on a Saturday morning with a couple who lived in Philadelphia.

Great. I get to lose a Saturday driving to Philly and back, probably to get my ears boxed by somebody telling me how little we knew about the needs of the infirm again. Shit.

I piled the chair into the van and headed down the Turnpike. Got there around eleven. It was a nice neighborhood, tree-lined and wide streets. Looked like most of the dwellings were townhouses.

I left the chair in the van to go hunt down my potential client. I found the place, rang the bell and was met at the door by a dour-looking guy in a suit and tie. A suit and tie on a Saturday morning?

OK, fine.

He was the husband and it looked like his face might have broken if he'd ever try to grin. Oddly, he was pleasant enough, just dour. His wife was obviously the one with the problem and my guess was that he'd been through a lot over the years. That'd make anybody dour.

"Where's the chair?", he asked.

"Oh, I left it down in the van 'til I found you. Hey – I have an idea. If it's alright with you, why don't you come down to the van with me? That way, I can show you how easy the chair is to move and you can test it outdoors, like on the sidewalks."

"Not a bad idea. I'll just go tell my wife we're leaving."

I don't remember the conversation we had walking back to the van, but if I know me, I was selling my little heart out.

I unlocked the van and had the thing unloaded and put together in less than a minute.

"Aren't those batteries awfully heavy?", he asked.

"Not individually, and that's how you move them."

I got into the chair and did a little routine for him on the sidewalk – forward, backwards, left, right, circles, the whole thing.

"Like to try it?"

"Okay."

He didn't do too badly. I had my eye on his kisser and noticed he almost – not really, but almost – cracked a smile.

"It's not very…..pretty, though, is it?"

"Well, it's a basic Everest and Jennings chair. And, I'll admit the batteries aren't all that attractive, but it certainly does the job, doesn't it?"

"It does at that."

He stared at it a minute, lost in thought. I knew he was trying to gauge what his wife'd think.

"Can we take it upstairs? I'd like my wife to see it, maybe try it out."

"Sure."

Up we went.

In the elevator, he asked me how much. "Nine hundred", I told him.

"Hmm."

He excused himself once we got into his house and took the chair somewhere deeper into the house, obviously to where his wife was situated.

A couple of minutes later, out they came, she sitting in the chair and him pushing it.

If he looked dour, she looked downright stone-faced. Pissed, almost.

"Oh, I don't know", she said dismissively. "Why do I need another chair? The one I have is perfectly good. I'm used to it." She seemed bothered by the whole deal.

Then it hit me.

She was bothered by the whole deal. She was very self-conscious about having to be restricted to a wheelchair, about having a couple of men talking about the way she moved across the Earth. Her pride had been ravaged along with her body and she was just plain unhappy. I felt very sorry for her.

"I'll tell you what. I'm going to run back down to the van for a few minutes. I got kind of lost getting here and I want to study the map a little before heading back. You guys try it out a little in here. You have plenty of room to put 'er through 'er paces. I'll be back in a little while."

I went back down to the van and just sat and thought how depressing this electric wheelchair business could be. I didn't want any more of it and fully intended to tell Dale as soon as I could.

A few minutes later I looked up and, lo and behold, there came the two of them, she guiding the chair all by herself and him walking alongside. Bingo.

"Hey", I said, "fancy meeting you two here."

She gave me a hint of a smile. I think she realized she had retained – or retrieved – a bit of her freedom. They could go for walks and out places with her being able to move along on her own at his side, not relying on him to push her everywhere.

"We'll take it", he said. "Nine hundred dollars, right?"

"Right."

He reached in his pocket and peeled nine bills off a considerable wad.

"Is there any guarantee?"

"Sure. We'll guarantee everything but the batteries for a year. We haven't run out of juice on a battery, yet, so I can't say how long they'll last. If one goes bad, just get the cheapest 12-volt car battery you can find. Any Sears."

He handed me the money and shook my hand.

"Can I help you guys take it back upstairs?"

"No", she said. "We're going to walk for a while."

Damn.

Now, I was thrilled to be in the electric wheelchair business. I'd made them really happy.

Maybe I wouldn't say anything to Dale just yet.

On top of everything, I'd just made ninety bucks. Not bad for a Saturday.

THIRTY-THREE

Sidney Zion was, and is, a friend.

Sidney was one of the regulars we hung with at Gallagher's.

He was tickled by the fact that PL called me "College Boy", so that's what he's always calls me, too. Not to be outdone, and because Sidney's a shyster lawyer at his core, I call him "F. Lee", as in F. Lee Bailey.

Back in the late '60s and early '70's, ol' F. Lee was a writer and reporter for the New York Times. He had one of the biggest moments in newspaperdom and blew it with a bonehead move.

He was the guy that broke the Pentagon Papers story, about the Ellsburg brothers finding the evidence that the government had done some very, very bad things in prosecuting the Vietnam War. The war had become hugely unpopular and the Ellsburgs had found the smoking gun. Essentially, it was the Watergate story of the Vietnam War.

The Times, in breaking the story, was to lead with it in a Wednesday edition. It was the kind of coup newspapers live for, particularly in the case of the Times, which had been solidly against the war almost from its inception. This would blow the roof off the administration. And the story was Sidney's and Sidney's alone. It was fucking huge.

On Tuesday night, as the presses were beginning to roll, Sidney was a guest on the Joe Franklin Show, a live talk show on one of the local independent television stations, Channel 9, if I remember correctly. It was really a kind of second-rate show on a second-rate channel, if the truth be told.

It was on Joe Franklin's show that Sidney, on the eve of one of journalism's greatest coups, pulled one of journalism's greatest blunders.

He told Joe Franklin and his viewers that he had evidence the government lied to the American public and the world about crucial aspects of the Vietnam War. Everybody could read about it in the next day's Times.

Instead of this massive story breaking in one of the great newspapers in the world, it broke on a little-watched talk show hosted by a mouthy little guy with the worst hairpiece known to man, Joe Franklin.

Oh, most of the world didn't know the story broke on the Joe Franklin Show, but the New York Times knew it.

And they skewered Sidney.

I think he was fired before dawn on Wednesday and was black-balled from ever setting foot in the door of the New York Times again, nor would anything ever written by him ever appear in its pages from that day until hell froze over. His name was even taken off the byline and some other reporter's name appeared.

Ol' F. Lee went from hero to pariah between commercials for Dick Gidron Ford ("at 1223 East Fordham Road in the Bronx!") and the Circle Line ("Circle it on the Circle Line, toot! toot!").

Not only that, he couldn't even show people it was his story – his name wasn't even on it. "Lookit the tape of the Franklin Show! Then you'll know!" Sure, Sidney, we'll get right on that.

Smooth move, F. Lee.

For the next few years, the only way Sidney could get his name in the New York papers was to buy an ad.

Lo and behold, though, he finally landed a gig with the Daily News to write a twice-weekly column about New York politics, with which he was very familiar.

F. Lee seemed to know everybody in local politics and everybody seemed to know him. He used to kind of hang out with Jimmy Breslin and he and Breslin would sit at the bar at Gallagher's and argue over every left-right issue they could think of.

If anybody else – any other mortal – tried to get into the conversation they were dismissed as being low-level know-nothings. Well, maybe not everybody, but I was dismissed as being a low-level know-nothing. How did they find me out?

F. Lee only dismissed me as a low-level know-nothing when he was with Breslin. All other times, we were very cool.

We were invited to F. Lee's birthday party at his and his wife, Elsa's, home on the Upper West Side in early November.

As soon as I walked in, F. Lee said to me, "College Boy! There's someone I want you to meet. You guys are from the same generation and both a couple of left-wing commie dogs. Jim, meet Jerry Rubin."

Jerry Rubin! Jerry Rubin of the Chicago Seven!

Jerry Rubin. Abbie Hoffman. Bobby Seale. Tom Hayden. David Dellinger. The other two guys. Heroes! These guys had single-handedly changed the world. As a result of the riots at the '68 Democratic Convention in Chicago, young people across the nation had banded together and brought an end to the fiasco in Vietnam. Nothing like Vietnam would ever, ever happen again. Until Iraq, but that's a story for another day.

"Hi, Jerry. Pleased to meet you. And thank you for everything you did and stood for. I was one of the kids that followed in your wake."

"Gee, thanks. Not too many people remember anymore."

"And that's a shame."

"It is what it is."

"Right."

As I made my way through the party, I spied Elsa. I walked over in her direction to thank her for inviting me and to tell her what a nice party, blah, blah, blah, and noticed she was talking to – Roy Cohn! The Roy Cohn. The lawyer Roy Cohn.

Funny, but he looked more like a rodent in person than he did on television or in photographs. He shook my hand like he was royalty and I lied to him about how nice it was to meet him and moved on.

This was a pretty cool party. At least there were some real movers and shakers here. Not Acuna and PL's guys and Billy Ruben. Oops. Billy Ruben was there, naturally, over by the food table.

Billy looked my way and waved me over, almost spilling his plate of food.

Between mouthfuls – well, almost between mouthfuls, he tended to talk with his mouth full – he said, "Jimmy, meet the man you and I toasted back on that Fourth of July a few years ago." He worked at swallowing what was in his mouth.

"Hi", I said, offering my hand, "my name is Jim." Billy was chewing furiously, but a little slow to make it comfortable between me and the small, intense man in front of me.

"Uri Dan", he said.

Uri Dan?!? The Uri Dan that led the raid on Entebbe?

"That Uri Dan?", I asked stupidly.

"That Uri Dan", said Ruben, mouth now empty.

He tilted his head in acknowledgment.

"Wow. Am I pleased to meet you! That was the most incredible thing I'd ever seen", I said.

"Thank you."

"Can you talk about it?"

"A little, but most of it is still classified."

Billy was shoveling and listening.

"You were in the command plane, right?"

"That's correct."

"How did you know exactly where the hostages were? You know, in exactly what part of the building?"

"That, I can't tell you."

"Ah. Were any other countries in on it, too? I don't mean in on it, I mean like standing by just in case."

"Can't tell you that, either."

"Well, is there anything you can tell me other than what I've read?"

"I'm afraid not. Sorry."

"Don't be. Okay – here's one. What are you doing now?"

"Well, I'm going to be writing for the New York Post."

"The Post!"

"Yes. Covering security and military issues and the like."

"Does that mean you've left the Israeli military?"

"That, I can't tell you, either", he said with a smile.

"Well, Uri, it certainly was a pleasure meeting you."

"The pleasure was all mine."

Sure it was.

I also met someone else very special there at F. Lee's party that night. The woman I would go on to live with for the next twenty-six years, twenty-five of them as man and wife. That's over now.

Manny was there. Bernard, too. Jim Lehner, the Magoo-voice guy, and his wife, Pat. The Lehners were a pair to draw to. Jim was about five-four and weighed about two hundred pounds. He had a little mustache. If he hadn't had the mustache, his nose would've started at his upper lip. He always wore a suit and tie, but his tie was never tied. He always looked like he just got off a terribly hard day at work, but he never worked.

Pat was a good head-and-a-half taller than he was. She was a nice woman, but had some kind of a nervous problem. Every once in a while, especially if she'd been drinking, which was the only time I ever saw her, she'd have a little fit.

Unless you were talking to her, you had no idea she was having a fit. What would happen is, she'd just freeze. She'd be sitting there talking and all of a sudden, she became a statue. Didn't or couldn't move a muscle. Couldn't speak. For like five minutes.

It was kind of unnerving because you'd be telling her something and she simply wouldn't respond. Just sit there, staring into space. Then, she'd snap right out of it. She'd feel lousy for a couple of minutes and then carry on as if nothing had happened.

Weird.

I always thought Lehner was an okay guy, but he was lazy and full of shit.

A month or so after F. Lee's party, Elizabeth Kennedy, the woman who owned the cute little frame company up on the nineteenth floor, told Dale she was looking to retire. She was up in her seventies and I was surprised she'd hung around as long as she did.

She wanted her frame company to live on, because she'd built up a pretty good little business and an excellent reputation, especially with those cute little shops that sold cute little shit. Places with names like The Quilted Bear or Aunt Bea's Attic or The Goose Down Shoppe or The Pleasure Chest (I'm just kidding about The Pleasure Chest).

Dale, in his infinite quest to rival the other Generals – Motors and Dynamics – decided to buy the business from Elizabeth.

So, that meant we now manufactured and sold water display fountains, submersible pumps, underwater lighting, electric wheelchairs and cloisonné picture frames – and we were landlords, to boot.

Unfortunately, I drew the short straw on the Elizabeth Kennedy project, too. For the most part.

Dale took over for getting the raw steel amalgam frames made. We had molds and ol' Elizabeth was having the frames poured (that's how they were made) in someplace in New England or something.

Dale found a foundry in Weehawken and had the molds shipped there. That way, you know who could drive over and pick up the raw frames and we'd save a ton on shipping charges. It was better hauling frames through the Lincoln Tunnel than a couple hundred gallons of high-octane fuel, though.

Elizabeth always had the frames gold-plated and we all agreed we should stay with that. It was part of the unique selling proposition. One of our tenants, a guy on the thirteenth floor, had a gold-plating operation. We gave him the business.

We kept the frame business in Elizabeth's old quarters, up on nineteen.

I spent a good part of the next six months making frames, developing the sales material and selling the goddam things.

Now, when I say these frames were "cute", they were cute beyond making your teeth hurt.

One of the frames had cute little bunnies all over it. One had teddy bears. One had ducklings. They came in blue for baby boys, pink for girls and yellow for 'I-don't-know-which-it-is-yet'. One had little bows. There was a golf-themed frame. A skiing-themed frame. A tennis-themed frame.

They were all the same size, about five inches by five inches, with a window for a photo that measured about two-by-two. They had a little thing on the back that would allow them to stand up.

To make the finished frame, we mixed up this epoxy-based solution, added in an appropriate amount of coloring, along with some hardener, and carefully poured the mixture into the frame.

If some dripped or you overfilled the frame, you had to clean it up with a toothpick or cotton swab, like the kind you clean your ears with. It was painstaking and really bad on the nerves and shoulder muscles.

A few hours later, the frames would be hard and ready to go. We'd generally pour twenty or thirty at a clip.

Each one then had to be wrapped in white tissue paper, placed on a little square of white cotton, with an accompanying little white cotton square laid lovingly over it and placed into a cute little white box. If you were going to sell this shit at a place called the Quilted Bear, everything had to be too fucking cute.

Working on the frames up on nineteen wasn't all that bad, though. For one thing, we had disconnected the phone and it now rang downstairs in the office. I'd just sit there and listen to ol' Big Wilson play country tunes and do commercials for Junior's Cheesecakes out in Brooklyn.

There were also windows! I hadn't seen daylight during working hours in years!

The only fly in the ointment up on nineteen was the presence of Lehner.

Lehner had taken to hanging around the office far too much. He was always yapping about this idea or that, but never did anything. He'd show up at the office around eleven, yap for an hour or so, then would mooch along with Jeanne and Dale when they went to lunch. Then he'd come back, yap for another hour or so, then announce he had to go on an audition.

This went on long enough to begin to drive everybody nuts. Why Jeanne and Dale didn't just chase his ass away was beyond me, but they never were ones to send hangers-on down the highway. That's just the way they were.

So, Jeanne decided he could earn some of his keep by working on the picture frame business. His actual work consisted of typing up invoices and labels, packing the right frames into the right boxes and getting the day's shipment ready for UPS.

I was happy that I didn't have to do it, but the sonofabitch needed help on every order.

"Jim, The Pregnant Panda ordered six bunny frames. Two each in blue, pink and yellow. I have the order ready except we have only one blue bunny in stock. What'll I do?"

"Look down in front of me. What am I doing?"

"Putting the back on some bunny frames."

"What color are the frames?"

"Uh, blue."

"Good. That means they're almost ready. Here's what I'd do. I'd get everything ready except for sealing the shipping box. I wouldn't write the info in the UPS book yet. If we're ready in time before the UPS guy gets here, we'll add it in. If not, it'll go tomorrow."

"Good. Sounds good. Good plan."

"Thanks." This went on every day.

We decided we'd do some direct mailings. We'd inherited Elizabeth's mailing and customer list and Al typed all the names and addresses onto Cheshire cards. We'd lay out the pages and I'd print them on the press the way I did with our fountain stuff.

Fortunately, Elizabeth had had professional photos taken of the frames; we didn't have to rely on Dale's photographic genius.

The only problem was, she didn't have any copy to accompany the photos. Jeanne voted me in charge of writing the copy.

My initial attempt was dismal, according to Jeanne. A little dry, I guess. I wasn't really into it.

"These frames are cute", she said.

Didn't I know it.

"And the places that sell them are cute."

"Right. Places like the Pimpled Ass."

"Stop it. Theses places want cute, cute, cute."

So?

"So our copy has to be cute, cute, cute, too."

"I'll try."

So, I decided to just lay on the treacle.

I made the goddam bunny rabbit frame's copy read something like, "Happy little bunnies romp playfully in fields of little boy blue, little girl pink, or bright sunshine yellow". What I wanted it to say was, "Horny little bunnies run around looking to, you know, fuck like rabbits."

"Now", Jeanne said, "that's what I'm talking about."

"Somebody shoot me."

"I'll shoot you if you try to slide a dirty description in there somewhere."

For the tennis frame, I wanted it to read, "Tennis rackets abound on this happy little frame, just looking for balls to whack."

We also decided to get a booth at the New York Gift Show. That was cool, I'd never been to the gift show and I was looking forward to scoping out all the crap that was about to hit the market. And, I thought we'd do gangbusters.

Unfortunately, I had a booth mate. Lehner. In his suit with the untied tie.

I didn't really mind Lehner all that much. Matter of fact, I kind of felt sorry for him. He really had no skills. And either his voice-over agent was lousy or he was a washed up voice-over guy, because he wasn't making any money doing the only thing he'd ever done.

Lehner drank a lot. Not that the rest of us drank any less, but his hands shook.

Watching him point at the romping little bunnies while he was demonstrating the frames to somebody whose name tag read "The Comfy Lap – Stroudsburg, Pennsylvania" and seeing his hands shake like a leaf was disquieting. Sad, even.

His shaking hands did provide me with a dose of hilarity one afternoon, though. He asked me if I wanted a cup of coffee. Sure. He went to fetch one for each of us.

As he was walking back to the booth, you'd have thought he was carrying live nitroglycerin, the care and focus he was displaying toward two free cups of coffee.

As he tiptoed into the booth and he went to hand me my cup, his hand started shaking. When his hand shook, the hot coffee slopped out of the cup onto his hand, burning it. This caused his hand to shake even more, and now his other hand, with his cup in it, started shaking, too. Now both of his hands were being burned by hot coffee. Between the shakes and burning hands, Lehner just stood there flinging coffee all over the place. The more he flung, the more he got burned and the more he flung some more. Shake. Burn. Fling. Shake. Burn. Fling.

By the time he settled down, both cups were no more than a third full. He handed me what was left of mine.

"You okay?", I asked.

"Yes, I'm all right. Why do they make that goddam coffee so hot? But, hey – the reason I was trying to hurry back here is that Ed Koch is walking down the aisle with a group of people." Koch was the mayor at the time.

I looked up to see Ed Koch standing right in front of me.

"Hello, young man. How's it going?" He stuck out his hand and I shook it.

"Fine, Ed. But don't you mean, 'How'm I doing?'" It was his catch-phrase.

"Ahaha. Good one, son. How am I doing?"

"You're doing just fine, Ed."

"Good. Well, good luck to you."

"Thanks."

Lehner just stood there, both hands dripping with coffee. No way in hell Koch was going to glad-hand him.

"Shit", he said.

"Oh, by the way, Jim", I said to him, "Ed Koch told me to say hello to you, but your hands were full at the time."

"Very funny. Goddammit, that coffee burns."

Good thing for Ed Koch that Lehner's hands were a mess. He had no idea how close he'd come to getting a "Magoo".

The show was just chock full of shit. Every stupid idea ever known to man was represented. Aisle upon aisle of trash and trinkets.

Frisbees with your logo imprinted. Dehydrated sponges that expanded when you put them in the water. With your logo. Those glow-in-the-dark things that are ubiquitous at fireworks displays. Ten thousand baseball hat manufacturers. With your logo. Pens with your logo on 'em.

The only company I'd ever heard of that had a booth there was the Michael C. Fina silver company. I didn't know Michael C. Fina silver even existed other than as a prize on The Price is Right.

On top of all that, our business sucked, too. I was used to writing ten thousand dollars in business with the fountains. If we did a grand at this show, it was because we'd double-booked something.

The only joy I had was in fucking with people's minds.

"Ooh, Leland. Aren't these the cutest frames ever? I'll take four."

Great. Thirty-six bucks.

"And please ship them C.O.D."

Cheap asshole.

"Let's see, now….four frames, thirty-six bucks, C.O.D. And I should ship them directly to the Wilted Pecker, right?"

"Pardon me?"

"Ship them directly to the Gilded Pepper, right?"

"Uh, yes. Right. C.O.D., please."

"And what's the zip code there in West Buttfuck?"

"Pardon?"

"What's the zip code there in West Bluffville?"

"Oh, it's four-five-one-two-eight."

"Got it. Great. Thanks again."

I hated the goddam frame business.

THIRTY-FOUR

There used to be a place where we'd go to brunch, up in the better part of town, up on the Upper East Side. I don't remember how we ever found it because it was just one of tens of thousands of restaurants in New York City. It was called the Lion's Rock and, if I remember correctly, was on 77th Street between First and Second.

It was new and the thing that made it really unique was, not that it had an outside patio, but towering over the patio was a huge mountain of stone that had never been removed when the neighborhood was originally built. It was very reminiscent of those huge rock formations found in Central Park.

It must've been two hundred feet long and ran behind three or four buildings. It was about twenty or twenty-five feet high. Huge. Massive. And it actually formed the back wall of the Lion's Rock patio.

We got to talking with the owner one day and suggested how cool it would be to have water running down the face of the rock into a pool at the bottom with a couple of small, non-obtrusive fountains in it. We could put a couple of underwater lights in the pool to make it really pretty at night, too.

How much?

We told him.

When can you start?

This week.

I was put in charge of the project and it was something I really relished. The idea of creating a waterfall on real rock would be a load of fun. Creating the pool at the bottom would be a little challenging because the owner didn't want to sacrifice any more seating area than he had to.

John and I went up on Tuesday afternoon to figure out exactly what we'd do.

"Not work", said John encouragingly.

"Why not?"

"Waterfall splash like hell. Have water all over floor."

I'd neglected to mention to John that I didn't envision a "waterfall", per se, but more of a slim sheen of water washing gently down the face of the rock (Christ, I was thinking like Jack Mohr!). Very little water volume.

"She still splash."

I could see what he meant in that the water would have to cascade over several rock outcroppings, meaning the water would fall several feet before hitting whatever rock was below it. Recipe for splash.

"John, what if I chisel away some of those overhangs so the water'll fall more smoothly?"

"Maybe she not splash so much then, but much work. Also, how you put pool at bottom when rock wall is not straight?"

"Well, it looks like we'll have to sort of customize the shape of the pool to follow the shape of the rock."

"Much work." John didn't like custom jobs.

He also didn't like anything new. No matter what new piece of equipment Dale brought in, John hated it to begin with. He used to be satisfied nailing our wooden crates together. Dale bought a powerful air-powered staple gun that sat on a shelf for six months.

"What we need new equipment for? Nail together in thirty minutes."

Dale would never argue with him. One day, he'd just pull together all the wood he'd need to build a crate, fire up the new staple gun and would snap a crate together in ten minutes.

"See if you can use this crate, John."

One day in the very near future, John would try out the new staple gun on his own, just to prove it wouldn't work and that Dale's crate was a fluke. He'd whip a crate together in ten minutes, too. From then on, he couldn't live without the air-powered staple gun.

It was just like that with everything new that John was introduced to.

That's why I took his negativity at the Lion's Rock with a grain of salt. I knew that once he started thinking about how to make it work and could make himself comfortable with the probable outcome, he'd figure out exactly what we'd need to make it work right.

"We measure. Make pool to fit along wall. But she have openings near rock and water run through openings. Make mess and we lose all water very soon."

"What if we bring some fiberglass with us and once the pool is in, we'll just run a few sheets of glass from the top of the pool to the rock? Glass and resin will stick to the rock, won't it?"

"Sure, she stick."

"What color we make pool?" Now he was starting to get into it.

"I figured black. Nobody wants to see the pool."

"Maybe grey to match rock."

"Can you do that? Match the color?"

"Sure. We bring color with us and mix into resin until same color as rock."

Ah, he was beginning to cook.

"I figure we can run clear plastic tubing up in the crevasses of the rock to the top and just point the open ends toward the rock face, so it'll just flow down, right?"

"Must have hose clamps to adjust flow of water."

"Yeah, of course."

"Just lit water coming down." He never said "little", it always came out as "lit".

"Right. No splash, then, right?"

"We see."

Over the next few days, John and his guys built the pool out of plywood and covered it completely with black fiberglass. We'd put a final coat of colored resin on at the site once we'd matched the color.

The rest was easy. Two good-sized submersible pumps would push the water up through clear plastic tubing to make the waterfall and we'd put three small stock pond type lighted fountains into the pool to complete the thing.

John and I and a couple of his guys delivered the whole thing on weekday morning. In four or five hours, the thing was finished. Except for the waterfall. The pumps were in and I'd run the tubing up to the top of the rock. John and his guys left and I was left alone to play on the rock.

I turned the thing on and realized I'd forgotten to put the hose clamps on the hoses at the top of the rock. We had a waterfall, all right. It looked like Springtime in the Rockies. It really looked beautiful but water was splashing everywhere. No problem, I'd turn it off, put the clamps on and get to chiseling.

Just then the owner walked out.

"Jesus Christ! What're you doing to me? I didn't ask for Niagara Fucking Falls!"

"Don't worry, it'll be fine. I'm just testing it. Still a lot of work to be done."

"I sure hope so."

Why is it that people always appear at the wrong time?

I spent the next day-and-a-half clambering over that rock face, hammer and chisel in hand, knocking off protuberances and smoothing out aberrations in the rock. I felt like the Michelangelo of the fountain world.

Finally, I was happy with the way the water cascaded down the face of the rock and had cut whatever splash down to almost non-existent. I called the owner to come look at it. He fell in love with it. "My God, I had never thought about that rock becoming a showcase for the place. And it is. It really is. Please, all of you come to dinner tonight as my guests."

"Great. Thanks. There'll be three of us – seven o'clock okay?" Just Jeanne and Dale and I would go, John and his guys would be rewarded in heaven or their paychecks, whichever came first.

We showed up right on time. Sober. Naturally, we sat on the back patio and the fountains were working perfectly. The owner came over and made a big deal over us. "Please, allow me to bring you a number of our specialties. Don't fill up on any one dish I bring you, though, I want you to try everything."

We had appetizers of every kind, plates of specialties of the house just kept coming. And going. Only to be replaced by more. Along with martinis.

By eight o'clock, the place was full and every table on the back patio was taken.

"Excuse me! Excuse me, everyone!" It was the owner and he was trying to get the attention of everyone on the patio and even the inside of the restaurant. "Excuse me!"

All the diners stopped eating and drinking and talking and gave him their attention.

"Thank you. I just wanted you all to notice our beautiful new fountains and waterfall cascading down the Lion's Rock. We've unveiled it all tonight and we think it helps make our restaurant unique in all of New York City."

Applause.

Wow.

"And – I'd like to introduce you to the artisans that have made it all possible. Jim, Jeanne, Dale – please stand up so everyone can see you and thank you for such exquisite artistry."

We stood up. Wow, again. Artisans?

People were actually applauding and toasting us.

It was great.

A few weeks later, the place was reviewed in the New York Times. The restaurant got an okay review. The food and the service were adequate, but as far as atmosphere and ambiance the back patio, with its waterfall and fountains, made the place something special for a New York City bistro.

On top of all that great stuff, the guy paid upon completion and his check cleared.

Didn't get much better than all that, huh?

****

I had been working full time for Jeanne and Dale for nine years. But I was still making dog squat as far as money. Still on an hourly wage, plus commissions. I was probably pulling down a whopping twelve grand a year.

I felt it was time to discuss my situation and my future.

Here's what I thought:

I thought I should be given a piece of the business. Not a big piece, but maybe ten percent or so. Jeanne and Dale had fifty percent each. I thought they'd each give up five percent.

They always talked in terms of "our" business, but really, it was still "their" business.

I didn't want a piece of the building, that would've been asking a bit much, I thought. Ten percent of the wheelchair business would've amounted to maybe seventy bucks and ten percent of the frame business wouldn't have meant much more.

But, ten percent of the fountain business seemed reasonable. Virtually all of its growth had taken place while I was there and I was a big part of that growth. And, lest it be forgotten, the growth of the fountain business had precipitated their ability to buy the building.

Jeanne and Dale were living pretty high on the hog by now. Two or three cars, a couple of months a year in Miami, an unlimited expense account, new toys left, right and center.

Me? Twelve grand.

I felt I had to broach the subject and broach it soon. After all, I was now in my late twenties and thought it was time to graduate from a three-steps-ahead-of-the-Polish guys existence.

But broaching the subject was something I dreaded more than anything. Neither one of them ever liked to talk about stuff like that. Neither did I, for that matter. As close as we were, the subject of money could still be a prickly one.

I devised all kinds of scenarios on how to bring it up.

I'd write down all the things I'd done to help grow the business and would hand it to them in the course of the conversation. Nah, too formal.

I'd keep dropping strategic hints. Nah, that's be an assholic thing to do. What would I say? "Boy, if I had a piece of the action, I'd sure work a lot harder and smarter." No, not even close.

I'd persuade some of our friends to act as an emissary on my part. Wait a minute. Who? Billy Ruben? Jim Lucey? Iz? John? Unh-uh. Besides, a lot of the people they respected were already doing that unknowingly.

Bernard Brill, for example. He'd say to Dale, "You'd better take good care of Jimmy. Your place would fall flat on its face if he ever left." Doesn't get much more direct than that.

Dale would say, "You're absolutely right, Bernard. We couldn't do it without Jim, that's for sure." And that would be the end of that.

True to myself and our lifestyle, I finally brought it up to Dale one night when we were both quite drunk and Jeanne had gone home to bed.

It was easy.

"Hey, Dale. How about giving me a piece of the fountain business? Not a big piece, but a meaningful piece of it."

He said, "You know, I've been thinking about that for a long time, now. I think you should get a piece and I think John should get a piece. We wouldn't be where we are without you two. Oh, I think you should get a bigger piece than John, but he should get some, too."

"Great. Lemme ask you – when?"

"Let me talk it over with Jake. Couple of weeks, tops."

"Wow, and I thought that was gonna be hard. You know, asking you that way."

"Hell, you deserve it."

I went home happy.

A couple of weeks went by. Then a month.

One night at Gallagher's I broached the subject again with Dale.

I got essentially the same answer as I had several weeks earlier.

Hmm.

Except this time, he said something along the lines of, "but Jake's dragging her heels".

Aha.

It was Jeanne. Jeanne was an odd one, even though she was one of my favorite people in the world. She always thought people were out to get her, to steal from her, to take something that didn't belong to them, at least in her eyes.

There was no way, though, that she could be thinking along those lines as far as I was concerned.

Could she?

Because I'd had those conversations with Dale, I felt I had courage enough to broach the subject with Jeanne. I'd have to do it during the workday, though, because once she got a couple of drinks into her, there was no telling what could happen.

In all actuality, the booze was getting the better part of her. After no more than two or three drinks, she'd be zonked, would begin acting somewhat irrationally, and head off to bed, if everyone was lucky. If everyone wasn't lucky, a real scene could ensue. And things could get real ugly real fast.

One morning when things were pretty quiet and stable around the office, I said, "Jeanne, can I talk to you for a minute?"

"What is it?", she asked formally, almost coldly. Uh-oh, the wall was going up.

"Well, Dale's probably mentioned it, but I'd like to talk to you about maybe my getting a small piece of the fountain business. He seemed to think it was a pretty good idea."

"Well, I don't. Dale and I have put everything into building this business. We've taken all the financial risks, suffered through some very bad times. Had to fight for everything we have. And nobody's going to take any of that away. Not you. Not anybody."

"Jeanne, I'm not trying to take anything away from you. I've been helping you with this business since I was a kid and have spent the last nine years helping it to grow. And I'm not asking for much. Just a small percentage. Enough to make me feel like the last nine years have meant something more than just a job."

"No, Jim. It's just not going to happen. At least while I have anything to say about it."

"Do you suppose the three of us can talk about it, together?"

"Talk all you want, but I have fifty percent of the vote and I say no."

And that was that.

Maybe I was a fountain tycoon, but it didn't mean shit.

My now-mother-in-law was in the newspaper business. Over the next weeks and months, I'd go on interviews she'd helped me set up with various newspaper companies.

It was funny. I wore jeans to work at 264, but I had to look good for the interviews. Sometimes, my wife would meet me on the corner with the car, I'd change my pants and shirt in the front seat and throw on the one tie I'd bought for five bucks from Tie City.

I finally landed a job offer at Gannett, one of the largest newspaper chains.

I was between a shit and a sweat. I knew the new job would put me on an actual career path, toward what I didn't know.

But it would also mean my leaving the only real job I'd ever known. And really loved, in spite of all the nonsense. I wondered if Bill Leith and Harry Hyatt had ever worked in the newspaper business and if their presence was even allowed. With a big company like Gannett, probably not. I might have to leave them behind at 264.

Did I want to leave? Really?

Hell, no.

But the writing was on the wall. If I stayed, I was at a dead end. I'd always be just an employee. Just an employee! That alone pissed me off. I was married now, too, with a stepdaughter, to boot. No way I could provide for even a piece of our lives on 12K a year.

It had to be done.

I had to leave.

Shit.

On a Monday evening, I accepted the job at Gannett. I would start in two weeks.

At least, I thought, that gave me two weeks to change my mind, if I had to.

It also just might give me a little bit of last-ditch leverage with Jeanne and Dale. Maybe Jeanne just needed to know I would really leave before she'd cave and acquiesce to parting with her five percent. Yeah, that was probably it. Once I told her I'd been offered another job – a position, really – she'd tell me they didn't want me to leave and maybe it was time for us to sit down and work something out. Yeah, that's what would happen.

I went in the next day, fully prepared for my scenario to play itself out.

"Jeanne", I said, "I have some news."

"You're leaving."

"Well, I've been offered a position at the Gannett newspaper company."

"Good. Great. Take it. You'll do a lot better than you'll ever do here."

What? That didn't go the way I'd envisioned. Not in the least. I'd try it again.

"They want me to start in two weeks. You know, I don't really want to leave." Give her an opening.

"No, Jimmy, I think you should go. Just finish up what you're working on and go."

"Well, there's nothing really pressing in the mailings right now that Al can't do without me. And I don't have any real big deals in the pipeline...."

"Then go. Just go."

And I went.

THIRTY-FIVE

Jeanne and Dale and I stayed fairly close but that life was gone.

My wife and I bought a house in Englewood, New Jersey and we'd get together with them at Christmas and other holidays. We'd get invited to parties on the roof with some regularity. They bought a weekend house out on Lake Hopatcong and we'd get invited there once in a while, too.

But something started to go south between the two of them.

Jeanne's drinking had gotten the best of Dale. Not that Dale's drinking had ebbed any, it's just that Jeanne's behavior, when drunk, was abominable. And that was pretty much every night.

Over the next few years, they broke up.

Dale took up with this woman who, I guess was nice to him, but the relationship was beyond me. He lived in Lake Hopatcong almost all the time and Jeanne lived in the apartment on Eighth Avenue.

I don't know all the gory details, but I do know the fountain business went completely to hell. I mean, within no more than two or three years, it was gone. Zip. Zilch.

They each still had money coming in from the building, so I guess they did alright in that regard.

One day, Iz called me and told me Dale had been diagnosed with liver cancer and had to have an operation.

I called him.

"Jim", he said, "it's the damndest thing. I went for a regular physical and somehow the tests showed that I have some exotic form of liver cancer that usually only manifests itself in Southeast Asia. The doctors asked me if I'd ever been to Southeast Asia. Hell, I've never been out of the country."

"So what's the prognosis?"

"Well, seems the liver is the only organ that can regenerate itself. If they can cut out the bad part, I just might be alright." He sounded scared. Never in my life had I ever heard Dale sound scared.

"What can I do?"

"Nothing. Wish you could, but you can't. It'll be fine."

He had the operation but, of course, it was more advanced than they'd hoped. He went on chemo and all that other stuff. I couldn't bring myself to go see him and he didn't seem to want any company.

Iz decided to throw him a big birthday party for his 65th birthday and we went. The funny part was, he always thought he was a year younger than he really was. He thought he was going to be sixty-four, but they'd found some records of some kind that revealed he was really going to be sixty-five.

When we got there, I couldn't believe it. I always knew Dale as a robust, great-looking, strong guy. Here was a bald-headed little old man who could hardly move on his own.

He was smoking a cigarette.

"Hey, I thought you quit years ago."

"Started again. What's it gonna do, make me sick?"

"Good point."

He asked me to help him to the bathroom. I had to hold him up. As we walked, he said in a whisper, "Damn, we didn't see this coming, did we, Jim?"

"No, Dale, we didn't."

Actually, we didn't see any of what had happened coming.

He died two weeks later.

Jeanne sort of existed in a netherworld for several years, in and out of the hospital for half a dozen ailments.

She kind of took up with this Russian guy who had put a restaurant called The Russian Samovar into the space where Jilly's once had been. He was a drunk with a capital "D". But he took care of Jeanne. Pretty good care of her, I guess. His name was Paul.

Jeanne still owned half of the building, along with the other half that was part of Dale's estate. The whole thing had become a major cluster fuck, with two or three lawyers suing Dale's estate to try and get their greedy, grubby hands on money that wasn't theirs. But, they were lawyers and had Jeanne over a barrel, especially considering her delicate condition.

The building pretty much ran on its own, though, and Jeanne got a monthly stipend from Newmark. Just barely enough to survive on, which was a crime in itself. She simply didn't have the mental capacity or physical ability to fight it.

In an interesting twist on things, I got involved with the building again for about six months.

I had left the newspaper business and had started my own bullshit little marketing company. I needed an office in the City, but didn't have any money. I called Jeanne.

"Hey, Jeanne. I have a little, minor proposition for you. If you'll let me have that real little space up on twenty, I'll manage the building for you. You know, put Newmark's feet to the fire, keep my eye on all the money coming in and going out and will try to see if it's possible to get some better, higher-class tenants. I don't want any money, just the space."

"Oh, Jimmy, I wish you would. Those rat-bastards at Newmark are robbing me blind and I just can't keep up with them anymore."

So, I took the little space up on twenty.

It had been fifteen years since I'd left 264 and though the building really hadn't changed, it looked and felt entirely different to me. Everything looked smaller. More rudimentary. The hallways seemed darker. Dale had upgraded the bathrooms, but that had been years earlier and in his signature wall paneling. The only thing that looked the same were the slop sinks.

General Fountain Corp. was gone. In the space where the office had been, there was a mess. A couple of desks piled high with bills and catalogs and that type of shit. Some of the correspondence was four years old, according to the post marks.

There was a dump of a workbench in the middle of the room with shit strewn all over it. Jeanne's friend, Paul, would hang out there, drunk, and talk about how he was going to start the fountain business up again. The only fountain that sonofabitch could've ever made was to stand in the middle of a pond and piss in it. I completely ignored him and didn't acknowledge his presence. He died a few years ago.

Bubniak was still around. He was now the super, with no real responsibilities, because Newmark had centralized the supers at most of their buildings and they kind of came and went as they were needed and called. None of them had any real on-site supers anymore.

John had aged. Not that I hadn't, it's just that I looked in the mirror every day and I hadn't laid eyes on him in nearly fifteen years. He was aging pretty well, though. Didn't limp, didn't complain and hadn't gotten fat. He had a few grandkids now, but his wife wasn't well. He seemed kind of sad. Had to be. He watched the thing disintegrate, piece by piece.

One day I went up to the roof, on the outside chance the bar and all would still be there. Everything was gone. It was just a roof again, as empty as it had been on that day in 1976 when Billy Ruben and I watched the parade of tall ships and drank warm beer.

I asked John about it. "What happened to roof?"

"Some building inspectors were over at McGraw-Hill Building on 42nd and look over here.

See bar, everything. They come here and say 'Show us roof.' We show them. They ask for permits. No have. Say, 'must have roof clean by tomorrow or ten thousand dollar fine'."

"What did you do?"

"Tore down roof and throw in garbage."

We had some new young hotshot from Newmark and I got involved with their bookkeeping and maintenance people. Maybe we could upgrade the building a little and attract some better tenants.

The new young hotshot's name was Mark. He kept pissing all over my idea to upgrade the building.

"Jim, this is the Garment Center. Fortieth Street between Seventh and Eighth. The Garment Center is broken down into its own little lots. Seventh Avenue has the fashion houses and, therefore, the highest rents.

"Thirty-Eighth Street is next highest because that's where most of those houses have their goods built.

"Thirty-Ninth is the pits because all that has is accessory and button guys.

"Fortieth has a few small seasonal designers, but they're here and gone, most of them leaving a big rent bill behind. Other than that, they're miscellaneous guys, just like you have here. Some sell cloth, some sell embroidery, all the stuff that's always in demand, but always at low prices.

"You have a few small designers in this building. I just make sure they're not seasonal guys or one-shots.

"264 is doing about as well as can be expected. Just know you're not going to be able to make much of difference in a short time. Over three or four years, maybe, we can begin to attract some better tenants, but look at this place."

He was right. 264 looked like shit. As I said, the bathrooms were old. The hallways were dreary. Dale had, at one point, tried to upgrade certain floors, but he'd had John do it in – what else? - cheap paneling, most of which had now been painted over and was dingy at best.

Even the lobby looked dismal. If Parker had still been there, I'd have had him put up one of his "Happy Chanuan" signs just to add some life to it.

When I told all of this to Jeanne, albeit in a gentle and not very specific manner, she simply thought the crooks at Newmark had gotten to me, too. I looked at all the books every month, though, and couldn't find any chicanery, just a nearly hundred-year-old, twenty-story building on West 40th Street, just east of Eighth Avenue. A few months later, I moved to Los Angeles. Jeanne didn't need me to watch over that building and, true to form, I wasn't making any money there, either. Newmark would do just fine.

Jeanne continued downhill and died a couple of years later.

Here's what happened then.

Jeanne had inherited all of Dale's estate. When Jeanne died, she left her estate to Iz, my mother and their sister, Betty.

They all hired a top-notch legal firm to sort out the problems with the shysters and, to the best of my limited knowledge, it was ultimately resolved.

264, again to the best of my knowledge, either was or is in the process of being sold.

For several million dollars.

Further pursuant to my limited knowledge, a portion of said profits will eventually make their way in my direction, thanks to my mom.

We'll see.

THIRTY-SIX

So there you have it.

It's funny how life works, you know?

When something's happening and you're in the middle of it, it's like a maelstrom. Vibrant. Crazy. Funny. Exciting. It seems as if whatever you're involved with will go on and on and on – because it's just all so real at the time.

For years, all hell was breaking loose at 264 West 40th Street. Characters came and went. Situations arose and spun away and new ones took their place.

We were living the life of urban cowboys. We didn't answer to anybody. Did whatever we wanted whenever we wanted. No rules. No barriers. No concrete expectations and no regrets. Just a constantly changing horizon.

No real vision for the future. And that was good. And bad. It was taking life as it comes and bring it on. We'll deal with it when it gets here.

As Dale used to say, "They can kill us but they can't eat us." Whatever that meant.

God, I miss those days.

Dale and Jeanne often visit me in my dreams. We're all back at 264 and the characters and situations are as real as the real ones seem now. Tiger's even there.

Bubniak. Acuna. Al. Parker. Billy Ruben. PL. Bernard. Even that goofy Ming.

They all show up, too.

And they're just as real as they were in 1976.

Look the same. Sound the same. Act the same. Are the same.

Because those dreams are so real, I sometimes wonder if those years really happened or if I just dreamed the whole goddam thing.

Ah, I know better. Yeah, they happened.

I think.

I used to see some of our fountains in places around the country now and then. Oh, they all needed work – work that I could have done with my eyes closed – but I just looked and remembered and moved on.

At least they were proof that those days once existed.

Now I don't see any of those fountains anymore.

Next time I'm in New York, if I'm ever in New York again, I'll go by 264 West 40th Street, between Seventh and Eighth. It'll still be there. I think.

But there's an awful lot of renovation going on in the area just south of Times Square, I know that for sure. Maybe 264 won't be there. Maybe it'll be the sweeping driveway entrance to a huge, fancy new hotel, where the driveway winds its way around a decorative island.

It would be only fitting if there were a huge fucking fountain right smack in the middle of that island.

With eleven dramatic color changes and three exciting water pattern changes a minute.

ABOUT THE AUTHOR

It's funny how life's trails can lead a person into strange and wonderful diversions before eventually leading him or her back home.

Jim Gath comes from a family of horsemen – his grandfather was a trick rider, trainer and horse trader, one of his uncles was a jockey and another was an owner of rather questionably talented racehorses. As a kid, horses were an important part of his life, but he began his adult life taking a different trail.

There was a time when the first thing Jim Gath did when he got to work every day 6:30 a.m. was look at the prior day's revenue figures

Now, the first thing he does every morning is walk around Tierra Madre Horse Sanctuary and makes sure that the 31 horses living there have spent a comfortable, quiet night. He tosses a little hay to a few of them – his day beginning at 3 a.m., 365 days a year.

Tierra Madre Horse Sanctuary in Cave Creek, Arizona, is a sanctuary rescue ranch – a "Forever Home" to 31 previously unwanted, neglected, injured or abused horses. Ex-racehorses, ex-show horses, ex-rodeo horses, ex-ranch horses, ex-trail horses – horses of all sizes and breeds have found their way to Tierra Madre.

The one thing they all have in common is that they had nowhere else to go and are now living out their lives in a happy, healthy, loving home.

Jim Gath was one of the founders of USA TODAY and eventually rose through the ranks to become the head of its advertising sales department. He moved on to Turner Broadcasting, where he worked with CNN, TBS, TNT and The Cartoon Network, before developing the marketing platform for the 1998 Goodwill Games.

He was the publisher of College Sports Magazine. He produced the first-ever Insight.com Bowl, a post-season college football game. He produced Phoenix 2000, a huge turn-of-the-century extravaganza in downtown Phoenix that drew tens of thousands of revelers. He became a concert promoter in Las Vegas producing, among other things, the first-ever major open air concert in the Las Vegas suburb of Summerlin, the country's largest master-planned community.

Jim finally decided none of those achievements – or the pursuit of them – was making him happy or satisfied. Upon reflection, he realized the best times in his life were spent around and among horses. So he took another, more fulfilling trail.

He worked at a Summer horse camp for kids. Gave riding lessons at the Los Angeles Equestrian Center. Guided trail rides through LA's Griffith Park. Got a few of his own horses. Moved to Phoenix. Found a ranch he and his family would take over. Trained horses. Trained riders. Boarded horses. Rescued horses. Cared for horses. He has never, ever met a horse he didn't like. "You just have to listen to them", he says. "They'll tell you everything you need to know."

****

Jim Gath donates all of the proceeds of his books to support Tierra Madre Horse Sanctuary. Tierra Madre is a non-profit organization – it has a 501(c)(3) status with the IRS – and must depend on donations and contributions to raise funds.

TIERRA MADRE HORSE SANCTUARY is simply a very nice, very loving home for horses who, through no fault of their own, have no better place to go. Good food, good care, a lot of room, a lot of love and understanding and a lot of treats – a place where horses can enjoy being horses. No pressure to perform just to assuage fragile human egos. To find out more about this great organization and to donate go to: www.tierramadrehorsesanctuary.org

www.ingramcontent.com/pod-product-compliance
Lightning Source LLC
LaVergne TN
LVHW051110080426
835510LV00018B/1987